GUERRILLA HOME RECORDING

HOW TO GET GREAT SOUND FROM ANY STUDIO

(no matter how weird or cheap your gear is)

BY KARL CORYAT

Backbeat Books
San Francisco

Published by Backbeat Books
600 Harrison Street, San Francisco, CA 94107
www.backbeatbooks.com
email: books@musicplayer.com

An imprint of CMP Information
Publishers of *Guitar Player*, *Bass Player*, *Keyboard*, and *EQ* magazines

CMP
United Business Media

Distributed to the book trade in the US and Canada by
Publishers Group West, 1700 Fourth Street, Berkeley, CA 94710

Distributed to the music trade in the US and Canada by
Hal Leonard Publishing, P.O. Box 13819, Milwaukee, WI 53213

Cover Design by Richard Leeds – bigwigdesign.com
Composition by Michael Baughan

Library of Congress Cataloging-in-Publication Data

Coryat, Karl.
Guerrilla home recording : how to get great sound from any studio / by Karl Coryat.
p. cm.
Includes index.
ISBN 0-87930-834-6 (alk. paper)
1. Sound—Recording and reproducing—Amateurs' manuals. 2. Sound studios. I. Title.

TK9968.C57 2004
781.49'0285—dc22

2004025016

Printed in the United States of America

05 06 07 08 09 5 4 3 2 1

Contents

Introduction

This book isn't for every recording musician. Some people will get angry reading what I have to say. Who? Basically, anyone who has spent too much money on vintage or otherwise expensive recording gear in the quest for a "professional" studio sound. These people don't want to hear that you can make excellent recordings without a $5,000 tube mic or a Massenburg EQ. *Guerrilla Home Recording* is for the rest of us: musicians who just want to create great-sounding recordings and, I hope, haven't read too many other books and articles on the art and science of recording sound.

Mind you, there's nothing wrong with reading about recording—except that in my opinion, most of this instructional material tends to steer musicians in the wrong direction. Recording books and articles are usually written by people who know too much for their own good. They forget what it was like to struggle with equipment, to flail away trying to get a decent mix of a song. They're way past that stage, to the point where only a tube compressor or vintage board is acceptable for their projects. They write about reducing reflections in the control room and building baffles and bass traps, and the subtle differences between mixing to analog and mixing to digital, because this is the level on which they operate professionally, every day. Simply put, they're out of touch with the masses—musicians who still haven't mastered the basics of getting a good sound, who can't afford to upgrade to the best, and who must make do with a bunch of strange and ill-matching gear they've pieced together over the years.

I have good news for you: Contrary to the newer/faster/better culture that exists among pro engineers and the musical-equipment manufacturing industry, you *can* record a really good-sounding CD with minimal tools. All you need are a few key pieces of inexpensive gear, knowledge of a handful of important concepts, and some experience learning to hear what does and doesn't sound good. Yes, there is a limit to what you can do with obsolete studio equipment, and yes, once you've reached those limits, you can improve your recording potential by upgrading. But in my 14 years as a music-magazine editor listening to reader-submitted solo recording projects, I have learned that the vast majority of musicians haven't come close to this point. Instead, they've bought into the hype that maybe with one more gadget, with just a few more thousands of dollars spent, they'll finally achieve the polished sound that professionals get—because, hey, pros use only the best gear in only the best acoustical spaces money can buy. But it's all a huge lie, fabricated to get you to spend your money. Look at it this way: The best-stocked kitchen with the most professional pots and pans won't magically turn you into a brilliant chef. You need to learn the basics of the craft first. And even though I'm not much of a cook, I'd swear that if I knew what I was doing, I could whip up one hell of a soufflé with 20 bucks' worth of thrift-store pots and pans and run-of-the-mill ingredients from a discount supermarket.

That's exactly what *Guerrilla Home Recording* is about: getting you to the point where you can record great-sounding songs using more or less the gear you already have. This book takes a different approach to home recording: It focuses on *sound* first, with gear taking a distant second place. You'll see very few mentions of specific equipment brands and models in this book. I even treat the multitrack recorder as a generic "black box" with input and output jacks, because let's face it, whether you record on cassette 4-track, ADAT, or Pro Tools, the sounds going in—and the sounds you want to come out—are more or less the same regardless.

Guerrilla Home Recording doesn't assume you know anything about the science of sound or recording technology. In fact, I'd like you to forget everything you've read about recording. I start with the very basics, and I tell you what you need to know—and *only* what you need to know. I break down the recording process into the management of three simple "dimensions of sound": dynamics, frequency content, and pan position. If you can properly manage these three properties for each sound you record in a song, and you mix the song with all of these properties in mind, you will make a recording that will dazzle all but the most critical listeners.

You and your studio have the potential to create music that most people, including most musicians, will judge as sounding thoroughly professional—and you don't have to spend a fortune on gear or a ton of time reconstructing your space. You just have to read this book.

Chapter 1

What Is Guerrilla Home Recording?

I'm not a big-name record producer or well-known engineer, and I'm not even a famous musician. I'm just a guy who records his own music at home in his spare time. So why am I writing a book about recording? Well, over the course of the last 20 years or so I've gotten pretty good at it, even though I've always had to make do with a meager budget, both time-wise and money-wise. Plus, as an avid student of home-recording techniques, I've devoured dozens of books and articles on the subject, both good and bad. Along the way I've either picked up or invented my own set of techniques for getting the most sound out of a little studio. So I decided to put it all together in a new method for home-studio owners, which I call Guerrilla Home Recording.

To help explain what Guerrilla Home Recording is, I'll tell you a story about how the term came about. In 1990 I was having dinner with Richard Leeds, then the art director of *Keyboard* magazine and later *Guitar Player*. Rich, a home recordist himself, was interested in knowing how I got a certain drum sound on one of my songs without using live drums. At the time I didn't own a sampler; I had one cheap drum machine (an Alesis HR-16), a Tascam 38 analog ½" 8-track, and a Yamaha SPX90 multieffect. I explained that I put together the drum pattern on the HR-16, used the drum machine to record sync code onto the tape, and then individually laid down one track per drum sound—each of which I had recorded (from LP records) into the SPX90's one-half-second of sample memory. I'd make one tape pass per drum sound, feeding the HR-16's audio out into the SPX90's audio in to trigger each sample at the appropriate times. Once I had laid down the kick, snare, hi-hat, and maybe a tom or two, I mixed the tracks—each one EQed properly, along with cymbals and other sounds coming out of the HR-16 in real time, and perhaps a gated reverb on the snare, again courtesy of the SPX90—and recorded the stereo blend onto two of the Tascam 38's open tracks. The result was a stereo submix of drums plus reverb, with six tracks available for other instruments. I didn't think this process was particularly innovative or special; I was just making do with the very limited gear I had, using a few creative ideas to get the best possible sound. But Rich was impressed. He suggested that I write an article on "guerrilla recording techniques" for *Keyboard.* I never did pitch the idea to his magazine (a few years later I did write a recording column for *Bass Player*)—but the term "Guerrilla Home Recording" has stuck with me ever since. It's what I do, and it's what I think every home recordist working on the cheap should do.

The *American Heritage Dictionary* defines a guerrilla as "a member of an irregular military force operating usually in small, independent groups capable of great speed and mobility." As unsigned musicians, we may not be military, but we are irregular, we're independent (for now), and, if we know what we're doing, we're capable of recording good music at great speed. Guerrilla warfare subverts a traditional military force in a low-budget, underhanded way: making the greatest impact with the fewest resources. As history has proved, guerrilla warfare can be highly effective under certain conditions. In coming years I'd love to see Guerrilla Home Recording musicians deliver the same kind of impact on the music world, by creating a lot of great-sounding music without relying on the industry's traditional, slow-to-react infrastructure. That's what this book is about. A revolution is afoot—musicians of the world, unite!

Get Over Yourself

Another tale: Sometime around 1994, I found myself in a modest project studio recording a demo for my band, Pillars Of Jeleaux. I was about to lay down a bass track when I noticed that I was going straight to tape, with no compression or any other processing on my sound. I asked the engineer why. "We'll compress you in the mix," he smirked in his condescending, self-impressed manner. "That's the way the pros do it!" The demo ended up sounding horrible (we never used it), and "that's the way the pros do it!" became an inside joke among my bandmates. The engineer in question was a classic wannabe: He was stuck on using traditional, "pro" recording techniques in his small facility, and the end result was a very unprofessional sound.

Although it's often said that there are no rules in recording, the first rule of Guerrilla Home Recording is: *Get over yourself.* You've probably already read way too many interviews, trade-magazine articles, or recording books for your own good. And if you've spent time in a really good pro studio, the place's glamour may have rubbed off on you, turning you into a wannabe as well. You have to get over this. Until you can afford to sink a million dollars into your facility, build acoustically treated performance and control rooms, and have a mic collection, console, and racks of outboard gear to match, you're like me: a musician who records his or her own music. That's not to say your goal should be anything less than a record that sounds 100 percent professional. It just means: Don't delude yourself along the way.

Consider the history of the recording studio. When the Beatles made *Please Please Me* in 1962, the folks working at Abbey Road Studios looked more like NASA engineers than Butch Vig or Bill Laswell. They wore white lab coats. They analyzed. They calibrated. To them, recording was a precise electrical- and acoustical-engineering process that required a serious background in calculus and physics. And even though most engineers today no longer look like Ed Harris in *Apollo 13*, the engineering culture still exists. (They are called engineers, after all.) This is fine in a pro studio—when you're in charge of a $500,000 mixing console, it helps to know what a positive feedback loop is. But this engineering culture has trickled down to project-studio wannabes as well as the authors of recording books and articles, and in my opinion that's not a good thing.

It's easy to take something you've read in a recording article as gospel, especially if it was written by someone with impressive credentials. But realize that many of these people live in a different world than we do. They can do things the traditional, "serious" way, because they have the resources. We home recordists, though, might have to perform a few tricks and pull a few strings to get the same great sounds. It might mean using a stomp box as a signal splitter, or using that circa-1980 curlycue Radio Shack "guitar cable" for an effect send because you're out of good cables, or not cleaning your tape heads one day because you've got an idea for a drum sound that needs to go down. The engineering establishment would scoff at such practices—that's *not* the way the pros do it! They'd like you to think the only real way to get a good sound is by using their skills and a facility that charges $150 per hour. But attitudes are changing—even among top musicians, many of whom have started recording their own "pro" tracks at home, without attending engineering school.

Bottom line: Believe in yourself. Trust that with experience, ear training, forethought, and, most important, an approach that acknowledges your studio's limitations, you *can* make music that for all intents and purposes sounds every bit as good as a professional studio recording. And you don't have to pretend you're a pro to do it.

Mix As You Go

In professional recording, it's standard practice to lay down all of the tracks, and then, at a later date, to "wipe" (reset) the mixing board and start mixing the song from scratch. That's fine if the board has endless channels as well as tons of sends and returns (and perhaps automation), the studio has a truckload of outboard gear, and the mixing engineer's ears are so golden he can throw together a sweet-sounding mix in 90 seconds or less. But we need to take a different approach. Part of Guerrilla Home Recording involves mixing as you go—making sure the instruments that are already down are balanced and sound right before adding the next instrument, and constantly tweaking levels and EQs as you listen to playbacks. In the perfect scenario, you could start running a mixdown five minutes after putting down your last track and be done with the song ten minutes later. That probably won't actually happen, but it's something to shoot for.

Why is mixing-as-you-go better than starting a mix from scratch, with fresh ears? The main reason is that with our limited resources, we Guerrilla recordists have to make calculated compromises during the recording process. Say, for example, you wanted to add a bit of short, dark-sounding reverb to the kick and snare drum. But you have only one reverb unit, and at some point you read that it isn't wise to paint yourself into a corner by "printing effects" (recording them along with the track). So rather than adding the reverb while you're recording the drum tracks to tape, you record the drums dry, with the intent that during mixdown you'll use a bit of the same reverb on the drums that you're using on the vocals. The problem with this approach is it results in a flatter sound. In the final mix, the vocals and drums don't live in their own unique reverb spaces; they're kind of mashed together. Plus, since both the drums and vocals are feeding into the reverb together, the resulting reverb sound is muddier than if the vocals went through the reverb's complex mathematical signal-processing operations by themselves.

To use another example, consider the project-studio situation I mentioned earlier. I was expecting to send my bass through a compressor before hitting tape (because that's what I did at home), but the engineer wanted to compress later. If my bass line went in compressed, from that point on it would be easier to get guitar, keyboard, and vocal sounds that fit really well with my bass sound, because my bass sound would be more representative of my sound in the final mixdown. If the engineer did have "golden ears" and therefore knew exactly what my bass would sound like post-compression, no problem. If I were a better bassist who could supply more even dynamics just with my performance skills, that would have helped as well. And if the engineer had the resources to go all the way with the big-studio approach, he might have recorded several separate bass tracks (say, one clean direct, one clean miked-amp, and one distorted miked-amp track), allowing for a lot more flexibility come mixdown time. But he wasn't; his ears were mediocre, and he was recording one overly woofy direct track with levels that were fluctuating all over the place—which didn't exactly inspire brilliant playing on my part, I might add.

These are only a couple of examples. The point is, you will maximize your sound if you plan things so that the final mixdown is as simple as possible, with minimal added effects, EQ tweaks, and level changes. When you lay down a track and then listen back, what you hear should sound as close as possible to an excellent final mix, minus the tracks you have yet to record. Sure, you give up some flexibility this way (if you "print" the reverb with the drums, you won't be able to reduce the reverb later), and it requires you to make some guesses. But these are the kinds of compromises you need to make in Guerrilla Home Recording.

Sample Those Drums

Home recordists can record live drums—plenty do. But the drum sound is perhaps a song's most sonically critical element, the part most likely to scream "amateur recording!" to the casual listener. Also, recording live drums introduces a slew of variables into the process. It's just very hard to do well. Therefore, I recommend using sampled drums. This can mean anything from using sounds straight out of a drum machine, to employing a high-capacity sampler and an extensive library of custom-built drum kit samples on CD-ROM. If you're a non-drummer or don't have a drummer friend, this is a good thing: With this method it's very possible to fool people into thinking you *do* play the drums. If you are a drummer, don't feel threatened. I'm not advocating just setting up a two-bar pattern and having your drum machine churn out an endless stock "boom-chuck" sound (although, of course, that can work well in certain musical styles). I do advocate *playing* drum parts, in real time, recording your performance via MIDI rather than audio. In Chapter 8 I'll discuss in detail how to do that. It's just that with today's technology, from a purely sonic point of view, it's much easier to get impressive results by creating your drum sounds electronically than using the traditional method of miking a drum kit. And if you do your drum tracks well, most people will have no idea that you never put sticks to real drums while creating your music.

Don't Sweat Acoustics

Live drums tend to sound amateurish unless recorded by an engineer with years of drum-miking experience. But also very important is the room they're recorded in. Sure, Rick Rubin captured great drum sounds on the Red Hot Chili Peppers' classic *Blood Sugar Sex Magik* with only four mics—but he also had the incredible rooms of a Hollywood Hills mansion to do it in. In the Guerrilla studio, the room is irrelevant—you should be able to move your gear into a gymnasium or a VW bus and still get just about the same sound. Our approach involves avoiding the problems acoustics can create. In addition to using sampled drums, this includes close-miking amps (with most ambience supplied by digital processors), and using near-field monitors at low volume levels to listen to your mixes. (More on how to do these things later.) Entire books have been written on how to perfect a control room's acoustics, but you probably don't have the time, money, or interest to bother with these details. That's okay—it'll be our secret.

Headphones Are Your Microscope

Among the pros, headphones have kind of a bad reputation; they're useful for musicians to hear the music they're recording to, but not a lot else. Me, I love a good pair of headphones. When I put on a set of great "cans," I know I'm hearing a perfect stereo image with no coloration from the room I'm in. Using the same pair of phones, a mix sounds identical whether I'm in my studio, the living room, outside—whatever. Even more important, good headphones allow you to hear subtleties and details of a mix that might be audible only with the best studio monitors, a well-tuned room, and a position at the "sweet spot" between the speakers. They're perfect for studying the craft of your favorite producers—how sounds move around the stereo field, how reverbs are brought up and back, how vocals are layered, and so on. On headphones, it's easy to hear if a sound is breaking up the wrong way, if there's a little unwanted click bleeding through on a track, or anything else that requires a really close listen. With practice, you can also get good at subtle sound-shaping on a pair of headphones you know well. When you want to hear the big picture, real speakers are better—but to zoom in close, grab the headphones. You'll be glad you did.

Sound-On-Sound & Bouncing

You might already use the techniques of sound-on-sound and bouncing. If you don't, and your recording system has a limited number of tracks, you should.

Sound-on-sound refers to recording a track, and then playing back that track while mixing in a new sound source, and recording the blend of the original track and the new sound. Many recordists-to-be got their first taste of "multitrack" recording this way: Perhaps they recorded an acoustic guitar and vocal on a cassette deck, and then they mixed in a harmony vocal and perhaps another guitar part as they transferred the sound onto another cassette deck. This can be done again and again to build up the "tracks," but of course there are disadvantages. In addition to the various performances being forever intertwined and inseparable, the sound of the original performances deteriorates with each pass—particularly when using analog tape, and most of all when using cassette tape. You can get away with a certain amount of sonic deterioration, let's say if you and a few friends are trying to create the sound of a couple dozen people partying for the background of a song, but you wouldn't want to build an important track (such as a layered lead vocal) this way. It would probably just sound bad.

Real sound-on-sound. Back in my cassette 4-track days, I actually used a technique that was a more literal form of sound-on-sound: I would lay down a track, and then I would *literally* lay down a little piece of masking tape over the 4-track deck's erase head. With the erase head disabled, I could lay new performances of the same part on the same

LOOK ■ OUT!

Bouncing & Track Feedback

On analog tape machines, sometimes you get unexpected howling electronic feedback when you're trying to bounce tracks. What's going on here? This often happens when one of the tape tracks you're bouncing *to* is physically adjacent to one of the tracks you're bouncing *from.* To the tape machine's record head, the source and destination tracks are just too close for comfort. The best solution is to leave a "guard track" between your source tracks and your bounce tracks, and always bounce to a track or tracks on the edge of the tape, not in the middle. So, if you plan to bounce drums to tracks 7 and 8, try to leave track 6 empty and use only tracks 1 through 5. Obviously on a 4-track this is impractical, and even on an 8-track it may not leave you enough tracks. Workaround: Put the quietest instrument—like the hi-hat in a drum arrangement—on the border track, and record it at full volume; when you turn down this track during the bounce, it'll be less likely to feed back. Another workaround when bouncing to stereo is to pan the instrument on the border track to the opposite direction of its neighboring bounce track. For example, if track 6 is a shaker and track 7 is for the left side of the bounced drums, keep the shaker panned toward the right during the bounce. That way, very little of the audio from track 6 will be pumped onto track 7, reducing the chance of feedback.

track, building it up in layers. How did it sound? Not great; with each pass, the record head messed with the already-recorded tracks somewhat. It wasn't a very good technique, but I got some interesting effects nonetheless, and it was easy to do.

Bouncing is a slightly more sophisticated version of sound-on-sound. Bouncing, or reducing as British engineers call it, means making a preliminary mix of existing tracks in order to free up new tracks. When I described my old technique of recording a different drum sound on each track and then mixing the drums to stereo on two tracks, that was an example of bouncing. The obvious challenge is to get the bounce mix right; if you bounce the drums to stereo and then you can't hear the kick drum after the bass line goes on, you can't go back and turn it up. (You could add some low end to the mixed drums, but that might just make the kick sound woofy and flabby, not necessarily more audible.) Bouncing works better on 8-track formats and higher, because if you're recording on 4-track, you can only bounce three tracks onto one mono track, or two mono tracks onto two tracks in stereo. On an 8-track, though, you can bounce seven tracks to one mono, or six tracks to two stereo (see Fig. 1).

Combining bouncing with sound-on-sound. If you're bouncing your drums to stereo and you anticipate a track shortage later on, you can take the opportunity to lay a bass line into the drum mix while you're bouncing the tracks. One advantage here is you'll get to hear what the bass and drums sound like together—if the bass is obscuring the kick, you can turn up or EQ the kick's sound, and bounce again while laying down another bass-line take. This is exactly what I used to do when I recorded

> GUERRILLA TACTIC
> ### *Big-Time Bouncing*
>
> Think bouncing is just for home recordists on a budget? Think again. The Beatles' *Sgt. Pepper's Lonely Hearts Club Band*, considered by many to be the greatest recording achievement of all time, was famously made on a 4-track machine using numerous well-planned bounces. Same for the Beach Boys' 1966 classic *Pet Sounds*. Queen achieved its hugely layered, operatic vocal arrangements on songs like "Bohemian Rhapsody" by filling tracks with a series of bounced vocal performances. Even today, on analog 24-track machines, bouncing allows producers to get huge masses of sound without commandeering all of the tape's tracks.

on cassette 4-track. Sometimes I also wanted to add a mono or stereo sound that didn't need to be synced to the music, like a long sound effect or party noise, so I'd cue that up on a cassette player and "hot roll" (let the tape run free) the non-synced track into the mixer along with the drums and the bass line I was playing. The result: Two tracks containing a good stereo drum mix (maybe with reverb on the snare), a bass line, and sound effects—with two tracks open for more.

Now add keyboards. Just before I got my 8-track machine and I was getting *really* desperate for tracks, I devised another trick. I would get the drum machine to play a simple keyboard part. Here's how: I'd assign a MIDI note to each of the unused drum-machine sounds, turn down the audio for those sounds, assign those sounds to a MIDI channel different from the ones being used for drums, and then connect the drum machine's MIDI OUT jack to a cheap keyboard's MIDI IN (see Fig. 2). With the keyboard set to receive the proper MIDI channel, the drum machine was able to

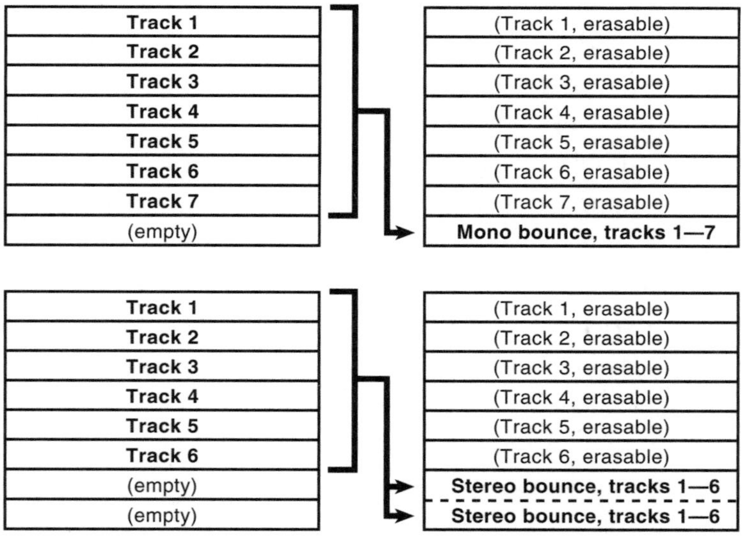

Fig. 1 Bouncing seven tracks to one mono (top), or six tracks to stereo (bottom).

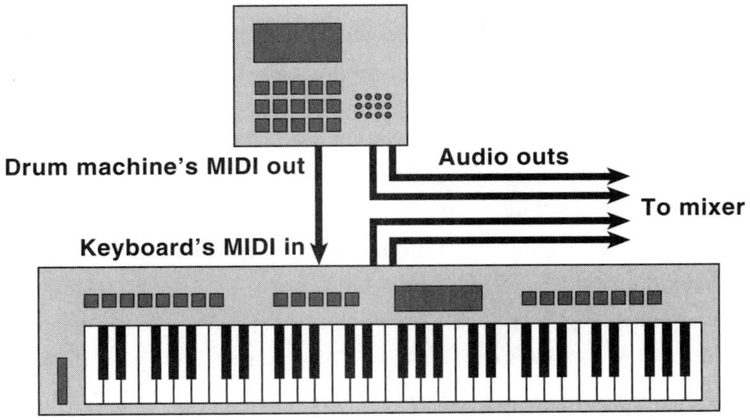

Fig. 2 Using a drum machine to "play" a simple keyboard part.

"play" the keyboard (albeit in a very limited, rudimentary way). I'd then mix everything together, maybe along with a bass line, and record all of it in stereo onto two first-generation tracks.

As you might imagine, when things get this complicated, you can easily run out of channels on your mixing board—something I experienced all too often. So how did I get it done? Any way I could, that's how! I believe I started with a 6-channel mixer, and when I ran out of channels, I started feeding signals into the board's EFFECT RETURN and AUX IN jacks. When I ran out of channels again, I found a bizarre 6-channel mixer for sale in the newspaper; it had no EQ or pan pots and looked like something out of a low-budget '50s audiology lab. Not exactly state of the art—but it got the job done. My point? As long as you get the sounds together and don't screw them up *too* much along the way, it doesn't matter if you use Y cables, stomp boxes, or your answering machine to do it. You just get it done. *That's* Guerrilla Home Recording.

Virtual Tracks

If you're recording with a fixed number of tracks and you're employing MIDI to "play" drum and keyboard parts, using *virtual tracks* is one of the best ways to expand your recording potential. Virtual tracks consist of performances where only the MIDI information is recorded, not the audio. Unless your system allows you to record both audio and MIDI (as most digital multitrack systems do), you'll first need to record a sync tone, which is a single track of audio that contains information about timing. This sync tone tells your MIDI gear when to start running, and how fast to run. Get it? On an 8-track deck, for instance, you can program drum machine patterns for your song, and then use the drum machine to lay down a sync tone on track 8. The sound of the sync tone can then drive (or "slave") the drum machine when you play the tape

Sync Tone Basics

All the gory details of sync tones are beyond the scope of this book, but briefly, the two most useful sync tones are *SMPTE timecode* (SMPTE stands for the Society of Motion Picture & Television Engineers) and *Smart FSK* (Frequency-Shift Keying). SMPTE timecode, the industry-standard sync tone, carries imbedded information about time, in the units of hours, minutes, seconds, and frames (as in video and film images). You'll probably need some kind of MIDI interface to create and read SMPTE and communicate it to your MIDI gear. Smart FSK, on the other hand, can often be created and read directly by drum machines and hardware sequencers without an interface. Rather than carrying time information, Smart FSK conveys units of bars and beats, along with where-are-we-in-the-song information called Song Position Pointer. The downside to Smart FSK is that once you decide on a song's tempo and length and lay down the sync tone, you're locked in. With SMPTE timecode, you can do things like extend the song or change meters, even after all of the audio tracks are down.

back, which means you can then fill tracks 1 through 7 with acoustic-instrument performances that remain in lockstep with the drums (see Fig. 3). Not only does this method leave you the option of changing the drum pattern, drum mix, and drum sounds right up until mixdown, the audio of the drums (and any other MIDI gear you might be slaving with the sync tone) is first-generation fresh when the mix goes to tape or disk. Before this point the MIDI gear's audio was never recorded—it was only "virtually recorded." (Note: Don't confuse this original definition of virtual tracks with another one now commonly applied to standalone digital recorders. A digital recorder may allow you to play back only eight tracks at a time but may have

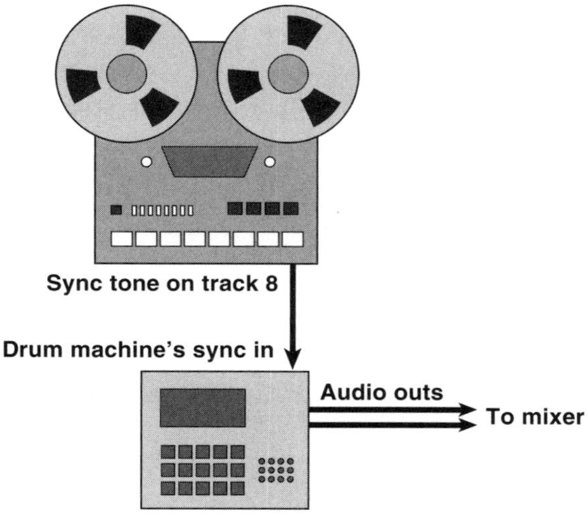

Fig. 3 Using a sync tone to drive a drum machine as a "virtual track."

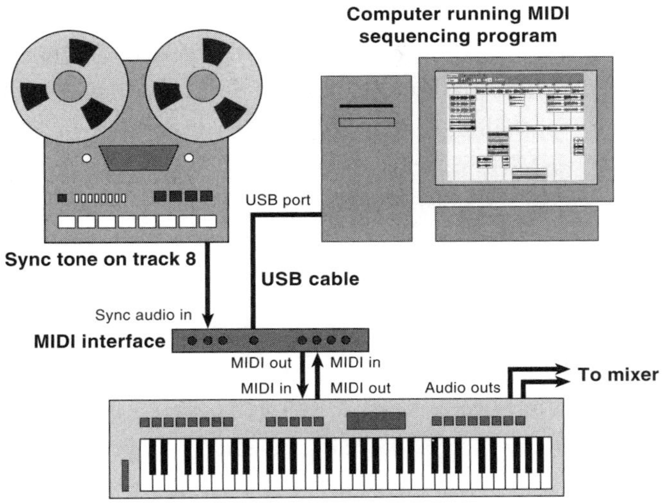

Fig. 4 Using a MIDI sequencing program to drive a drum machine and keyboard as virtual tracks.

dozens more virtual tracks, or alternate takes, available on disk to swap out. This kind of virtual tracking is a powerful feature—but so is the original definition of slaving MIDI gear to a recorded sync tone.)

Recording a sync tone is unnecessary on many of today's standalone digital recorders, which can create or read SMPTE timecode without using up one of the audio tracks. This is an obvious advantage, as an 8-track digital deck will allow you to record a full eight tracks of audio, and it will slave your MIDI gear.

Sequence this. Whether you're recording on a digital standalone machine or on tape, you can really expand your potential by incorporating a software MIDI sequencing program, slaved to the sync tone, into your setup (see Fig. 4). For this system you will need to use SMPTE timecode and a MIDI interface. Here's how it works: In the software program, you write your arrangement of a song's MIDI instruments: drums, keyboards, and perhaps a sampler. When you play this sequence on the computer, the

LOOK ■ OUT!

SMPTE From The Devil

As with bouncing, on analog formats it helps to put your sync tone on an edge track, with an unused "guard track" between it and those tracks used for actual audio. Otherwise, the sync tone can bleed onto the next track—and believe me, there's nothing musical about an audible sync tone. Also, certain audio signals on adjacent tracks can mess with a sync tone, particularly if they have a lot of sharp attacks, thereby potentially compromising your song's timing. If a guard track isn't feasible, at least use the track for an audio signal that will be at low level in the mixdown (to help prevent sync tone from bleeding over), and don't record the border track's audio at too high a level—record it at only a moderate level to reduce the chance of the signal contaminating the sync tone.

software "plays" the arrangement you just made by sending MIDI information to the various MIDI instruments. When you're ready to start laying down audio, you "stripe" an edge track with SMPTE timecode. (You probably won't need to stripe SMPTE on a digital standalone machine.) Alternatively, and usually a better option, you can stripe the entire length of tape with a single SMPTE track ahead of time, and specify, in each song's sequence file, when (in SMPTE terms) the song begins. Now you can set the sequence program to sync mode, roll your recording medium, and *voilà*—the program magically "chases" and synchronizes with your tape or digital machine. When you stop the recording medium, the sequencer program stops. You can even start in the middle of the song and the program will figure out where you are and catch up. It's quite thrilling the first time you experience this, especially if you've been held captive by only four or eight rigid audio tracks for a while.

Going Digital

There's an awful lot you can do with an analog system and a heap of cagey creativity. But nothing will supercharge your Guerrilla Home Recording power more than going digital. Sure, there are naysayers who insist analog sounds better and always will. That may or may not be true—but forget about them. The level of sonic distinction between a "warm" analog recording and a "sterile" digital one is so fine, it's not even worth talking about here. Suffice it to say that unless you're recording on some ancient 8-bit medium or overloading your system with nasty digital clipping, as far as you're concerned, *no one will know* what medium you're using. It won't make the difference between getting signed or not getting signed, or getting that coveted gig at the local 1,000-seat club. The benefits far outweigh the possible downsides. So there.

Digital Bouncing

Even though digital systems are generally powerful, you can still run out of tracks. Here's where bouncing can come in handy. By bouncing, say, 12 background-vocal tracks down to two, the machine doesn't have to work as hard to output the same mass of sound. And with digital recording, you can always keep the original performances on disk, ready to be called up again should you need to adjust the bounce's mix or EQ.

There are times when bouncing is useful even when you aren't going from a large number of tracks to a small one. I recently had a situation where I had made many rapid-fire edits to a track—too many for my computer to handle while it was dealing with all of the other audio, which caused it to lock up each time the sequencer got to that section of the song. So I soloed the troublesome track and simply bounced it to another track. Whereas the audio previously consisted of many tiny audio clips edited together (the hard drive had only a few hundredths of a second to find each of them), the bounced audio consisted of a single, continuous audio file—same sound, but much easier for the computer to handle. End of lock-ups.

A few of the plusses of digital recording:

Editing capability. In my analog days I used to have fun splicing together sections of tape and "flying in" parts off a DAT machine when I decided to rearrange a song late in the game. But I'm really glad those days are gone. When you're recording digitally, it can take mere seconds to double the length of a verse or tack the intro back onto the end of a song. These are things most analog recordists probably wouldn't even consider as options. Recording digitally gives you options—tons of them.

Cost. A reel of tape for an analog 8-track can cost $50. The same amount of audio, recorded digitally, can fit onto two CD-R discs, at a cost of about 50 cents. Case closed.

No erasing required. Since digital storage is so cheap, you almost never have to erase a digital track. That guitar solo might have been *almost* perfect—but do you really want to record over it in the hope that you'll nail the next take? These are the kinds of decisions you often have to make on analog. On a digital system, you can just mute that near-perfect take and try again—and keep on trying until you do nail it.

Track flexibility. On a digital system, the number of tracks you can record is limited by the speed of your computer's processor, its memory (RAM), and your hard drive's speed—so the system doesn't have a fixed number of tracks like an analog machine. I have had as many as 15 audio tracks (plus many more virtual tracks) playing at once on a system that's now about five years old, without it missing a beat. Perhaps even more important, even if you don't plan on having a lot of tracks playing back at once, the *total* number of tracks a song can have on a digital system is virtually limitless. You can have eight tracks going during a verse, and if you want entirely different sounds for the chorus, eight different tracks can start playing when the chorus begins (see Fig. 5). On an analog machine, trying to get that same verse-chorus

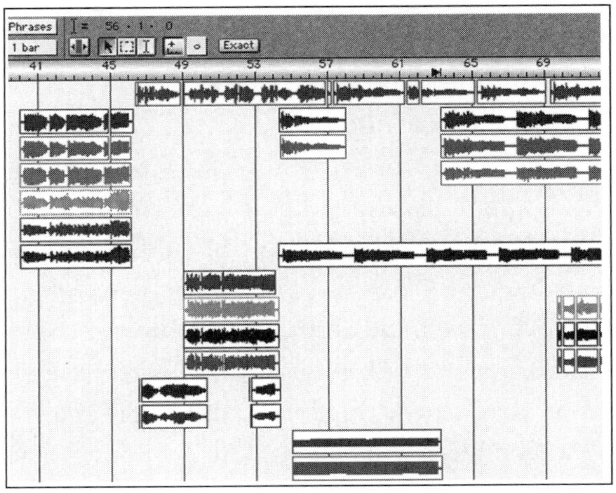

Fig. 5 Even if a digital system can play only eight tracks at once, its total number of tracks can be much higher.

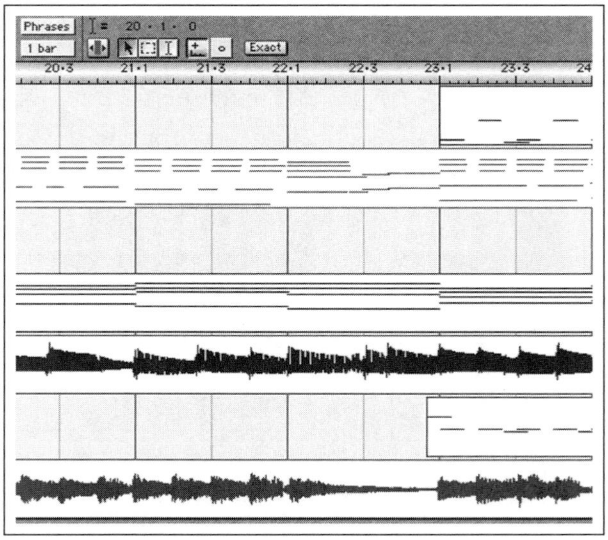

Fig. 6 MIDI tracks (top) and audio tracks (bottom) synced together in a digital recording program.

transition would make for a very tricky mix—you might have to mix the song in sections and edit together the parts later. (This technique is discussed in Chapter 10.) But if you're recording digitally, the transition can be both seamless and easy to accomplish. What more can you ask?

Digital doesn't degrade. I love listening to songs in progress over and over while I try to come up with ideas. But I hate the idea that with every pass of analog tape, a tiny amount of oxide sloughs off and the tape demagnetizes just a bit, making the sound just a tiny bit worse with each listen—not enough to hear, just enough to make me paranoid. With digital recording, you know that the 1,000th playback sounds *exactly* the same as the first playback. Just remember to back up your work; otherwise the current playback could be the last—forever.

Seamless integration of audio & MIDI. With an audio/MIDI digital recording program, your audio tracks lie side by side with your MIDI tracks (see Fig. 6), making it much easier to build up massive arrangements of virtual MIDI tracks, which you can then move around along with the audio tracks to your heart's desire. When you're slaving a MIDI sequencer or drum machine to analog tape, sometimes it seems that the planets need to be aligned in order for everything to work together. This is rarely the case with an integrated program; usually, either it works or it doesn't.

Automation, anyone? Pro recording studios often have consoles that memorize every move that was made during mixdown, allowing the producer and engineer to get very fine with their mixing moves, with the board automatically reproducing them time and time again. Even some of today's semi-pro boards have a certain amount of automation built in. But with a good digital recording program, full automation is part of the package. Incorporating "virtual console" windows that look like mixing

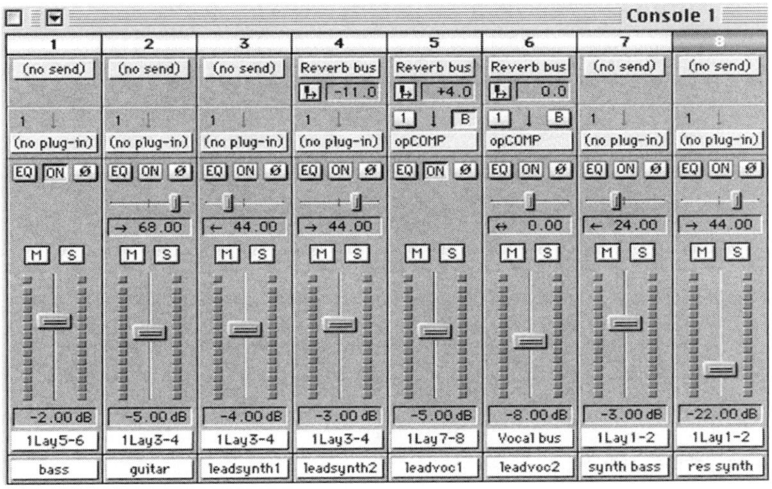

Fig. 7 A recording program's "virtual console" window allows you to automate mixdown moves.

boards (see Fig. 7), the programs let you click a track's RECORD button, play the sequence, and move a fader up and down. The next time you play the sequence, check it out—the onscreen fader moves all by itself. Many programs even allow you to automate EQ and effect-level changes. This capability works perfectly with the mix-as-you-go concept I discussed earlier.

Plan Ahead

You'll get a lot more mileage from your Guerrilla studio if you plan your course of action *before* you start a song. This isn't always possible; sometimes a song starts as a spontaneous idea, and you just want to start getting your ideas down without getting out graph paper and making a flow chart. And that's absolutely what you should do in this case; nothing can squelch a creative idea faster than having to tediously plan a step-by-step course of action. But if you *do* know exactly what a song will need—say, if you've already roughed out a quick sketch version, and now you want to polish the tune—sit down and plan it out. Planning is particularly important on analog formats, and extremely important on 4-track formats. Sure, you can throw a song together and hope for the best; this is how most people do it. But in Guerrilla Home Recording, where your goal is to get a pro sound, such forethought pays big dividends.

A key tool for session-planning is the *track strip*. A variation of the track sheet familiar in pro studios, a track strip is like a graph, with tracks indicated along one axis and time along the other axis. On a track strip you plan the order each instrument will go down in, on which tracks, also indicating steps like bounces and sound-on-sound passes. Fig. 8 shows an example of a track strip for a complex session on analog 8-track. A track strip allows you to see into the future and stop conflicts and

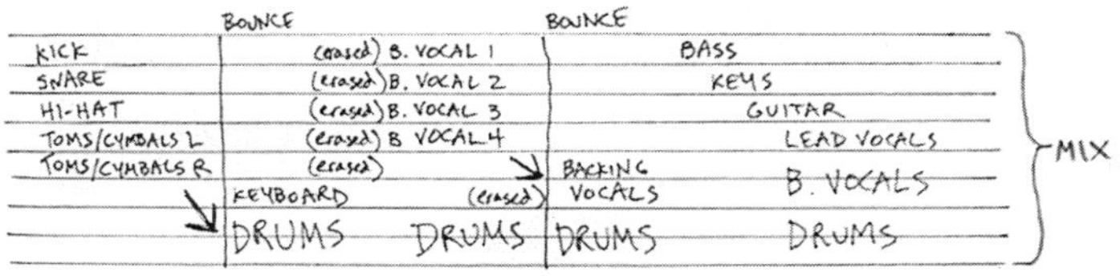

Fig. 8 A track strip can help in planning a complex course of action.

other problems before they occur. You may learn that your intended arrangement won't be possible if you don't have a friend play shaker while you play acoustic guitar, for instance, and you'll learn this before you need to compromise some other aspect of your recording in order to realize your vision for the song.

Document Your Work

You've probably experienced getting the "perfect" mix of a song, only days later deciding that something needs to be louder or quieter in the mix. So maybe you went back and banged out another mix. Often this is easy enough, but sometimes the mix is so complex you'd rather just live with a less-than-perfect mix than try to improve upon it.

If a mix is complex, document it immediately afterward, while it's still fresh in your mind. Write down all the fader and EQ settings, including all special moves to be made during the course of the song. Don't forget to note all effect send and return levels, as well as the master-fader output levels, and write down (or store) all of your effect parameters. If you have a digital camera, photograph the board with everything at its top-of-the-song position. You might even want to make a video of the mixdown. Who knows—if you come up with a song like Beck's "Loser" (which he recorded on analog 8-track), your footage might end up on a VH-1 special someday!

Essential Guerrilla Home Recording Tools

As you may have guessed, this book is not about trying to get you to upgrade to the latest, greatest gear. I believe that you can make a great recording using gear that's inexpensive or outdated; your ears and your approach are your most important tools. That said, though, there are a few pieces of hardware that I think are essential to creating a good recording:

At least two mics. You should have one decent dynamic mic and one decent condenser mic (see Chapter 3). By "decent," I just mean one that's designed for music, not dictation or some such thing. If it doesn't have a detachable cord, or if it has a built-in desk-stand or a little "mini" ⅛" plug, it's not worth using. Spend a hundred bucks on eBay for something a little better.

A mixing board. It doesn't need to be fancy or have dozens of channels, but you will need something that takes in signals of varying levels, allows you to shape them a bit, and blends them together.

Direct box. This will allow you to plug an electric guitar or bass straight into the mixer, without an amp, when you want a very clean sound. If you plug an instrument directly into a mixer's ¼" input jack, you'll get a sound, but not a good one. You need a direct box to record directly; that's all there is to it. Direct boxes are discussed in Chapter 3.

Compressor. This will give you much more control over levels. If you currently don't use a compressor, your recordings will improve markedly once you get one and learn to use it. Avoid the "easy to use" kind with just one or two knobs; these don't give you enough control. Look for one that at least allows you to set the threshold, ratio, and output levels—and be sure it has an LED or something that tells you when the compression is kicking in. Units without "compressor active" LEDs or meters are harder to use. Compressors are discussed in Chapters 3 and 4.

Expander. Often built into compressors (they're called compressor/expanders), an expander will greatly clean up your recording by eliminating hum and other noise when no signal is present. A "noise gate" is a heavy-handed type of expander; make sure you can at least set the expander's threshold and ratio parameters. Expanders are discussed in Chapters 3 and 4.

One good reverb. Since the room is irrelevant in the Guerrilla studio, you need a good reverb to create your room sounds. Digital reverbs vary from awful to great—and this isn't always proportionate to price. For instance, throughout this book I don't mention many specific pieces of gear, but I will say that the Yamaha SPX90 is a terrific old reverb that's still used in many pro studios. Introduced in the mid '80s and manufactured by the thousands, it can also perform other effects such as auto-pan, pitch change, and modulation effects. You can find SPX90s (and their later-model derivatives) for sale for as cheap as $100. More about reverbs and how to choose them can be found in Chapter 6.

One good pair of headphones. Since the Guerrilla studio room may be far from acoustically neutral and uncolored, you may want to do a lot of your tracking work through headphones. Some models being manufactured today for studio use are excellent—and in addition to being a necessary recording tool, good headphones are a great way to rediscover your favorite CDs. So invest a little money in a good pair.

The essential tools: A mixing board; compressor/ expander and reverb (top); direct box, condenser mic, and dynamic mic (left); and headphones (right).

CHAPTER 2

Principles Guerrilla Recordists Need To Know

Just about every recording book has a chapter like this—the one where you see diagrams of sine waves and graphs showing the sensitivity of the human ear to various frequencies, and so on. I'm going to take a slightly different approach and provide *only* information that's critical to understanding recording from a Guerrilla perspective. I'll try not to make your eyes glaze over; rather than paraphrasing stuff from a physics textbook, I'll try to relate everything to the music you hear and the music you make, or want to make.

I hope you won't skip over this chapter. It's important to get a firm grounding in the principles behind sound and capturing sound. Otherwise, you might find yourself flailing away aimlessly in your studio, fingers crossed as you hope to recreate the sounds you hear in your head. Understanding the important principles will also help you create Guerrilla Home Recording tricks of your own. After all, anyone can follow a set of directions, but understanding the principles *behind* those directions can make following them—and perhaps even more important, deviating from them—easier and more effective. Look at it this way: You can do a decent job of brushing your teeth by just doing it the way you've seen everyone else brush. But if you really want to keep your teeth clean, you'll pay attention to the dental hygienist's little lectures. You'll understand that plaque and tartar build up at the gum line, and holding your brush at a certain angle and brushing in a certain way for a certain amount of time will maximize the removal of that stuff. If you should switch to an electric rotary toothbrush, you'll be able to apply your knowledge to this new tool with maximum benefits. Lame analogy? Perhaps, but at least I hope I convinced you to keep reading. (By the way, don't forget to floss.)

Basics Of Sound

All music consists of sound, and all sound consists of sound waves. These waves can be traveling through the air, as in the case of live music, or they can be fixed on a medium that stores these waves, as in the case of a CD. Our job is to be able to enable a transition between these two worlds: translating sound waves that are traveling through the air into those fixed onto tape or disc. That's all recording is.

Sound easy? Well, here's where it starts to get a bit more complicated. The human ear and brain are so unbelievably good at making another translation—turning sound waves in the air into a conscious perception of that sound—that they put to shame every man-made invention dealing with sound. You probably know what it's like to sit in a concert hall and listen to a live orchestra. In a perfect world, we'd be able to set up two microphones (one representing each ear) in the concert hall and record the sound, and the resulting recording would be a perfect recreation of what it's like to listen to the orchestra from that same position. But in reality, this isn't possible. Even the best microphone in the world is inadequate at replacing the human ear in this fashion, and even the best recording media, amplifiers, and loudspeakers have weaknesses that further weaken the ability of such a setup to perfectly recreate the concert-hall listening experience.

The art and science of recording, by sheer necessity, is a process of compromising and compensating for the inadequacies of recording and playback technologies. In the concert-hall example, this might mean carefully placing five, ten, or more mics closer to the orchestra, and blending the signals just right, perhaps shaping each mic's sound a bit and giving it the proper place in the stereo field. Even though two $10,000 mics out in the middle of the hall might create a great-sounding recording, using ten of these mics—along with some skill—would create a recording that sounds *more* like what you'd hear if you were actually sitting there in the middle of the hall. Strange, isn't it? That's the world of recording!

Okay, enough about concert halls and $10,000 mics. I'm just giving an example. Using cheap mics and blending "real" sounds with electronic sounds, not to mention tricky instruments like electric bass, makes things even tougher for the Guerrilla recordist. But you need to know what we recording musicians are up against.

Dynamic Range

You've probably heard of decibels (dB), used to describe degrees of loudness. You may have learned in high-school biology that 0dB (zero decibels) is defined as the threshold of human hearing, or the point where sound *just* begins to get audible. As sounds get louder, the dB number used to describe them goes up. I remember my biology teacher, Mr. Forbes, writing on the board what the other end of human hearing was: 120dB … THE WHO. From complete silence to concert-level rock & roll—these are the extremes between which live music exists. Degrees of loudness are referred to as *dynamics*, and the territory between the quietest and loudest extremes is called the *dynamic range*. Dynamic range expresses the difference between the extremes. Pain typically begins to set in at around 120dB, but ears are said to have a dynamic range that is greater than 120dB.

Here's where problems with recording start: None of our conventional recording/playback technologies can capture and reproduce sounds with such a broad dynamic range as that which exists in nature, or even at a Who show. That's because recording requires the use of electronics, and electronics inherently have some degree of background *noise*, a blanket of hiss caused largely by electrons moving at random. Think of the hiss that you hear when you turn up a stereo, even when nothing is playing. (Sometimes this is called the *noise floor*; like the floor of a room, you can't go any lower, try as you might.) This noise establishes the lower limit of recorded music's dynamic range, which is always less than 120dB; on a CD, the dynamic range is around 90dB.

Because of the technological limitations, when music is recorded, its dynamic range must be *squeezed* between the lower and upper dynamic limits of whatever medium is being recorded onto (see Fig. 1). Otherwise, the music might get either too loud to be recorded without distortion, or too quiet to be heard under the noise floor. Squeezing the dynamic range in this way is called *compression*; we'll discuss it in detail in Chapter 4.

There's another factor working against us: If you decide to record a song that makes dramatic use of the entire dynamic range—the proverbial whisper to a scream—the song won't be able to compete in the rock & roll world, where everyone else's songs sound much louder overall. Radio listeners might change the station because they can't hear a thing in certain places, and record-label execs will eject your

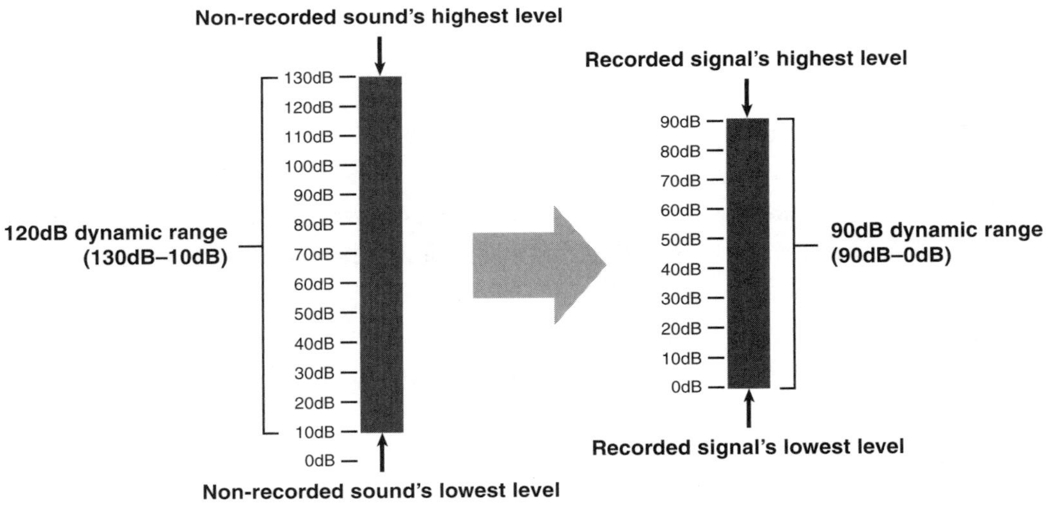

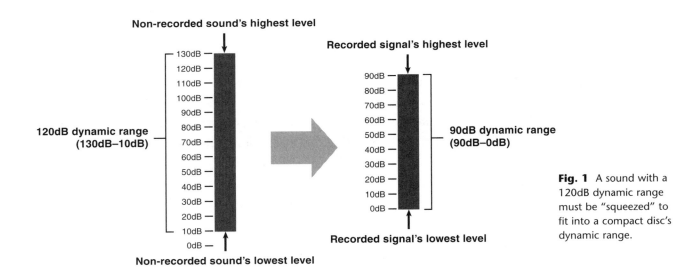

Fig. 1 A sound with a 120dB dynamic range must be "squeezed" to fit into a compact disc's dynamic range.

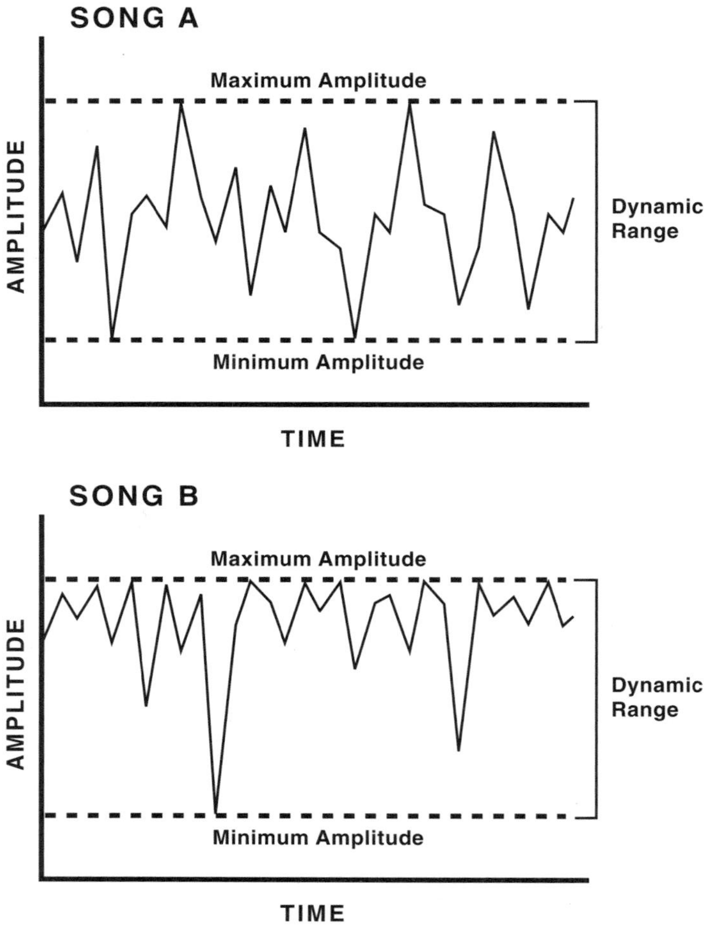

Fig. 2 Even though both songs have the same dynamic range, song B will sound louder overall—and therefore generally better—than song A.

CD. Your song will be left in the dust, simple as that. Let's look at a more subtle example: If the loudest moment of a song you've recorded is 20dB louder than the rest of the song, but the loudest moment of your arch-rival's song is only 5dB louder than the rest of his song, when played back, most of your arch-rival's song will sound 15dB louder than yours (see Fig. 2). And in rock & roll, that kind of relative quietness is no good. It makes music sound wimpy, and because human ears are less sensitive to bass frequencies and treble frequencies than they are to midrange frequencies, the bass and treble are the first frequencies to seem to disappear as music gets quieter. Result: Your arch-rival's song is big and rocking and thumping, while your song sounds little and tinny, with no definition.

Don't get discouraged. Your arch-rival may not know how to use things like moving faders and mastering to optimize his music's place in that restricted window of dynamic range. But armed with these techniques (which we'll discuss in Chapter 10), when you bust out your next song, you'll blow his out of the water.

What's The Frequency, Kenneth?

Our ears aren't perfect. We can't hear all sounds—like the sound of a dog whistle, or certain kinds of communications between elephants. The dog whistle is called *ultrasound*; it's too high for us to hear. The elephant rumblings are called *infrasound*; they're too low. Music, and anything else that's audible, consists of sounds with frequencies in between these ranges. People use terms like a "high voice" or "speaking low" all the time, though these phrases can be misleading. Highness and lowness can refer to either loudness or frequency, and it's an important distinction. Right now we're talking about frequency, or what many people call pitch (although that can be a little fuzzy as well).

With regard to sound waves, frequency refers to how many waves are reaching your ears per second. When a car with a subwoofer in the trunk goes by, you hear a *boom boom*; those are low frequencies, meaning the waves emanating from the car are long and widely spaced—maybe only about 30 of them pass per second. In this example, we say the sound has a frequency of 30 Hertz (Hz), "Hertz" being the unit that's used to describe frequency. But imagine that the same car's driver suddenly slams on the brakes to avoid something, causing the tires to screech. That's a high-frequency sound, at maybe something like 4,000Hz, or 4kHz (kilohertz). A lot more waves of this sound will be produced, and heard, per second than from the subwoofer.

You might notice, though, that even while the tires are screeching, you can still hear the subwoofer. (It's one loud subwoofer.) How can high-frequency and low-frequency sounds travel through your walls, and be heard by your ears, at the same time? Because a sound wave can carry many different frequencies at once. Think of it in terms of water: If you go to the ocean, you'll see waves crashing at a certain rate; this rate is the frequency of those waves. But throw a rock into one of those big waves, and you'll see a lot of smaller, closer-together waves propagating outward from where the rock hit the surface. The other waves are still going, only with smaller waves on top of them. This is exactly what happens with sound, too (see Figures 3a–3c).

In fact, almost all sound waves *do* consist of more than one frequency; the only sound that doesn't is a simple sine wave generated by a synthesizer. To get an idea of what a sine wave sounds like, pucker up and whistle—that sound is about as close to a sine wave as you can produce without a synth. Dull, muted sounds like these are said to have fewer *harmonics* or *overtones* than bright, complex sounds like brass instruments and cymbals. Harmonics or overtones are frequencies that are blended in

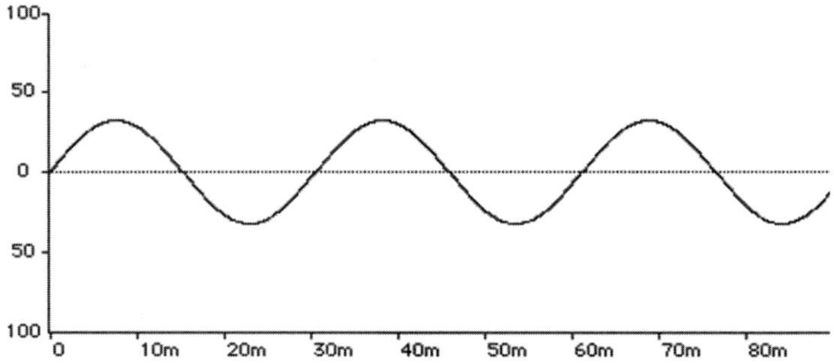

Fig. 3a A low-frequency sound (about 33Hz).

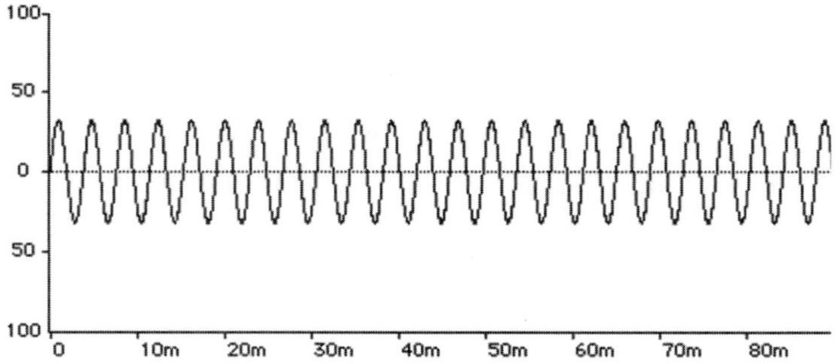

Fig. 3b A higher-frequency sound (about 250Hz).

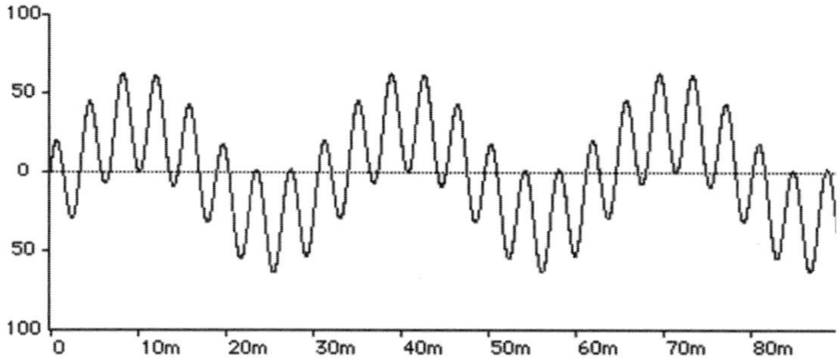

Fig. 3c A sound wave carrying both frequencies—what you'd get if you added Figures 3a and 3b together.

with the sound's lowest frequency, which is called the *fundamental.* The ratio of the amount of the various harmonics to the fundamental, as well as the frequency ratios between the fundamental and the harmonics, are largely responsible for determining a sound's character—a trumpet versus a clarinet, for example.

Often the frequencies of harmonics exist in whole-number multiples of the fundamental frequency; for instance, a sound might have a fundamental at 100Hz, with harmonics at 200Hz, 300Hz, and so on. These sounds tend to be tonal or pitched, like that of a woodwind or brass instrument. In some sounds, however, the harmonics are more randomly related to the fundamental. These tend to be more "clangy," like a bell or ride cymbal; in extreme cases the sounds are noisy, like a cymbal crash or woodblock. (Hear a cymbal crash and I bet it won't inspire you to think of any note in particular.) The noisiest sound of all, not surprisingly, is called just that: *noise.* "White noise," for example, is by definition a sound containing all frequencies mixed in equal proportions. (The term makes an analogy with white light, which comprises all of the colors of the spectrum.) White noise is a random wave; there's no repeating pattern, because a repeating pattern would suggest that it has a fundamental frequency, which it doesn't. But if you blended in, say, a 50Hz sine wave, the resulting wave would have elements of both the repeating 50Hz pattern and the random noise pattern. And if you listened to that sound wave, you'd hear a wash of noise with a 50Hz hum blended in.

The Frequency Spectrum

So far we haven't talked a lot about music, but here's where it starts getting a little more interesting—and useful. The area between infrasound and ultrasound is the spectrum of (audible) audio frequencies, which is analogous to the frequency spectrum of visible light, a.k.a. the colors of the rainbow. The most common numbers given for the ends of the audible frequency spectrum are 20Hz on the low end (anything lower is considered infrasound) and 20kHz on the upper end (anything higher is considered ultrasound). The majority of recorded sounds exist between these endpoints, from 20Hz to 20kHz, and the roles that different sounds play in this frequency spectrum—as well as the frequency *components* of individual sounds—is one of the most important concepts for a recording musician to grasp. The better a handle you have on this concept, the better equipped you'll be to make wise decisions when making recorded music.

It helps to look at the frequency spectrum not as a whole but in terms of frequency *bands*. Many people are familiar with the terms "bass" and "treble" from the controls on their stereo, but this is much too vague and broad for our purposes. In Guerrilla Home Recording we're better off thinking in terms of at least five bands: lows, low

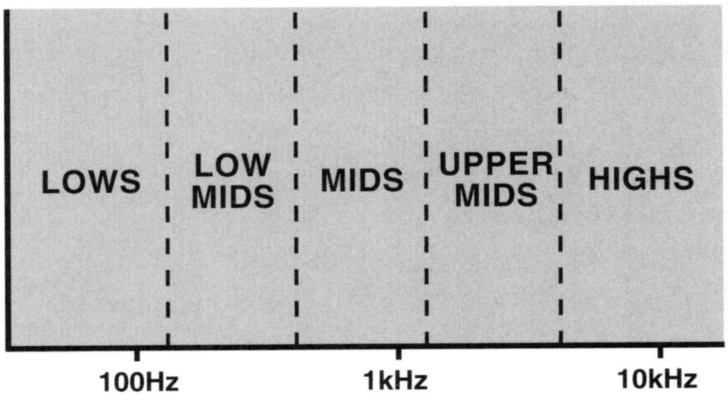

Fig. 4 The audible frequency spectrum is easier to understand if we break it into frequency bands.

mids, mids, upper mids, and highs (see Fig. 4). Engineers break this down further into as many as 31 bands, but let's start here for now. Here's the significance of each of these bands, and their approximate boundaries, with reference to a rock & roll recording:

Lows (roughly 20Hz–150Hz) are the domain of the beefy part of the kick-drum sound and the bass guitar's fundamental. A lot of lows tend to make a recording sound powerful, even if they appear only now and then. The downside of lows is that they can get in the way of other sounds if not managed properly, because the lower in frequency a sound is, the more efficiently it "masks" (covers up) other frequencies. Lows also carry the most energy of all frequency bands.

Low mids (150Hz–600Hz) are often where you'll find the frequencies that give the bass guitar its note definition, as well as the *oomph* of a snare drum or distorted electric guitar, and the "body" of an organ, electric piano, or acoustic guitar sound. Low mids give a recording a certain fullness. They're like the meaty or fibrous portion of a meal—without them, you're left feeling a little hungry. However, if overdone, low mids can muddy up a mix. Frequencies in the low and low-mid ranges (and within these ranges) don't get along very well with each other and are tough to keep in check, so too much energy down in this area can make a mix sound like a gooey, muddy mess.

Mids (600Hz–1.5kHz) are the frequencies that the ear is most sensitive to; they're the frequency spectrum's heartland. If you listen to music coming out of a small transistor-radio speaker, or particularly through a telephone, you're hearing mostly mids, because these systems aren't very good at reproducing low and high frequencies. Hold a paper-towel tube up to your ear and you'll hear what it sounds like when mid frequencies are emphasized. Because our hearing is naturally tuned to this band, these frequencies tend to catch our ear; not coincidentally, the fundamentals of many melodic instruments tend to be found here. (You might not be surprised to learn that the parts of the human voice important in discerning speech are heavy on the mids—it's why you can often hear what someone is saying through even a lousy cell-phone connection.) Lay the mids on too heavy, though, and your music will tend to "honk." The trick is keeping these frequencies in balance and proportion with the other bands.

Upper mids (1.5kHz–6kHz) affect what is commonly called "presence": If these frequencies are muted, a sound will tend to seem more distant, whereas if a sound has a lot of upper mids, it will seem more in-your-face. But pour on the upper mids too much and your song can be fatiguing to the ear, even irritating. Up in this range, we're hearing almost entirely harmonics, with few if any fundamentals (unless your song happens to have a triangle or piccolo part). Overly hyped upper mids are common in amateur recordings; an inexperienced producer might want each sound to pop out, so all of the upper mids are enhanced everywhere. The result is just an ear-numbing wash of harshness, with no instrument particularly "present" in the mix. Upper mids, like all the frequency bands, need to be managed with discretion and taste.

Highs (6kHz–20kHz) create a "bright" sound; they tend to be the first frequencies to go away in a low-fidelity recording. But as with upper mids, trying to compensate for lost highs can have bad-sounding results. It's best to get a recording that faithfully captures highs first. Perhaps more so than any of the other bands, highs can be divided into several other sub-bands that are useful to think about. The lower end of this band is responsible for run-of-the-mill brightness, like most of the frequencies from a cymbal crash. Higher highs (say, in the 10kHz range) are responsible for crispness in a sound, like the "zing" of new acoustic-guitar strings. The highest highs (above 12kHz) are perhaps the hardest to describe; many people use the word "air" to describe these frequencies. When they're there, a sound can have a certain lightness or clarity; when they're missing, a sound might seem lifeless or empty. If you use the wrong kind of microphone, a sound's highest highs may not be captured, and you won't be able to create them after the fact. But too much of this sub-band can make a recording sound brittle. This is particularly true if you're recording digitally, because where analog media might tame and sweeten those uppermost highs, digital systems tend to capture them as is, which might end up being too much of a good thing.

So, what does it all mean? Basically, every band has its good features and bad features: Too much of any one of them, and not enough of any one of them, will usually make a recording sound not as good as when they're all balanced with each other. So, what's "balanced"? Isn't that subjective? It is—but today's recorded popular music has certain standards that have evolved over the years. You probably won't turn on the radio and hear a song that's a relentless blast of highs with a thin bottom end, because such a sound would probably be too extreme for contemporary pop-music sensibilities. So, your best bet in learning about how your own recordings stack up to those of the pros is to put them up against professional recordings. It's a sobering thing to create a setup where you can "A/B" your music against a recording that you admire, but that's a great way to listen closely and try to hear weaknesses in your recordings. For instance, even after 20 years of making music, I sometimes notice that the low mids in my music are deficient. When this happens, I might turn up the organ, electric piano, or rhythm guitar slightly in the mix (particularly if the part is played in a low register), and that often provides a fullness which fixes the problem.

Equalization

You've heard of equalization, or EQ, before—hey, I mentioned it a few times in Chapter 1. It refers to the electronic alteration of a sound in order to adjust the preponderance of certain frequencies relative to the others. EQ circuits are built into almost all mixing boards, and there are also outboard rackmount EQs, and good mic

EQ Types

An equalizer circuit can be as simple as a single knob—a guitar's tone knob is a type of EQ—or it can have several dozen controls. EQs are classified by how flexible they are in shaping the frequency content of a sound. Here are some types of EQs you're likely to encounter:

Shelving EQ. You've known this one since you were a kid: The BASS and TREBLE controls on a home stereo are shelving EQs. These affect all frequencies above or below a certain frequency (see Fig. 5). For example, a BASS control, when turned down, might cut or "roll off" frequencies below 100Hz; when turned up, it will boost the same frequencies. In this case, the lower a frequency is below 100Hz, the more it will be affected by the control. The maximum effect that a shelving EQ can have is expressed as a "slope" in units of decibels per octave (dB/oct). The higher the figure, the more potentially extreme the EQ. Shelving EQs are most useful when a sound just has too much highs or too much lows and needs to be tamed. They can be used to enhance highs or lows, but use them judiciously—particularly when boosting lows, because of the way low frequencies carry so much energy. Two types of shelving EQ are the *lowpass filter* and the *highpass filter*; lowpass filters cut high frequencies (passing the lows through, hence the somewhat counterintuitive name), while highpass filters cut lows, allowing highs to pass.

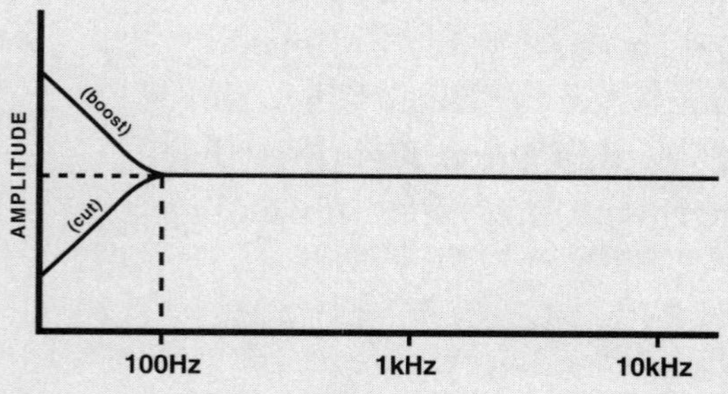

Fig. 5 Shelving EQ, highpass type, with a 100Hz cutoff frequency.

Bandpass EQ. Also sometimes just called "mid EQ," a bandpass EQ affects midrange frequencies but leaves highs and lows more or less alone (see Fig. 6). A mid EQ is most useful when it's either parametric or semi-parametric (see below). You might also run across the term *notch filter*; this is a kind of bandpass EQ that only cuts a specific frequency range. This kind of EQ is especially useful in live sound systems, as it can help eliminate feedback squeals at the precise frequencies where feedback occurs.

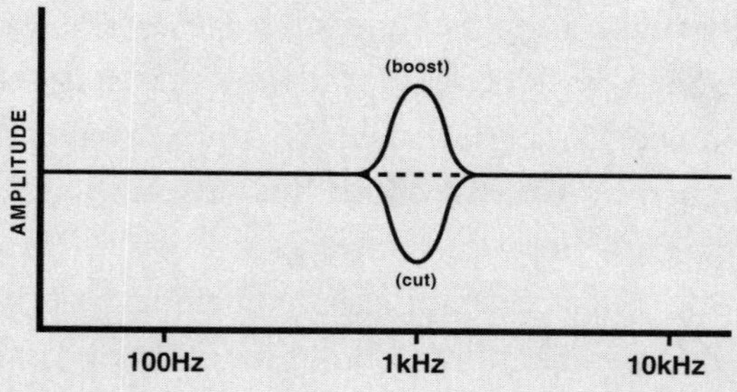

Fig. 6 Bandpass EQ.

Graphic EQ. You've seen this on home stereos or instrument amplifiers: It's a number of sliders arranged together, any one of which can cut or boost a band of frequencies. Each slider controls a bandpass EQ circuit, except for the highest and lowest ones, which control shelving circuits. Graphic EQs are named because the pattern formed by all of the sliders represents, more or less,

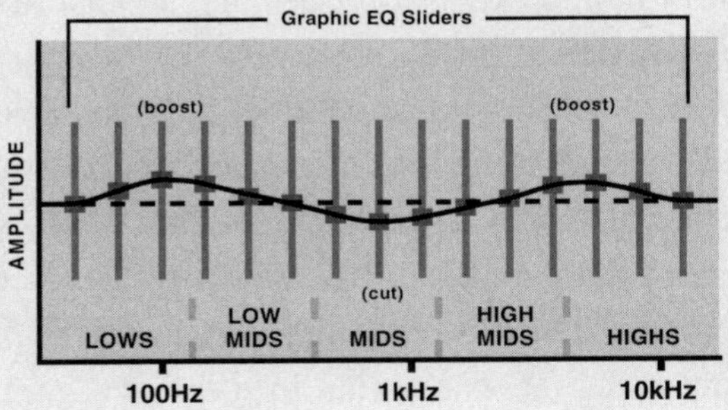

Fig. 7 A graphic EQ can affect all of the frequency spectrum's bands at once.

a graph of the EQ's effect on the sound, with frequency on the horizontal axis and degree of boost or cut on the vertical axis (see Fig. 7). A graphic EQ is often useful for subtle, overall shaping of a sound; for instance, with some practice you might learn that your singing voice benefits from being boosted a little here, cut a little here, boosted a little there, etc. Graphic EQs sound best when you build a smooth, curvy contour on the sliders, but some cool effects can be produced by boosting or cutting only certain sliders by a large degree. (Always listen for distortion anytime you're radically boosting frequencies.) There are wonderful graphic EQs out there as well as horrible ones. In general, more sliders is better, because they allow more precise tone shaping, and because each slider affects a more narrow range of frequencies. The 31-band graphic EQ, which has three sliders for each octave (doubling of frequency), is a fairly standard piece of studio gear. You'll hear this type of EQ called a *one-third-octave* graphic EQ.

Parametric EQ. This is the kind we Guerrilla recordists (as well as most pro engineers) like the most. A parametric EQ is so named because each frequency band allows three parameters to be set: amount of boost or cut, the center frequency, and the bandwidth (also called "Q"), which is how wide a chunk of the frequency spectrum, on either side of the center frequency, is affected (see Fig. 8). With a parametric EQ you can make broad contour on a sound by specifying a wide bandwidth, or target a specific frequency range. If a snare-drum sound has an annoying ring, for instance, you can locate where in the frequency spectrum that ring is occurring, and soften it. A pro studio might have one or more dedicated outboard parametric EQs in a rack, but most home recordists encounter parametric EQ on their mixing board, in the form of "sweepable mid" EQ knobs. This is a valuable tool for the Guerrilla recordist to have; it's especially useful for enhancing instrument separation, which is covered in Chapter 5.

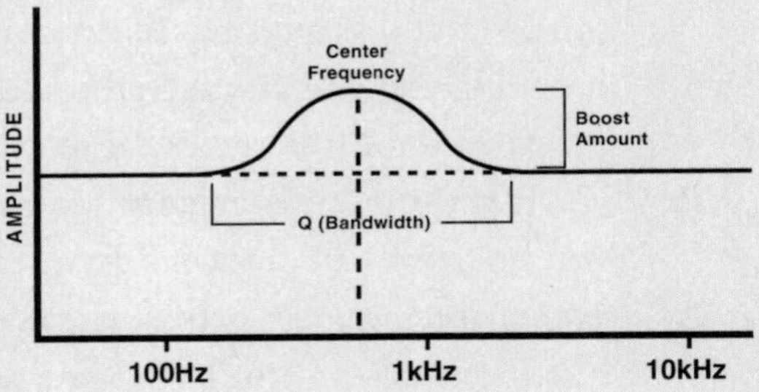

Fig. 8 A parametric EQ allows you to specify three different parameters to shape a sound: center frequency, amount of boost/cut, and Q (bandwidth).

A **semi-parametric EQ** is just like a parametric EQ, except it has a fixed (non-adjustable) bandwidth. Budget mixing boards' mid-EQ controls commonly use these less expensive circuits, but that's okay; being able to sweep the frequencies is much more important than being able to set the bandwidth.

preamps also often have EQ circuits built in. Equalization is one of the Guerrilla recordist's best friends, along with compression and expansion (see Chapters 3 and 4). EQ comes in handy because rarely in the home studio do we capture a sound with just the right frequency proportions for the recording we're making. At some point, those proportions will likely need to be adjusted, the way you might add salt to a soup you're cooking as the other ingredients go in. A highly skilled engineer might be able to get a sound just right at the outset by, say, using a certain microphone and placing it a certain way. In the Guerrilla studio, though, we're not quite that good. So EQ helps us make corrections as the recording takes shape, keeping in mind the "mix as you go" idea mentioned in Chapter 1.

Overall, it's better not to have to use EQ. Depending on the quality of the EQ circuit you're using, it can lend a plasticky, non-musical artificiality to the frequency region where it's being used. But even if you don't have the greatest EQ, you can get away with using a little (for any particular frequency band, for any particular sound), with basically no harm done. However, if you find yourself turning a knob or sliding a slider halfway or more past the center point, it might be time to consider re-recording that part or using a different sound altogether. Finally, it's usually better to cut frequencies rather than boost them, whenever this is an option. Cutting often results in a more natural sound (and it sounds less like, um, an EQ boost)—plus, cutting doesn't boost your mix's overall levels, which can lead to other problems down the line, as we'll see.

Shelving EQs (see EQ Types sidebar) are useful for adjusting highs and lows, but you'll get more mileage out of a *sweepable mid* EQ. "Mid" means that the circuit lets you boost or cut a range of frequencies somewhere in the middle of the spectrum, and "sweepable" means you can select the center frequency of that range. This is useful because it allows you to target a specific aspect of a sound that might need emphasis or taming. Say you have a kick-drum sound that's nice and beefy, but you can't hear the "snap" of the beater hitting the drumhead very well. Boosting the lows will just make the kick beefier—maybe too beefy. What you want to do in this case is crank up that mid control to a much higher level than you'd probably want to use, and slowly sweep the frequency control across the mids and upper mids while the kick-drum sound is going through the EQ. If the EQ is fully parametric, meaning it has a bandwidth (Q) control as well, set the bandwidth to be moderately narrow. At some point as you sweep, you'll hear the "snap" of the kick drum being dialed in. Once you've found the key frequency for that attack, back off on the boost and tweak the bandwidth parameter until it sounds more appropriate in context.

By the way, toying around with a sweepable-mid EQ on all sorts of sounds is one of the best ways to train your ears about the effects of boosting and cutting certain frequencies. And training your ears is a very good thing. I'll talk in more detail about how to use EQ in Chapter 5.

Mono, Stereo & Panning

When you play back a CD, you're actually hearing not one recording but two: one for the left speaker, and one for the right. These two recordings can be called *channels* when spoken of individually, or together as a *stereo pair*. They're locked together in time on a CD, but they're otherwise independent; if you wanted to, you could make a CD that plays a different song out of each speaker at the same time. In the early years of recording, music consisted of only one channel, because home playback systems had only one speaker. This is called *monophonic*, or "mono," sound. In the 1950s, music started being commercially released in the two-channel *stereophonic* (stereo) sound that we know today. Stereo provides a more realistic, interesting listening experience, because it allows sounds to appear to exist in different places in space and to move around. It also helps us Guerrilla recordists, because being able to place sounds in different parts of the stereo field—that imaginary listening space encompassing both the left and right channels—makes it easier for us to separate the sounds. And separation, as we'll see in Chapter 5, is an important feature of a well-made recording.

You can record a sound in stereo that plays back as a mono sound, simply by making the left and right channels identical. When the same exact sound is playing out of both speakers, the sound appears to come from between them, or to come from both of them as a whole. But if the sound is louder in one speaker than in the other, it will appear to be coming more from that speaker. If another sound is playing at the same time but is coming more from the other speaker, the two sounds will be separated somewhat in the stereo field: One will be kind of on the left, the other kind of on the right. And if a sound begins to decrease in volume in one speaker while it gets louder in the other, the sound will appear to move across the stereo field. This placement in the stereo field is called *panning*—a sound can be "panned" to the left, or it can "pan" from one side to the other. (The word is short for "panorama" and is derived from the

The Three "Dimensions" Of Recorded Sound

Throughout this book, you'll see three terms being used over and over to describe sound: dynamics, frequency content, and pan position. If you think of every recorded sound in terms of these three "dimensions," it becomes easier to understand how that sound fits into a mix with all of the other sounds. For example, if you want an instrument to be a focal point, you'd probably record and mix it so that it's loud, bright, and panned to the center. When we discuss the principle of instrument separation in Chapter 5, you'll see how this approach to sound management can give each sound its own unique place in a mix, which—when applied to all sounds—generally makes a recording sound better and more professional.

terminology of cinema, where a camera can "pan" across a room as it points to different things.) Along with dynamics and frequency content, panning is one of the three most important factors determining a particular sound's place and function in a recording. Panning also creates opportunities for artistic expression, as the way you pan a sound, and the way its panning position changes over time, is a choice you make during the recording's creation—one that has a distinct effect on the way the finished recording sounds.

Tracking Vs. Mixing

Recording usually consists of two phases: *tracking* and *mixing*. When you're tracking, you're recording individual sounds (or perhaps several sounds at once, or, in the case of live recording, a whole band) in a form that is not yet a finished stereo (two-channel) recording. Usually, this means that for any particular sound, you're taking one mono channel or two channels (if you're recording that sound in stereo) and recording the sound to one or two tracks of a *multitrack recorder*. A multitrack recorder is a device that keeps four, eight, or more audio channels (usually called *tracks* in this context) synchronized together but otherwise separate, very much like the left and right channels on a stereo CD. After all of the tracks are recorded, they are all played back at the same time and "mixed," or "mixed down," to two channels in stereo and recorded somewhere else. During mixdown, the level, EQ, and pan position of each sound determine its role in the final mix. For example, you could make two versions of a song by doing two mixdowns: one in which the rhythm guitar is playing softly and off to one side, and another in which the rhythm guitar is panned to the center, extra-bright, and loud. Obviously, these song versions would be quite different, which is why mixing decisions are important, both technically and artistically.

Digital Vs. Analog

Recording systems come in both *analog* and *digital* varieties. The distinction is important in terms of the recording process, so let's take a brief look at how each technology works.

Analog recording has been around for well over a century. Thomas Edison famously developed a way to record sound onto wax cylinders, and if you were to take a microscope and look at the grooves even his earliest contraptions left in the wax, they would look like sound-wave diagrams, with repeating patterns that represent the frequency components of the sound that was recorded. Whether we're talking about wax, vinyl LPs, or magnetic tape (which captures sound in magnetic form, not in a way we could look at with a microscope), we say that the waves that are recorded are *analogous* to the original sound waves that traveled through the air (see Fig. 9). By this

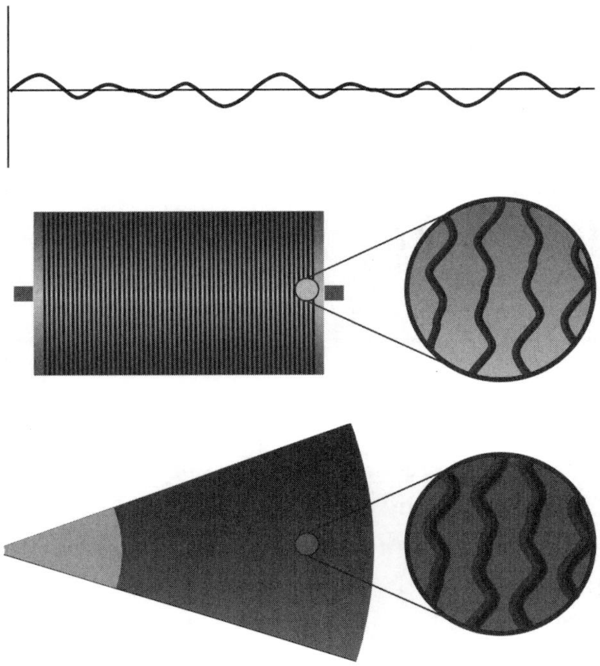

Fig. 9 If a sound wave (top) were recorded onto an old-fashioned wax cylinder (center) or pressed onto a vinyl LP (bottom), you could see the wave's shape in the grooves under a microscope. For this reason, the grooves are said to be an analog representation of the sound wave.

we mean the recorded waves are identical (well, almost) to the original sound, with peaks and valleys and smaller wavelets in all the same places.

Digital recording is very different. A digital recorder converts an analog electrical signal (meaning a signal with electrical waves that are analogous to those in the sound that was recorded) into a set of numbers that can be written onto a hard drive or some similar medium. It does this by analyzing, or *sampling*, the position of the wave many thousands of times per second, and assigning a number to the wave's position at each sample point. This isn't a perfect process, though, because a real sound wave (and its electrical analog) is continuous, defining an infinite number of points. The digital version is limited by how many samples were taken per second (called the *sampling rate*), as well as the *resolution* of each sample. Resolution refers to how many numbers are used in each sample to define the position of the wave at that point. Resolution is expressed in *bits*, a digital measurement unit. If more bits are used in a digital recording, the recording will be more accurate than if fewer bits are used (see Fig. 10). Early digital recording systems used eight bits per sample; slightly better systems used 12 bits. Commercial CDs use 16 bits, which today is considered the minimum bit resolution for digital recording. Today's superior systems use 24-bit resolution, which results in quieter, less grainy recordings, particularly at low levels. CDs contain 44,100 samples per second, which is referred to as a 44.1kHz sampling rate. This, too, is

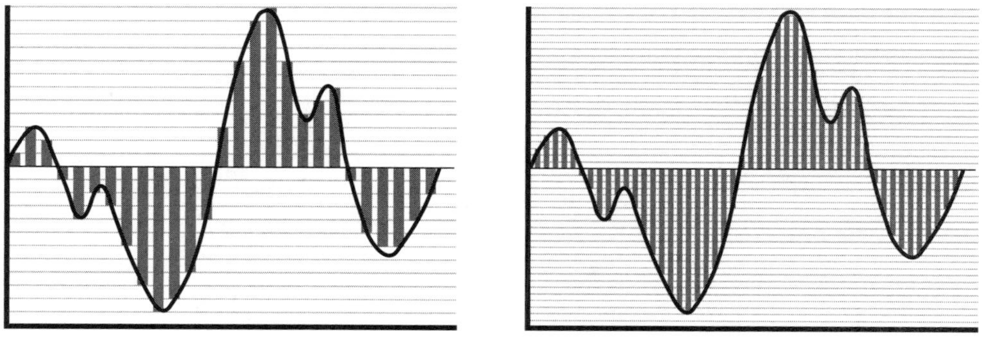

Fig. 10 These diagrams represent two approaches to expressing a wave shape (black curve) digitally via individual samples (gray bars); the horizontal lines represent bit resolution. A digital system with a higher sampling rate and bit resolution (right) will more faithfully capture a sound wave's shape than one with a lower sampling rate and bit resolution (left).

considered the minimum for high-fidelity music; some recording and playback systems can operate at 48kHz, 96kHz, and even 192kHz.

There's an endless debate about the sound quality of digital vs. analog recordings. Analog systems are prized for their "warm" sound and gentle, natural-sounding compression of volume peaks, while digital tends to "color" (alter) the sound less; analog freaks often say digital systems sound "cold" or "clinical," perhaps because they record *too* faithfully. Even digital enthusiasts argue about how valuable higher bit resolutions and sampling rates are with regard to the resulting sound. For Guerrilla Home Recording, digital sounds just fine. And yes, you can make a slightly better recording by employing a higher bit resolution and sampling rate—but for our purposes, 16 bits and 44.1kHz sampling is plenty.

There is one critical thing to understand when you're recording digitally. Analog systems are somewhat forgiving at the maximum end of the dynamic range; as I mentioned, analog tape is known to gently compress a recording's loudest moments. Digital, though, is not. Since it uses a range of numbers to describe a sound at any given moment, once it hits the top of the range, there's nowhere to go. A digital system can't magically create new numbers to describe the sound. As a result, if you go over the top of the range, the sound will distort in a really ugly way. Unlike analog distortion (a distorted electric-guitar amp is a type of analog distortion), digital distortion is horrible, unmusical, and useless. So while you can get some cool effects by "baking the tape" on an analog machine, you absolutely must stay under that upper limit on a digital system. All digital systems help you to do this, for instance lighting an LED that stays lit if you reach the "over" point. (If that happens, you'd better go back and redo the part.) You don't want to be *too* safe with your levels, but you simply want to reach a happy medium—or perhaps "a happy moderately loud" would be a better way to put it. More about maintaining good levels in Chapter 3.

Signal Levels

Recording would be a lot easier if there were only one type of cable, all plugs and jacks fit together, and all equipment operated at the same signal level. But things are more complicated than that, and it's essential to get a handle on all of the differences and what they mean in the Guerrilla studio. The explanations that follow are a bit simplified and loosey-goosey. Technical audio geeks don't like to simplify things or leave out details, which is why some recording books include lots of dazzling formulas and rigorous explanations. I'll spare you the technical details and just tell you what you need to know to make a good recording.

An analog audio signal requires at least two wires (conductors) to be carried by a cable: One conductor, called "hot," carries the actual signal, and the other, called "ground," completes the circuit and provides a place for the electricity to return. Keep in mind that since the current is an alternating one, the electrons aren't actually going anywhere other than back and forth—but the signal is being fed into the cable at one end and being detected at the other, so the signal *is* traveling, in the form of waves. That's why you'll read about "signal flow," or hear that "the signal goes from point A to point B." Anyway, a signal can travel down a cable at different intensities, depending on where it's coming from and where it's going. That's where volts come into play: We describe the signal's maximum strength as a voltage. It's a reference number to help us understand how pieces of audio gear fit together; it isn't necessarily a direct measurement of the signal.

The signal coming from a microphone is the weakest kind of audio signal. A microphone picking up a loud sound generates only a few dozen millivolts (thousandths of a volt)—very small. This is called a *mic level* signal, and a signal that small is pretty useless for most audio gear unless it is first amplified by a circuit. Amplification refers to "stepping up" the voltage, or making it much larger, while maintaining the integrity of the sound being represented. Some amplifier circuits are better than others at doing this; good ones are clean and quiet, while bad ones introduce noise and/or distortion, which is an alteration of the sound waves' shapes. If the circuit changes the wave shapes, the sound will change—sometimes in a good way, but often in an unwanted way.

Amplifiers designed to accept mic-level signals are called *microphone preamps*; engineers often call them "mic pre's" for short. A mic pre boosts a mic-level signal to *line level*, which is the signal level that operates inside most mixing boards, rackmount effects, and analog tape machines. In a line-level signal, the maximum voltage reached is somewhere in the order of one volt. Most mixing boards have built-in mic pre's, and some of them are pretty good. There are also external mic pre's, some of which are incredibly expensive. (Until I win the lottery, I'll stick with my board's mic preamps.)

A third kind of signal level, called *instrument level*, is generated by electric guitars and basses. Instrument level is usually weaker than line level but stronger than mic level. I say "usually" because instrument level varies quite a bit; some guitar pickups are much more powerful than others, and some instruments contain onboard preamps that boost the signal even before it leaves the output jack. Guitars and basses are either plugged into amplifiers designed to accept instrument levels, or they're recorded *direct*, meaning the signal remains electronic all the way through the signal chain to the recording. But first, a direct-recorded guitar or bass must go through a direct box, which I mentioned in Chapter 1. A direct box changes something called the *impedance* of the signal. But many direct boxes don't actually amplify the instrument level up to line level, so you still need a preamp to do this; a mixing board's mic preamps are often fine for the job.

Synthesizers and drum machines output yet another kind of level; often it's lower than line level but much higher than instrument level. Generally, though, you can treat this kind of signal like a line-level signal, although it may need to be boosted a bit as it comes into the board to bring it up to true line level.

I've spoken of signal level in terms of voltage so far, but actually, recording engineers rarely use voltage to describe signal levels. More often, they use the decibel—the same unit to describe sound intensity. But in this context, decibels aren't absolute as with sound (where an 80dB sound corresponds to a specific loudness that's more or less universally agreed upon). Regarding electrical signal levels, decibels are relative, meaning they describe a level as it compares to some other constant or standard level. For instance, that standard might be the maximum signal allowable on a digital recorder; a signal that reaches exactly that maximum can be described as 0dB—zero decibels—with lower levels described in negative numbers, such as –3dB or –10dB. (And you thought 0dB was *quiet!*) To complicate matters, engineers have invented different kinds of decibels, specifying them with a letter at the end of the abbreviation, such as dBV or dBu. I'll mention these again a little later, but don't worry about the distinctions between them. Let the techies worry about that stuff.

Signal-To-Noise Ratios

Since line level is the recording studio's most "universal" type of signal level, you generally want to bring mic- and instrument-level signals up to line level as early as possible in the signal chain. The weaker a signal is, the more susceptible it is to being corrupted by noise. If the same amount of noise is added to two signals—one weak and one strong—the strong one will be less affected overall, because when the weak signal (plus the added noise) is amplified to match the stronger signal's level, the noise will be amplified, too. The concept of the *signal-to-noise ratio* is important in understanding this and anything having to do with noise. It's another decibel measurement, again of the relative kind: It expresses the *difference* in strength between the signal, meaning the good stuff, and the noise—the bad stuff. The higher the number (in decibels), the greater the difference between the signal and the noise—in other words, the less significant the noise is compared to what you want on your recording. We say a recording with a high signal-to-noise ratio is a *quiet* recording; one with a low ratio is a *noisy* recording. In studio contexts, "quiet" and "noisy" normally refer only to the noise, not the signal.

Naturally, in the studio, we like high signal-to-noise ratios, because unless your goal is actually to record noise (and sometimes it is), quieter is always better. For example, 90dB is a very good ratio, about what you get from a high-quality digital recorder. A vinyl-record turntable, on the other hand, with its surface hiss and rumble, affords us something closer to 50dB. With today's technology—or even with 15-year-old used gear—we're better than that. In making a good recording it's important to maximize the signal-to-noise ratio every step of the way, as we'll see.

Cable Types

Naturally, line-level signals need to be able to go from one place to another, such as from a mixing board to a recording deck. But weak mic-level and instrument-level signals need to go from one place to another as well, because often a microphone or instrument doesn't contain a preamp. So, there are different kinds of cables to carry different kinds of signals—and they're all designed to prevent noise from being added to them.

The simplest kind of cable is the one that connects a table lamp to the wall outlet: Two conductors—"hot" and "ground"—running right alongside each other. This kind of cable has almost no use in carrying audio. Why? Because, particularly around electronic equipment and fluorescent lights, there's energy constantly buzzing through the air at the rate of 60 cycles per second (60Hz)—that's the frequency of the alternating current of 110-volt wall-socket electricity in the U.S. This energy tends to creep into wires, so it shouldn't surprise you that if this stuff gets into one of your studio cables, you'll hear a hum at the frequency of exactly 60Hz mixed in when the cable's signal is turned into sound. The longer the cable, the more likely this is to happen. This can destroy your precious signal-to-noise ratio, so it needs to be prevented.

Shielded cable is an effective way to do this. In this kind of cable, the ground conductor is in the form of a tube-like sheath that surrounds the hot conductor for the cable's entire length. (This is the form that cable-TV cable comes in. If it didn't, you wouldn't be able to see a picture—too much noise would be picked up between the cable company and your house.) When a cable is shielded, 60-cycle hum is

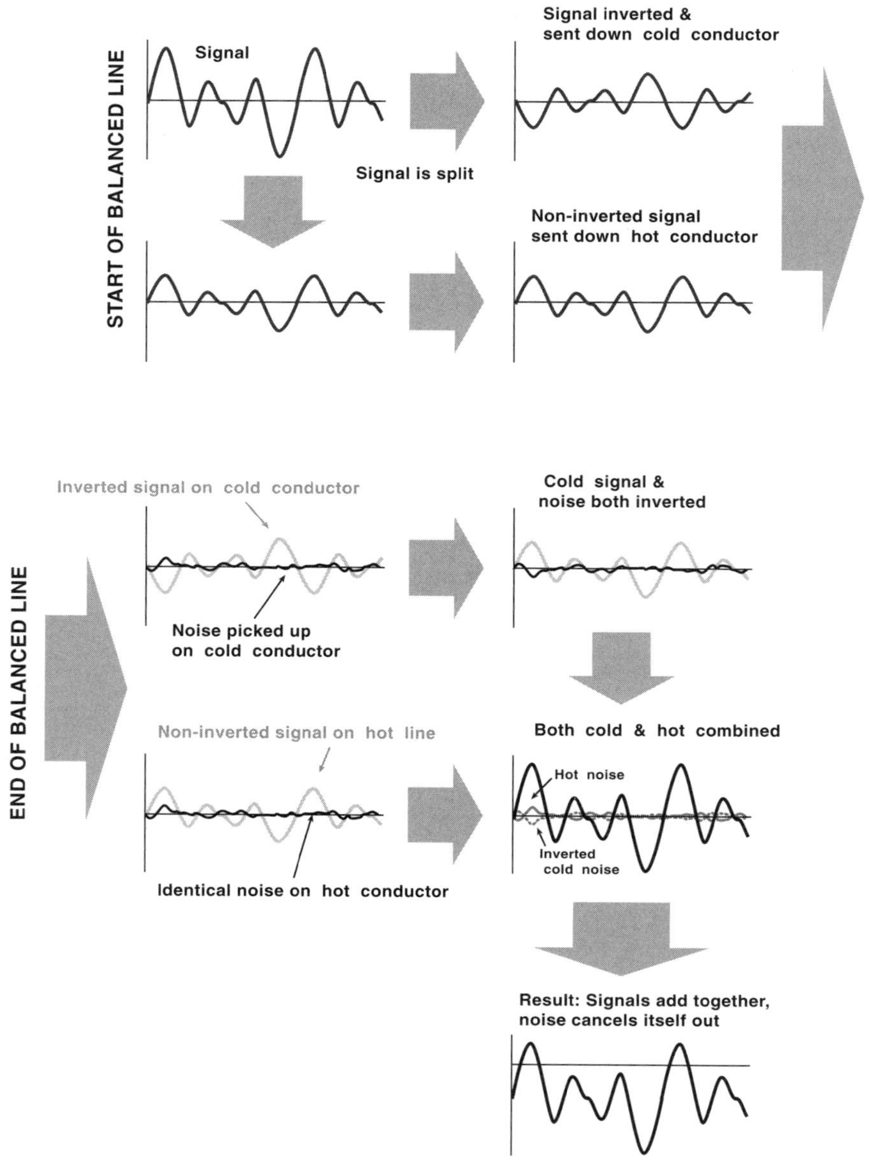

Fig. 11 At the start of a balanced line, the signal is split, and one of the two conductors is phase-inverted (top). At the other end of the cable (bottom), the inverted side is reversed again. When the two sides are then re-combined, noise picked up along the cable's run cancels itself out.

intercepted by the ground conductor and never makes it to the hot conductor, so the signal remains pure and quiet.

Shielded cable is fine for line-level signals and even not-too-long cables carrying instrument signals—but what about mic-level signals? These weak signals are extremely susceptible to being corrupted by noise, so even shielded cables won't cut it. The solution is a third conductor in what's known as a *balanced line*. A balanced line carries two copies of the signal: one on the hot conductor, and a mirror-image version of that signal on what's called the "cold" conductor. The third conductor is a shielded ground. If any 60Hz noise makes it past the ground (and a little bit always does), it goes into both the hot and cold conductors equally. At the end of the cable, the cold conductor's mirror image of the signal is flipped again and combined with the hot signal—and magically, the noise on both lines cancels itself out (see Fig. 11). This is a brilliant invention, and even though you didn't really need to know how balanced lines work, they're so cool I had to share it with you. Guitarists will recognize this noise-fighting approach; it's similar to the way humbucking pickups work.

Most mic signals are carried along balanced lines, but not all; some cheaper mics use regular shielded cables. Try not to use mics like these; they're just too noisy—and anything that cheap will probably sound bad, anyway.

Plugs & Jacks

As there are different types of cables in the studio, there are different types of plugs (the "male" ends of cables) and jacks (the "female" sockets that accept plugs). Collectively, plugs and jacks are known as connectors (see Fig. 12).

¼" connectors. The bread-and-butter of home-studio connector schemes, the ¼" plug and jack are also archaically called "phone" connectors, because they were originally developed for telephone operators. The inputs and outputs of most semi-pro (and some pro) studio gear use ¼" connectors. They're easy to use, and shielded cables with ¼" connectors are widely available as guitar cables or higher-quality studio cables. You should always have plenty of these available, of different lengths—they'll always come in handy.

¼" TRS connectors. TRS stands for "tip-ring-sleeve," describing the parts of the plug itself. These connectors can accommodate three conductors. You see them on headphone cables—that's one hot conductor for the left channel, one hot conductor for the right, and a single ground conductor for both sides. If you ever need to split the signal coming from one stereo jack into the two separate channels (and this is the kind of thing that often happens in the Guerrilla studio), you'll need a "Y" adapter. These often have two standard ¼" jacks along with the one ¼" TRS plug. Radio Shack

LOOK OUT!

Speaker Cables

Even though a cable looks like a shielded cable, it might not be one. Except when you're connecting a power amplifier to a speaker, never use a cable with SPEAKER CABLE printed on it. These are heavy-duty cables that aren't shielded—the signal meant to be carried is so strong, any noise it picks up will be meaningless. Conversely, never use an instrument cable to connect a power amp to a speaker; it's not built to take strong current and could overheat and melt.

sells them, but you're better off going with something more reliable, bought from a music store (read: something that costs more than five bucks).

Another common place you'll find TRS connectors is on a mixing board's insert section (see Chapter 3). A TRS jack allows a piece of gear to send a signal on one hot conductor and receive another signal on a second hot conductor, with the third serving as a ground for both. Again, to use one of these jacks, you'll need a "Y" adapter, although there are also "Y" cables made just for this purpose. In either case, one end of the fork goes to a jack that needs to receive a signal, and the other goes to a jack that's sending a signal.

Since they have three conductors, ¼" TRS connectors can also form the end of balanced-line cables. Balanced cables that have a ¼" TRS plug on one side and an XLR (see below) male or female plug on the other are also common. These allow you to send signals, for example, from a DI or preamp to the balanced ¼" analog input of a digital recording device.

⅛" connectors. Also called "mini" or "mini-phone" plugs and jacks, these are the kind found on a Sony Walkman, personal CD player, and Walkman-style headphones. As with ¼" connectors, if they're dealing with a stereo signal, they'll be of the TRS variety. You'll want to stock up on adapters that go from ¼" to ⅛" and back, both TRS (yes, they do exist) and regular. For instance, if you wanted to split a Walkman's stereo signal into left and right, you could plug a ⅛"-TRS-male-to-¼"-TRS-female adapter into it, and then plug a ¼" TRS "Y" cable into the adapter. Some headphones have built-in ¼"-to-⅛" adapters that snap or screw on, enabling you to use them on different kinds of equipment, large and small. Of course, as a Guerrilla recordist you can use one of these as an adapter for other functions—just don't lose it!

RCA connectors. Also sometimes called *phono* or *coaxial* connectors, these are widely used on consumer stereo and video equipment, as well as on some older semi-pro studio gear. An RCA plug consists of a small rod surrounded by a sleeve. Even if you have no RCA connectors in your studio, they can still serve a function: Shielded consumer cables with RCA plugs on both ends are a lot cheaper than cables with ¼" plugs, and if you find yourself short a cable or two, they're as near as the local Radio Shack or Circuit City. They conveniently come in lengths of three feet, six feet, and longer. And since they're usually stereo, they're two cables in one—just stick on four RCA-female-to-¼"-male adapters, and you've got a handy double-cable for about ten bucks. Tripled cables (for audio + video) and even quadrupled cables (for hooking up tape decks) are available as well, and you can chain them together with RCA-female-to-RCA-female connectors—those always come in handy, so buy a bunch. You can never have too many adapters in the Guerrilla studio.

XLR connectors. This is the standard plug and jack for microphones and mic cables. Unlike most cables, those with XLR connectors usually have one male end and one female end, so they can be easily daisy-chained. Balanced XLR connections are also preferred on pro gear, even for line-level signals. Some mixing boards offer XLR balanced master outputs, but unless you're feeding a power amplifier or powered speakers with built-in balanced XLR or ¼" connectors, you might as well stick with the unbalanced ¼" outs.

There are also such things as XLR-to-unbalanced-¼" adapters called transformers, but these adapters incorporate extra components that change the impedance of the signal. This may or may not audibly affect the signal, depending on the situation.

Nominal Operating Levels

In a couple of places I've mentioned the terms "semi-pro gear" and "pro gear." I'm not making arbitrary value judgments here; these are actually two established divisions of audio equipment. Whether a piece of gear is considered "pro" or "semi-pro" (the latter is also sometimes called "consumer") depends on something called its *nominal operating level*. This refers to the maximum voltage at which its circuitry is designed to operate. Think of it as the difference between a professional race car and a regular sports car: Pro-level gear is designed to run at "hotter" internal signal levels than semi-pro gear, so the potential signal-to-noise ratio is greater on pro gear than on semi-pro. The specification used to describe pro gear's nominal operating level is +4dBu (often referred to simply as "+4"), and the spec for semi-pro is –10dBV (or just –10). (The letters *u* and *V* after dB specify exactly what kind of decibel it is.) I mention the numbers just so you'll recognize them in ads and user manuals. Suffice it to say that pro gear runs considerably hotter than semi-pro gear—electrically speaking, that is, not necessarily temperature-wise.

Some gear allows you to specify whether you want it to operate at +4 or –10 (as the nominal levels are often informally called). My Mackie 8•Bus mixing board, for instance, has a switch on the back for this purpose. I leave it set to –10, because pretty much everything else in my studio operates at –10. With the switch set here, the

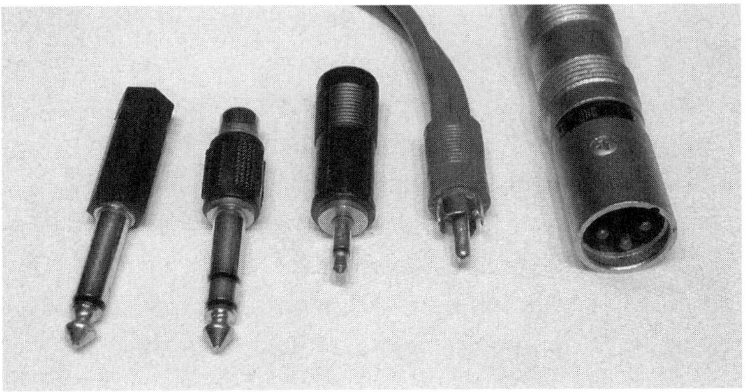

Fig. 12 Left to right: A standard ¼" plug, ¼" TRS plug, ⅛" plug, RCA plug, and XLR plug.

output through its unbalanced ¼" master-out jacks. However, ›wn to a professional-level DAT recorder, I would change would cause the board to send its stereo output through ut jacks instead. That would work out well, because the ›nly XLR balanced inputs, which are designed to accept the

… & Loops

…ryone knows that some electrical wall outlets have two slots and some have the two slots plus a hole, and most people know that the latter variety is said to be *grounded.* This is a little confusing, because earlier I said that "ground" is one of the two conductors in an audio-signal cable, but bear with me. Electrical power in the form of 110-volt alternating current comes out of one of the outlet slots, called "hot" (as in an audio-signal cable). The other slot, in the context of a home's electrical power, is called "neutral"; it serves the same function as the ground conductor in an audio-signal cable: It completes the circuit and provides a place for the hot conductor's electricity to return. The third conductor on a grounded outlet, called "ground" in this capacity, is normally not used—it provides an *alternative* path for electricity to travel in the event that something goes wrong with the circuit. This makes the outlet safer, because if there isn't a direct alternative path to ground (which, for many homes, literally means a long copper stake driven into the earth near the electric meter), a wayward electric current might have to go through you instead. Ouch.

So grounding is good, right? In terms of safety, definitely—but grounding can also cause annoyances in the studio. Most studio gear needs to be grounded (which is why the power cords' plugs have three prongs), but if you set up your studio in certain ways, this can cause pieces of gear to add that 60-cycle hum to the audio going through it. This hum can easily become unacceptably loud, and the uninformed recordist can go crazy trying to figure out how to get rid of it.

The cause of this mysterious hum is called a *ground loop.* Ground loops happen when there are two or more different paths to ground among all of your studio gear. For example, if your mixing board, computer, and effects rack are all plugged into different outlets—and all of this stuff is connected together via audio cables—you're asking for ground loops to occur. This is particularly true if the outlets are connected to different electrical circuits in the building.

The key to preventing ground loops is to provide every piece of gear one and only one path to ground—for instance, by plugging everything into the same power strip. This technique is called "star grounding"—think of the electricity's source as the center of the star, with all of the power cables coming out of that one source. You may have learned that it isn't safe to plug so many things into one outlet. Except for power amplifiers and powered monitors, studio gear doesn't suck up that much power—not as much as, say, a toaster, a coffee maker, and a microwave oven all plugged in together. As long as your home's fuses or circuit breakers are proper and sufficient, it shouldn't be a problem. (I have never blown a fuse or tripped a breaker with my studio gear.)

Even if you practice star grounding, you can still have problems with hum. If you want to take an audio feed from a VCR, for example, you'll want to disconnect the cable-TV signal going into it. The cable's shielding provides a path to ground that's entirely independent from your home's grounding, so the audio from the VCR will hum like crazy if it stays connected. But sometimes you just cannot figure out why a piece of gear is humming. In that case, sometimes it's necessary to defeat the ground on that piece of gear by using a three-prong-to-two-slot grounding adapter. This should be absolutely a last resort, though, because it is potentially dangerous. When the ground is defeated this way, *you* become the only path to ground in the event that a problem develops with the neutral conductor—and that can be deadly.

Some pieces of gear (for instance, bass amplifiers with direct-out jacks) have GROUND LIFT switches on them. If you're having a problem with hum or even radio sounds coming from such a piece of gear, try flipping this switch. The noise will probably disappear.

MIDI Basics

MIDI, which stands for Musical Instrument Digital Interface, is a protocol by which electronic instruments can "talk" to one another. MIDI's first attraction was that it allowed you to play multiple synthesizers with just one controller keyboard. It was such a success it became an industry standard. MIDI allowed for the proliferation of the digital sequencer, a piece of hardware that recorded and played back MIDI data. The robotic, perfectly timed rhythms of sequencers—which could be synchronized with drum machines, also then a fairly new invention—created a sound that's now forever identified with '80s music. Music has changed a lot since then (although some styles still retain that robotic feel), but MIDI is more important to the recording studio than ever.

A MIDI signal does not carry any audio data; rather, it specifies details about note-related events, for example: "note 71 on" (the keyboardist played a *B* above middle *C*), "velocity 125" (the note was played very hard), and "note 71 off" (the player released the key). This is pretty cool, because unlike audio, which eats up a lot of hard-drive space, all of the MIDI for one song can fit into a very small computer file—maybe just 100 kilobytes or so. MIDI also allows us to record a performance and then completely change the instrument's sound. Changing from a piano solo to a harpsichord solo can be as simple as changing the program on your synth—in terms of MIDI, the notes are the same regardless. It also allows you to change the performance after it's recorded, for instance changing the key, adding fills, etc., all without compromising the initial performance's quality. This allows for tons of after-the-fact flexibility—and flexibility is a very good thing in the Guerrilla studio.

The way you implement MIDI depends on your studio. If you record on analog tape and don't have a sequencer, you might not have much use for MIDI, except maybe to thicken up keyboard sounds by having one synthesizer "slave" (control) another. In this case, you'd just plug a 5-pin MIDI cable into the MIDI OUT jack of the synth you're playing, and plug the cable's other end into the other synth's MIDI IN jack. Then you'd set up the second synth to receive MIDI data (check the manual), feed both synths' audio into your mixer, and blend the audio signals there. If you wanted to add a third synth, you'd plug another cable into the second synth's MIDI THRU jack, which spits out an exact copy of the MIDI signal coming into the unit, and plug the other end into your third synth's MIDI IN jack.

These days, though, many home recordists have some kind of MIDI sequencing going on in their studio. For most, this means a computer program is recording and playing back MIDI information—sending it either to another program that generates audio (such as a software synth), or out of the computer to some kind of MIDI interface, which sends and receives both data from the computer and data from your external hardware (synths, drum machines, etc.). The manner in which you set up MIDI in your studio is beyond the scope of this book; it varies widely and can get quite complicated if you're coordinating numerous pieces of external hardware with several software programs. There are plenty of resources out there to help you choose and configure your MIDI gear. In Chapter 8 I'll explain how you can harness MIDI's flexibility not only to make your recordings sound more "real," but also to make you sound like a better musician than you really are.

MIDI jacks, which allow pieces of electronic gear to communicate with each other, on (top to bottom) a keyboard, MIDI/computer interface, effect box, and MIDI drum controller.

CHAPTER 3

A Guided Tour Of The Signal Chain

In order to wrap your head around the principles of recording, it helps to think in terms of the *signal chain.* This term describes the path that an audio signal (or electrical sound waves, if you prefer) takes in your studio as it goes from its originating source to a version that's fixed on a recording medium (analog or digital). A common and useful way to visualize this path is to imagine the signal as water flowing through a series of pipes. Of course, this is just a visualization aid; as we saw in Chapter 2, electrons in an alternating current don't actually flow like water, but in effect, a signal does flow from one place to another. We say the signal travels *down* the signal chain (the way water flows downhill), and we may speak of an effect box *downstream* (later in the signal chain) or a mic preamp *upstream* (earlier in the chain).

Recall from Chapter 2 that unless you actually want to record noise, you always want signal-to-noise ratios to be as high as possible: more signal, less noise. That's true for any particular point in the signal chain, which means making the signal as "hot" (high in level) as possible without causing distortion at that point. But you also have to make sure your hot level isn't creating distortion at any point downstream in the chain. Complicating this is the fact that a signal chain is made up of *stages*, with signal amplification or attenuation occurring at each stage. A signal's level can go up several times in different stages of your chain, and it can also go down at certain stages, and perhaps up again later still. As a recording engineer, your job is to properly manage the signal-to-noise ratio at every stage of the signal chain (see Fig. 1)—making sure the signal is hot enough to keep noise at bay, but not so hot as to create distortion downstream. This management process is called *gain-staging*, "gain" referring to the amplification (or attenuation, which is negative gain) that occurs at each stage.

Let's follow the path a signal might take in a Guerrilla studio—first in a tracking session, and then in a mixing session.

Microphones

As you know, sound waves in the air need to be converted to electrical sound waves in order for us to do anything with them, and the microphone is our tool to do this.

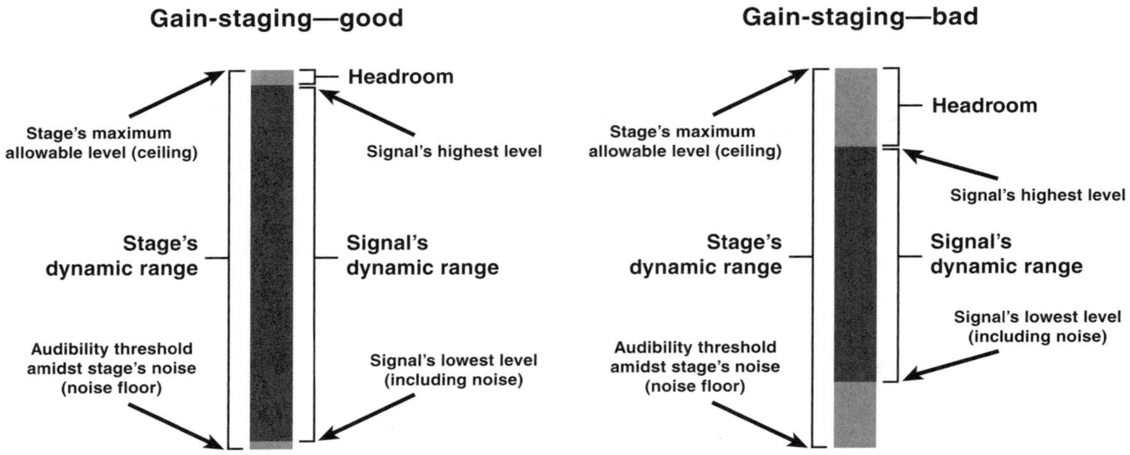

Fig. 1 Good gain-staging means making the most of each stage's dynamic range. At left, a signal's dynamic range (darker) is almost as large as the dynamic range of the stage it's passing through. At right, the signal is both too weak and too noisy—too much headroom remains at the top, and the signal's noise level is well above the noise floor. Result: A noisy recording with little dynamic impact.

Microphones come in several varieties. A *dynamic* microphone is the oldest design: Basically, it consists of a wire coil suspended in a magnetic field. When sound waves strike the coil, the coil moves along with the sound waves like a cork in the ocean. You may remember from high-school physics that when a wire coil moves in a magnetic field, a current is induced in the coil. If the coil moves one way, electrons in the coil flow in one direction; when the coil moves back, the electrons reverse direction. You know where this is going: Because of this action, with the flow of electrons matching the coil's movement, a small AC current is generated in the coil—one that's analogous to the sound waves in the air. So the sound has been converted to an analog electrical audio signal.

Dynamic mics are durable and can handle high SPLs (sound-pressure levels)—meaning they're great for loud sounds—but one problem is that the coil has a certain size and mass, which makes it not terribly sensitive to the tiniest sound waves: high frequencies. Since the highest frequencies are responsible for "air" or "transparency" in certain sounds, dynamic mics aren't the best at capturing these qualities in sounds that are rich in the highest harmonics. For that task, we turn to another class of mics: *condenser* mics. In a condenser mic, a tiny plate is given an electrical charge, and any physical changes in the plate (as a result of encountering sound waves) create a tiny current—an electrical audio signal. But unlike a dynamic mic, a condenser mic requires electricity to operate. This creates the charge in the audio-sensing plate and amplifies the resulting signal, which is considerably weaker than a dynamic mic's signal. This electricity can come from an internal battery or from *phantom power*, which is a direct current—usually 9 to 48 volts—sent to a microphone from a power source over the same cable. (Because it is a fixed voltage, phantom power doesn't interfere with the audio signal coming from the mic.) Many mixing boards and mic preamps provide phantom power. If you don't have a device that offers phantom power, you can purchase a standalone unit to power your mic. Some microphones—particularly expensive tube mics—come with their own power supply that takes care of this.

Choosing A Mic

So when do you use a dynamic mic, and when do you use a condenser? It depends on the sound you're recording. When choosing, think about each type's characteristics versus the sound you're capturing. Is the sound loud? How bright is it? In your song, will it be used in a subtle way, or should it convey force and power? For instance, vocals are almost always recorded with condenser mics; they're a major focal point in a song, so you want to capture every detail, and the "air" at the top of a vocal's frequency range adds to its intimacy and emotional impact. A crunching guitar amplifier, though, is best captured with a dynamic mic, which will provide more low-end punch and is less likely to distort under loud conditions. Even if you lose a bit of the highs, that's okay—other instruments have plenty of highs, so listeners may never know what they're missing.

In addition to dynamic vs. condenser, mics are classified by another factor, their *directional pattern* (see Fig. 2). A mic can be *omnidirectional*, or "omni," meaning it's

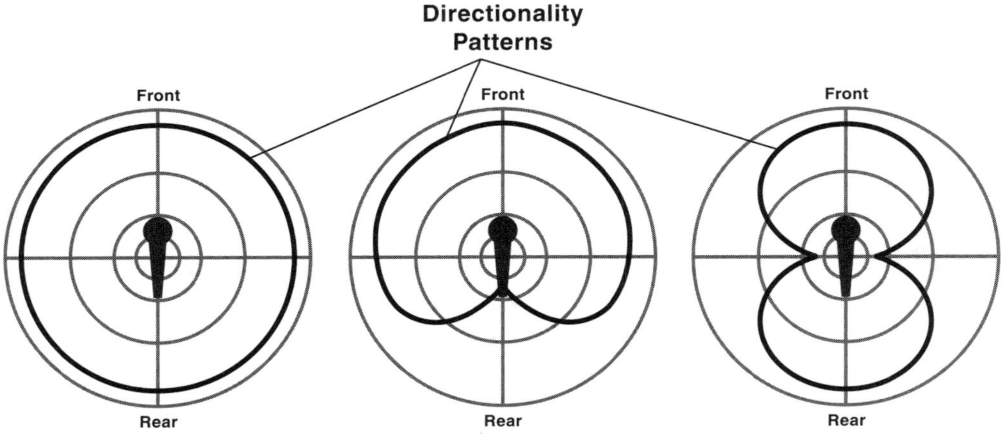

Fig. 2 Omnidirectional (left), cardioid (center), and figure-8 (right) directional mic patterns. Notice that the cardioid mic doesn't pick up sounds that are directly behind it. The figure-8 mic rejects sounds from the sides.

> **GUERRILLA TACTIC** *Break The Rules!*
>
> Many years ago, I got a great "bass" sound by detuning a guitar's bottom strings and overloading the hell out of the mixer's input. As I recall, that board, which I bought for about $600 at Guitar Center, didn't have XLR mic inputs—just ¼" ins with a switch for mic-level signals. That's the position I chose, with the trim knob cranked all the way up. I picked the "bass" line hard, the overload LED lit up bright, and I got a great, wacky fuzz tone that was very useful after a little EQing.
>
> Even though the "rules" are here to help you get a clean sound for most audio applications, sometimes you can get amazing sounds by just throwing the rules to the wind and simply abusing your equipment. Use common sense—but know that on most occasions, your gear can handle it. Remember that you won't know what an unusual, unorthodox recording technique sounds like unless you give it a try. In many cases it will sound like crap, but on the occasion that it works artistically, the result can be pure magic.

equally sensitive to sounds coming physically from the front (straight into the mic) as from the sides and rear. *Directional* or *cardioid* mics, which are more common in studios, are most sensitive to sounds coming from the front ("on-axis" sounds), less sensitive to sounds coming from the sides, and least sensitive to sounds coming from the rear (the latter two called "off-axis" sounds). In general, cardioid mics are a good choice for the Guerrilla studio, because we care only about the source of the sound—not the room's sound. Another pattern is called *hypercardioid*, which is similar to cardioid but even more directional. And some mics (such as the perennially popular AKG C 414) allow you to switch patterns. The C 414 includes a less-common figure-8 pattern, which is equally sensitive from the front and back but rejects sound coming from the sides. This is a good choice if you're recording vocals with another person: One of you stands in front of the mic and the other stands behind.

So, let's say you've hooked up a microphone to a balanced-line cable by way of its XLR connectors. You could plug the other end into a dedicated mic preamp, but let's assume you're like most Guerrilla recordists and don't have an external mic preamp. In that case you'd plug into the mixing board and use one of the board's mic preamps to bring the signal up to line level.

Mixer Channel Inputs

Here's where we begin a close look at the mixing board, the studio's equivalent of Grand Central Station. I love the way non-musicians react when they see my 24-channel mixing board, with its hundreds of seemingly identical knobs. They think I must be a genius—or at least a mad scientist—to know how to operate it. But a mixing board is easy to understand if you break it down into its components. A board has

> LOOK ■ OUT!
>
> ### Powering Up Phantom Power
>
> Get into the habit of switching on the board's phantom power *after* the board is switched on and the mic is connected. Due to possible electrical surges, it may be bad for the mic if you power up your board with a mic already connected and the phantom power on, or to plug the mic into a powered-up mixer with the phantom power already flowing. The safest power-up order to follow is: (1) Turn on the mixer with the mic disconnected, (2) make sure the phantom power is off, (3) plug in the mic, and (4) switch on the phantom power. When you're done with the session, turn off the phantom power first; then it's safe to disconnect the mic and/or shut down the board.

a number of vertically oriented *input channels*, each of which is divided into a number of sections with separate functions (see Fig. 3). The board processes these channels separately, and then it blends them to two (or more) output channels. Mixing boards are designed to make sense: The signals start at the top (meaning the part farthest away as you stand in front) and "flows" toward you, section by section, so that's how we'll look at an input channel's various components.

A signal's journey within the board, naturally, begins with the inputs. Input jacks vary from board to board, but most boards have at least one ¼" input jack, and usually an XLR jack, at the top of each channel. Older models may have RCA jacks in addition to, or instead of, the ¼" jacks. In most cases the ¼" jack represents the channel's input for line-level sources (i.e., its line input), but since the output of units like synthesizers and drum machines are close to line level (and usually have ¼" output jacks), this is where these signals normally enter the board. The channel's XLR jack is for an incoming microphone signal or a signal from a direct box—more on that in a

> LOOK ■ OUT!
>
> ### Maximize Your Levels At The Source
>
> Anytime you're using an electronic unit (synth, drum machine, etc.) as a sound source for recording, make sure its volume control is turned all the way up. If it isn't, you'll need to bring up the level later in the signal chain—and that means any noise picked up along the way, such as in the cable or at the input stage itself, will be boosted along with the signal. Assuming the manufacturer hasn't made a product that can accidentally self-distort (which would be pretty lame), there's no risk in turning it up full blast. In the unlikely case that the unit does self-distort (i.e., if you can hear the distortion even when you plug your headphones directly into the unit), just use trial and error, getting the most undistorted sound out of the unit that you can.

moment. Ordinarily, a switch determines which jack is active; if you're plugging in a microphone, the appropriate setting might be labeled MIC IN.

Many boards have an additional TAPE input jack on each input channel, along with a switch that selects between MIC/LINE and TAPE (or something similar). This allows the channel to have different roles during the tracking and mixing phases of recording. During tracking, you might set this switch to MIC/LINE and use the mic or line input jacks as appropriate. Then, during mixing, you might set these switches to TAPE and feed your multitrack system's outputs into the TAPE input jacks. This is convenient, because you can leave the multitrack's outputs permanently plugged into the TAPE inputs and use them only when you need to. If you have enough board channels, you can dedicate certain channels to the multitrack's outputs and use the others for tracking. If you don't have this luxury, though, you'll be doing a lot less plugging and unplugging by taking advantage of the board's TAPE inputs and switches.

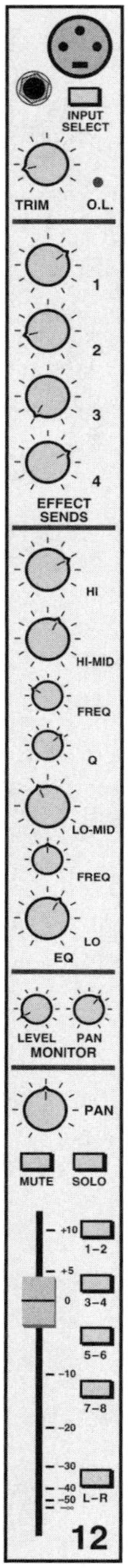

Fig. 3 A typical mixing-board input channel. A signal starts at the top and flows downward to the fader.

Gain-Staging At The Inputs

Setting up the input stage is critical—it's the board's "first impression" of a signal, and if the signal gets screwed up here, it will remain screwed up for the rest of the signal chain, all the way to CD. To help you, most if not all boards have a knob, switch, or both for setting the input's sensitivity to the incoming signal. Here's your first chance to practice gain-staging: The idea is that no matter what the signal is, you want to bring it up to line level right here. The input-sensitivity knob is called the *trim pot*, "pot" being short for potentiometer, the electronic component that the knob is physically connected to. The switch is called a *pad*. If a signal is too strong for the chosen input, we need to *pad down* or *trim* (attenuate) the signal. How do we know if it's too strong? If it is overloading the input, it's too strong. Most boards have an LED on each input channel to indicate overload; it might be labeled OL or PEAK, and it might be located at the top of the board (in the input section) or farther down. On my board, in addition to the red OL LED, there's a green LED labeled –20DB, which lights up when a signal entering that channel's input is 20dB below the overload point. When that green LED just barely lights, I know I have 20dB to spare before I run into problems with overloading the input. If your board doesn't have these input indication LEDs, you'll just have to use your ears. Headphones are a useful tool for listening closely to hear whether distortion is setting in—but usually if a mixer input is overloading, it's immediately obvious.

Let's say you are using the channel as a mic input. Plug the microphone cable into the XLR input, assuming your board has one; if not, you'll need to use a transformer adapter. If the mic is phantom-powered, turn on the board's phantom power. If the board lacks phantom power, you'll have to use an external phantom-power device, or switch to a mic that uses battery power or comes with its own power supply. As a last resort, you can use a dynamic mic.

Once you're sure the mic is active—here's where a green –20DB LED comes in handy—shout "check!" into the mic a little louder than you think you'll get in the performance you're about to record. If you're recording something else, like a guitar amp, play a little louder than you will during the recording. Now, as you do this, watch the overload LED. If it lights already, turn down the trim control a little and try again. If the trim control is down all the way and the input is still overloading, you'd better hope there's a switch that will add another level of pad; if not, you won't be able to record that source with that mic without putting something in between the mic and board to cut the signal.

If, however, your mic signal is not overloading the input on your first mic check, grab that trim control and turn it up a little. Keep going and see if you can get the input to overload a little. If it does, back off the knob about one-twelfth of a turn—that's one "hour" if you think of the knob's position as a clock's hour hand. (If you hear someone say something like "turn the knob to 3 o'clock," this is what they mean.) In the case of input overload, safe is definitely better than sorry. You don't want to be singing the vocal performance of a lifetime, only to have it ruined by a blat of distortion at your peak moment. Similar to what I said in Chapter 2 regarding digital recording levels, shoot for sending a *moderately hot* signal to the mixer's next stage. You definitely don't want the input to distort, but you don't want it to be 20dB below distortion, either. If you're –20dB here, you're losing 20dB of your signal-to-noise ratio right off the bat. Why? Because eventually you *will* need to bring that signal up to line level, and in doing so, you'll boost the noise floor 20dB higher than it needs to be. And in the recording world, 20dB of noise is way too much—especially when it could have been prevented with a quick, simple pre-recording procedure.

If you're recording a synth, drum machine, or some other not-quite-line-level device, use the ¼" input and the exact same procedure. The levels of electronic sources are more predictable than miked-up acoustic sources, so you can afford to get a slightly hotter signal from them without worrying about mixer-input overload.

Before we go on to the mixer channel's next section, let's step back a bit and consider another source: the direct input.

Direct-Input Instruments

In the mid 1960s, engineers discovered something interesting: Electric guitars and basses could be recorded "direct," meaning straight out of the instrument, without an amplifier. Up to that point, all instruments had been recorded with microphones only, including electronic instruments. It was revolutionary when engineers figured out a way to eliminate the middleman—where instead of miking up an amplified electric guitar, they could plug the guitar straight into the mixing board. This technique required the invention of the direct box, one of the Guerrilla recordist's Essential Tools listed in Chapter 1. Without getting too technical, a direct box—also called a DI, short for either direct input or direct injection, depending on whom you ask—makes the translation between the guitar's electronics and the mixer input's electronics. To hear what it sounds like to record direct without a direct box, try plugging a guitar or bass straight into the mixer input's ¼" jack and listen through headphones. Pretty crappy sound, right? All the highs get rolled off when you do this, and you usually don't want to start off with a sound that's been compromised so much. A direct box allows all of the instrument's frequencies to pass through to the next stage, the same way a guitar amp's own input is designed to work.

Direct boxes have balanced XLR output jacks. Treat a direct-box signal the same way you would a mic signal: Plug it into either a mic input on the board or an outboard mic preamp if you have one. The signal will likely be stronger than a mic's, so you may need to turn down the channel's input trim pot to prevent overload. And speaking of overload, it's possible to overload the direct box itself if your guitar or bass has a built-in preamp or if the direct box is the *active* kind, meaning it contains its own preamp and requires a battery to operate. Electronics can be either active or *passive*; active electronics require power to operate and include some kind of amplification circuit, whereas passive electronics require no power. The difference shouldn't be terribly important to you, except that if you know a circuit (such as a direct box's) is active, the circuit is capable of overloading. A passive direct box, when fed by a passive instrument—such as an electric guitar with standard pickups and no internal preamp—will not be overloaded, no matter how hard you play. We say the circuit has unlimited *headroom*, the word used to describe the "loud" end of the dynamic range. (Not surprisingly, headroom is kind of the opposite of the noise floor.) But as soon as an active circuit enters the picture, the headroom has a definite limit, and you need to keep your signal under this threshold. How do you know where this threshold lies? In the case of a direct box that has no kind of overload indicator, you have to use your ears. It's as simple as that. If you're playing guitar, slam an open *E* chord and listen for distortion on headphones. If you're playing bass, pound the open *E* with your thumb or pop the *G* string. The resulting sound should be clean and full, not gritty or grainy. If you do hear distortion, turn down the instrument's master volume knob and try again; if the direct box itself has knobs, try tweaking those instead. Find a setting where you're certain you won't overload the circuit while you're fully rocking out, but not so much that you'll have to amplify your signal—and the noise—greatly in the next stage.

Mixer Inserts

Most decent mixing boards provide an *insert* jack somewhere near the channel's input jacks. This insert is usually a ¼" TRS jack. The idea behind inserts is that plugging something into the jack breaks the signal chain at that point, in effect "siphoning" or "shunting" the signal away. Insert jacks are incredibly convenient; I don't know how I could record without them. If you're familiar with effect-loop SEND and RETURN jacks on amplifiers, you know how inserts are used: They allow you to run the signal through external processing gear and then return the signal to the main circuit to continue on. This external processing gear can be anything you need for a particular task (see Fig. 4).

When I'm tracking, I use the insert on practically every signal that goes into my board—and for Guerrilla Home Recording, I recommend that you do the same. After trying numerous approaches, I've settled on using the insert to run the signal through a compressor/expander (see Chapter 4) followed by a 31-band graphic EQ, which is often set to bypass mode. This way the graphic EQ is essentially out of the circuit, but it's instantly available should the need arise. So, I have one TRS "Y" adapter, which is connected to my compressor/expander/EQ sub-chain, hanging around the back of the board ready to be stuck into an insert jack. During tracking I usually use only one or two board channels as inputs, so this "Y" adapter usually remains in place in one

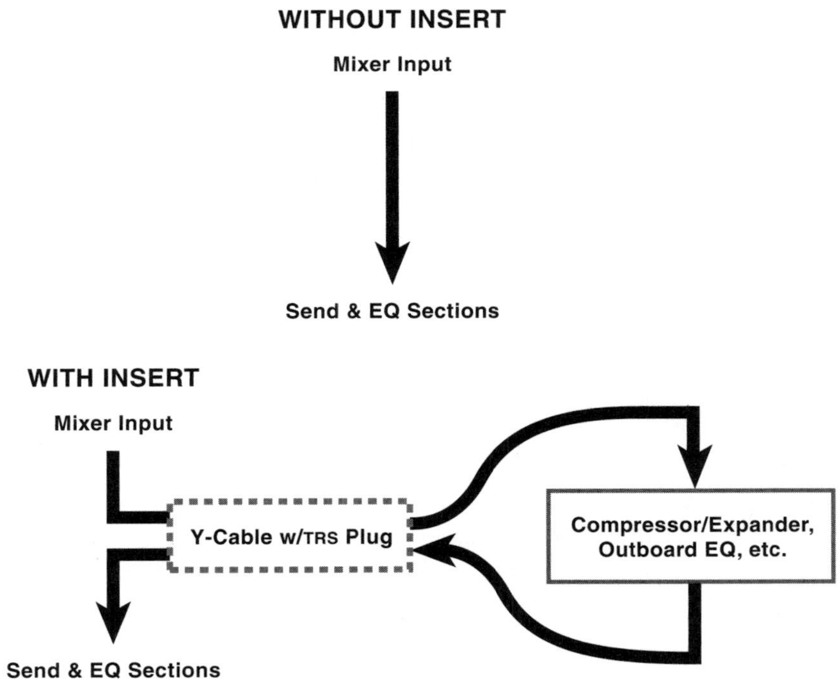

Fig. 4 An insert point breaks into the signal chain with a single ¼" TRS plug, allowing you to shunt the signal out of the board for external processing. A "Y" adapter, along with the TRS plug, provides both outgoing and returning paths for the insert.

of the insert jacks. If I need to take the insert sub-chain out of the main signal chain, or if I need to use the sub-chain on a different channel, or if I'm mixing a song and I need to run one of the tracks through the sub-chain again, I can just yank the adapter out of its "home" and plug it into a different insert jack. I also have two more inserts representing the left and right channels of a stereo exciter/enhancer sub-chain (see Chapter 6), but I don't use these nearly as often as my main insert sub-chain.

One last point about inserts: Think of an insert as a proper signal-chain stage. Amplification may very well be going on somewhere in the insert sub-chain, so watch your gain-staging to avoid unwanted distortion or undue noise. If you're close to running out of headroom at the input stage, it's certainly possible to overload the main signal chain's next stage with just a slight boost in the insert sub-chain. Most external effect devices have a master-out level control as well as a BYPASS switch, so a good way to gain-stage in the sub-chain is to bypass the effect(s), watch the board's meters, and compare the resulting signal with the non-bypassed version. If you find that a sub-chain device is boosting the signal level, turn down its master-output control until it more closely matches the bypassed version. If there is more than one device in the insert sub-chain, perform this procedure for each, in the order that the signal flows. The good news: This is pretty much a "set it and forget it" situation; I haven't had to tweak the output levels in my insert sub-chains for years. But be aware that there's always potential for trouble in the sub-chain. For example, to prevent distortion from happening after the signal gets a radical EQ boost, try to cut some frequencies to balance the ones you're boosting—that way, the overall level won't be very different. (Remember that low frequencies carry more energy than high ones.)

Effect Sends

On most boards, immediately after the inputs and/or inserts is the EFFECT SEND (sometimes called AUX SEND) section. An effect send is kind of like a partial insert: Instead of interrupting the signal chain and shunting away 100 percent of the signal, an effect send takes only a portion of the signal to be used for some purpose, usually to send to an external effect whose sound will be mixed back in at some later point in the chain. Actually, "takes" isn't the most accurate word here, though, because an effect send doesn't remove any of the signal from the signal chain; the signal remains unchanged as it passes through the effect-send circuit. Imagine if a water engineer could build a dam that diverted some of a river's water into a pipe without reducing the river's flow downstream—that's exactly what an effect send is like.

Your mixing board likely has at least one row of effect-send knobs (one per channel), and it probably has a master effect-send knob off to the right of all the input channels, as well as an effect-send output jack on the board's back. If your board has two, three, or more rows of send knobs, each row probably has its own master send knob and output jack. More rows of effect sends means more flexibility—but for simplicity's sake, let's assume for now that your board has just one row. If a signal is coming down channel 1 and that channel's effect-send knob is turned all the way down, there will be no signal at the effect-send jack. But turn it up a little, and a low-level version of the channel's signal will begin to come out of the jack. As you turn up the effect-send knob, the signal at the effect-send jack will get louder and louder. Now imagine that a different signal starts coming through channel 2 as well: If you turn up channel 2's effect-send knob, coming out of the effect-send jack will be a blend of the signals coming through channels 1 and 2. The proportion of the signals in this blend depends on where the effect-send knobs are set; if you want more channel 1, turn the channel 1 knob higher than channel 2's. The idea is that this blend will be sent to an external effect—reverb, for instance—and since you rarely want reverb added equally to all instruments, you use the effect-send knobs to determine which channels get a lot of reverb, which get only a little, and which get none at all. The master effect-send knob sets the overall level so you can get the right amount of signal going into your external effect—not enough to overload the effect, but enough to keep its signal-to-noise ratio high. (Does this sound familiar?) You could set this level by moving all of the individual effect-send knobs up or down by the same amount, but this would be inconvenient and imprecise with a lot of channels. The master knob just makes life a little easier for us.

As I mentioned, most boards have more than one row of effect sends. (You might read that a board has "four effect sends"; that means four sends per channel, not four knobs overall.) If you have only one external effect, more sends won't really help you—but most people have more than one effect. You can create some very nice spatial sounds by having two different reverbs going at once during a mixdown, which pretty much requires two sends to accomplish (although you could get around it with some creative rigging). Still, you can make an excellent mix with just one good reverb and careful use of those individual effect-send knobs. More on how to use reverb in Chapter 6.

One clever feature employed on some boards' effect-send sections is a SHIFT button on each channel. This allows you to split, say, two rows of effect sends into three: Depressing the SHIFT button causes one of the two effect sends to pass a signal to a third master send knob and output. By shifting the sends on only some of the board's channels, you can create three entirely independent effect-send blends with only two rows of effect-send knobs. (Of course, each channel can contribute to only two of these blends—one for each send knob.) If a board has four sends, a SHIFT button can split those four sends into six.

If you send a signal to an external effect, at some point it has to return to the main signal chain, right? That's where *effect returns* come in. But effect returns are usually located at the end of the board's signal chain, so we'll get to those a little later.

EQ Section

We don't need to pause here for long, because we discussed EQ in Chapter 2. You'll usually find the board's EQ section after the effect sends. The simplest (and least useful) board EQs have two knobs: high shelving and low shelving. If there's a third knob it's for mids, and if there's a fourth knob, it's probably for specifying the mid knob's center frequency. Some semi-pro mixing boards have as many as seven EQ knobs: high, low, high-mid, high-mid frequency, high-mid Q (bandwidth), low-mid, and low-mid frequency. If you paid attention to the previous chapter, you'd know that this means the highs and lows are the typical shelving types, the high-mids are fully parametric, and the low-mids are semi-parametric. This setup is highly flexible and rivals the EQ capabilities on pro boards—but I'm not going to tell you that you need to upgrade to a board with so many EQ knobs, because you don't. Having only shelving high and low EQs, plus a single semi-parametric (sweepable) mid, can work fine. To reiterate, a sweepable mid is perhaps the most important feature on a mixer channel. If you have only shelving high and low EQs, you'll improve your sonic potential by upgrading to a board with a sweepable mid. But if you can't do that right now, with practice, you can get a lot of mileage out of an external EQ in an insert sub-chain, as described above. I believe that by paying your dues in this way with less flexible gear now, you'll really improve your ear and make your recordings that much better later—when you *are* able to upgrade.

As with the insert sub-chain, you should regard the EQ section as a proper gain stage as well: Boosts here can create unwanted distortion in the next stage. Don't boost too much, try to cut frequencies as well where possible, listen closely (good headphones are always useful for detecting the first signs of signal breakup), and, if you run into trouble, trim the signal a bit at the board's input stage. The price of a clean, quiet signal is eternal gain-staging vigilance!

Monitor Section

Not all boards have this section, which may be called something else (my board calls it "Mix B"). A monitor section is similar to the effect-send section: It allows you to create at least one independent mix of the signals going through the board's input channels. However, unlike mono effect sends, the monitor section often lets you create a *stereo* mix that's separate from any other mix that the board might be creating. This is useful during tracking, especially if two musicians are playing at the same time: a bass player may want to hear more drums, while a singer may want to hear more guitar. Being able to set up two entirely different mixes allows you to give each musician what he or she wants. If you're recording a whole band live, the board's main function will probably be to deliver a line-level signal of each instrument to the multitrack—and since it's almost certain that the musicians won't want to hear all the instruments up full in their headphones while they're playing, the monitor section lets you set up a musician-friendly monitor mix without affecting the levels going to tape or disk. There are other ways to use the monitor section as well, even if you're recording by yourself; I'll get to them a bit later in this chapter.

Pan Pot & Fader

We've come almost to the bottom of the board as the signal travels down the channel; it will eventually have to go somewhere. The *pan pot* and *fader* play important roles in determining where the signal goes, and how much will go. Since all mixing boards you're likely to see are manufactured to mix sound in stereo (two output channels, left and right), we need to be able to tell the board how to distribute all of its various input channels between the left and right output channels. That's what a pan pot does: It specifies where in a two-channel stereo output—or any pair of channels, really—the signal should be placed. If the pan pot is straight up in the 12 o'clock position, the signal will go to both channels equally and therefore will appear to be in the center of the stereo image. If you slowly pan a sound from 9 o'clock to 3 o'clock, the sound will appear to move from left to right. If you turn the pan pot all the way to the left, the signal will go only to the first of the two channels. If it's a stereo signal, we say the sound is "panned hard left" in this case: It will come out of the left speaker only.

The fader, right at the bottom of the board, is that all-important control that sets the signal's level as it leaves the channel. Think of it as an output valve: The higher it's set, the hotter the signal will be going to wherever it's going. Some faders are labeled arbitrarily, for example 0 through 10; others use decibel markings, with 0dB up around the three-quarter mark, positive numbers above 0dB, and negative numbers below. On these boards, you'll find -∞dB at the very bottom, representing "signal completely off." The 0dB point represents what is called *unity gain*—it means the signal at this stage is neither boosted nor cut. It's merely passed through at the same level that it entered the fader.

The faders are a mixing board's most sexy feature, and some faders are definitely nicer than others. Expensive boards have faders with a smooth, syrupy feel that's conducive to flawless fade-ins and fade-outs; cheaper boards have faders that feel lightweight, rough, or otherwise just cheap. Some boards are advertised as having "long-throw" faders, meaning they have a longer travel from one end of their range to the other, which allows for more precise and subtle level settings. Sweet faders are a nice luxury, but they're by no means necessary to create a good recording. In fact, after I converted to a digital system and started doing much of my mixing within the computer's recording program, I cut back on my fader usage by probably 90 percent.

Digital recordists could theoretically get by with a board that has no faders at all, although faders always come in handy.

Busses & Assigns

Up to now, all of the input channels have remained more or less separate, but here is where the mixing board combines things. The simplest boards have just two output channels—the left and right sides. If a board has eight input channels and two output channels, we describe it as being an 8x2 board: eight ins, two outs. In that case, each input channel is sending its signal to the two output channels, balanced between them depending on the pan pot's position—pretty simple.

More flexible mixing boards offer *busses*, which are additional output channels, each with its own output fader and output jack. On a board with busses, an input channel's destinations are designated by *assign switches*, which are usually located near the channel's fader. Each assign switch represents a pair of busses (busses 1 and 2, busses 3 and 4, etc.), and there's also a switch for the master stereo output (sometimes labeled simply L/R or MIX). These switches allow you to send an input channel's signal to the master stereo output channels, to any pair of busses, or any combination thereof, for maximum flexibility. The input channel's pan pot determines how the signal is balanced in each pair of channels. For example, say you assigned input channel 8 to send its signal to busses 1 and 2 plus busses 3 and 4, as well as to the master stereo output channels. In this case, turning channel 8's pan pot all the way to the right would send the signal to bus 2, bus 4, and the stereo output's right channel, with nothing going to busses 1 or 3 or to the left channel. Got it?

When you're tracking, busses are normally set up to send signals to your multitrack system, completely independently of the master stereo output channels. A mixing board with four busses is ideal for recording to a 4-track system; one with eight is ideal for an 8-track. In this arrangement, you'd use a cable to connect each bus's output jack to the corresponding input on the multitrack. This way, if you had a mic plugged into input channel 8 and you wanted to record it onto the multitrack's track 1, you'd press the bus 1/2 assign button and turn up the bus 1 fader. (If you wanted to make sure no signal was going to bus 2, you could also crank channel 8's pan pot hard-left, or make sure the bus 2 fader was all the way down, but this would be unnecessary if you weren't also recording onto track 2.) So here's what's happening: You sing, and the mic's signal enters input channel 8, goes through the effect-send and EQ sections, goes through the fader, and then gets sent to bus 1. Bus 1, in turn, sends the signal to the multitrack's track 1, causing the multitrack's meter to react with your singing. Fig. 5 shows a schematic diagram of this signal chain.

That's great—but how do you hear yourself to make sure you're singing with the tracks that have already been recorded? One way would be to assign the input channel to the master stereo output as well as bus pair 1 and 2; when you plug your headphones into the board, you should hear yourself. It's more flexible and convenient, though, to create a monitor mix using the monitor section, if your board has one. If so, there will be a way to get the monitor mix to your headphones—check the manual. It's usually just a matter of hitting a button over near the headphone jack.

Each bus may also have its own switch for assigning the signal to the master stereo outputs. If you activate it, you'll hear the signal from the bus blended into the stereo output signal (without affecting the signal going to the bus's output jack). This is another way to monitor yourself while tracking.

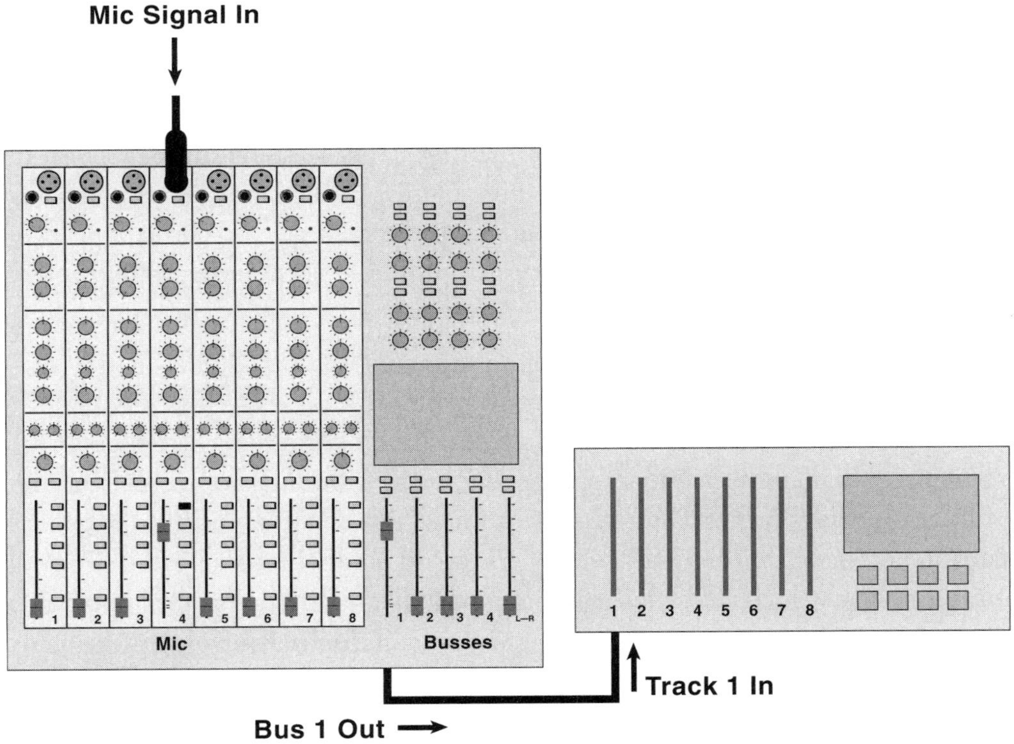

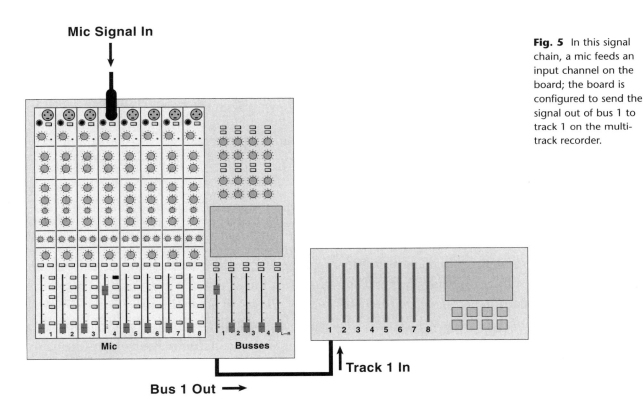

Fig. 5 In this signal chain, a mic feeds an input channel on the board; the board is configured to send the signal out of bus 1 to track 1 on the multitrack recorder.

By the way, if you hear a mixing board described with three numbers, the middle number refers to how many busses it has. For example, "8x4x2" means the board has eight input channels, four busses, and the usual master stereo output.

Pre/Post Switches

These switches, which often appear on input channels, let you choose *where* in the signal chain something happens: pre-fader, meaning before the fader, or post-fader, meaning after it. For example, if an effect send is set to be pre-fader (the button may be labeled simply PRE), then the send circuit will do its thing before the signal hits the fader. In this mode, changing the signal's level at the fader won't change the level going to your effect. For example, if you have a vocal coming through the channel and the effect send is feeding a reverb, pushing the PRE button lets you fade out the vocal until nothing is left but pure reverb. But if you want the reverb level to follow the signal's overall level (which is usually preferable), set the effect send to post-fader mode. That way, the effect-send circuit will encounter the signal *after* it has come out of the fader, so bringing down the fader will also bring down the level going to your reverb—instant reverb fade, perfectly matched to your vocal fade.

Mute, Solo, Lo-Cut & Phase Switches

Most boards offer a MUTE switch near each input-channel fader; this simply turns off that channel, as if you pulled the fader all the way down. Pushing this button, and then pushing it again to un-mute the channel, is a handy way to eliminate noises that you don't want between passages that you do want—for example, throat-clearing between vocal verses. Some recordists prefer to simply erase any portions of a track that would otherwise be muted; the decision is up to you.

A SOLO switch is kind of the opposite of MUTE: It mutes every channel *other* than the one you're soloing. Soloing a track is usually done more as a diagnostic procedure than as a part of actual tracking or mixing; for example, if you're hearing some gritty distortion in a mix but you're unsure of what track it's on, soloing tracks one by one usually points out the culprit—and it's a lot easier than trying to do the same thing with the MUTE buttons.

Some boards have a LO-CUT switch on each channel. This is essentially a shelving EQ with a sharp rolloff of the lowest lows. It's most useful to engage when recording vocals or other mic sources, where there may be rumbling sounds picked up through the mic stand, or "P-pops" or other breath noises, that you don't want on the track. Just remember to disengage this switch before you record a bass or kick-drum track, though—otherwise those critical frequencies will be filtered out, and the track will be ruined.

Pro boards and a few semi-pro boards also incorporate a PHASE switch on each input channel. This may not seem to do anything when you try it, but actually it flips over the audio signal so it becomes a "mirror image" of itself. If a sound starts with its wave shape going up, then you hit the PHASE switch, it will start with its wave shape going down (see Fig. 6). This button isn't of much use for Guerrilla recordists; it's used mostly in multiple-mic tracking situations. For instance, if you have two mics on a snare drum (one on the top and one on the bottom), you would want to reverse the phase of one mic so it will reinforce, rather than partially cancel out, the other. This is because while the top drumhead is going down (away from the top mic), the bottom head is probably also going down (toward the bottom mic)—and you want the wave shapes from the two mics to always be going in the same direction. Otherwise, the sound can be weakened considerably. But even if your board has these switches, as a Guerrilla recordist you may never use them.

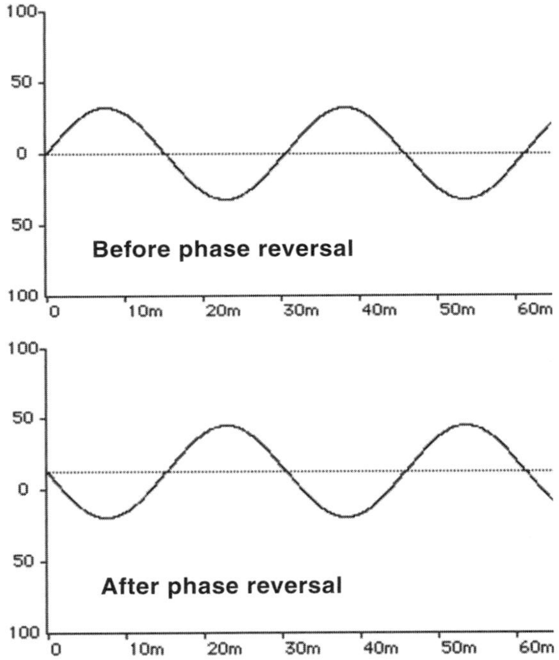

Fig. 6 A board's PHASE button inverts the audio signal so the wave shape becomes a mirror image of itself.

Effect Returns

As far as I know, every board with effect sends also has effect returns. Effect returns can be either mono or stereo. A mono effect return usually has one input jack, one level knob, and possibly a balance (or pan) control. A stereo effect return usually has two input jacks (one for each stereo channel), one level knob affecting both channels equally, and perhaps a BALANCE knob, which can tip the stereo effect-return signal to the left or right relative to its stereo destination. If the board has a bus section, there will invariably be assign buttons for each effect return as well: These allow you to assign the returning effect signal to a bus, the master stereo outs, or both.

LOOK ■ OUT!

Audio Vs. Data Compression

Don't confuse audio compression with data compression. Audio compression—that's the kind performed by outboard compressor/limiters and compressor/expanders—refers to intentionally reducing a sound's dynamic range to improve a recording's quality (explained in detail in Chapter 4). Data compression, on the other hand, is a necessary evil in some systems to increase the total duration of sound the system can record. Data compression involves running the digital data through an additional encoding process on recording and then decoding it on playback. Less disk space is used as a result, but it's a compromise: Inevitably there's some loss of sound quality.

An effect return is essentially a separate channel or pair of input channels, although it's not as flexible as an actual input channel. It usually has no EQ, and naturally it doesn't have its own effect sends. This may seem like a no-brainer—but I've often wanted to take an effect-send line from the signal coming back from an effect. Suppose you have one effect send going to a delay and another going to a reverb. The signal coming back from the delay will have no reverb on it—so blending it with the original signal plus the original's reverb may not sound very natural. There will be a sound with some reverb on it, and then a delayed version of that sound with no reverb on it. This may not be what you want. For this reason, I rarely use my effect returns. Instead, I run the returning signal into one or two input channels of its own. This way I can EQ the returning sound (maybe I want the echoes to sound more muffled), and I can also take pre- or post-fader effect sends from the returning signals. In the reverb-plus-delay example above, I'd simply take a reverb send from both the original sound and the returning delay. The reverb unit would receive a blend of the original plus the delayed sounds, and it would output a reverb for that blend. The result is that both the original sound and its delayed version end up with reverb on them, giving you a more natural effect.

I've also gotten some cool special effects by intentionally creating a positive feedback loop using effect sends: I might have the return from a delay or reverb feed back into itself, resulting in an interestingly chaotic, almost-out-of-control buildup of effect, which can be faded up or down (perhaps "encouraged or discouraged" would be a better way to put it) by working the return line's effect-send knob.

Effect returns are a great way for the Guerrilla recordist to get more signals going into the board—but if you have extra input channels available, consider using them instead.

Patchbays

A *patch* refers to any temporary signal chain set up (usually with cables) for a specific purpose. A *patchbay* can make creating patches easier for Guerrilla recordists, who can often be found reaching behind gear to plug and unplug stuff. A patchbay is simply a box with a bunch of jacks on the front and back, the goal being to put a bunch of inputs and outputs all in one convenient place. You can connect the jacks on the patchbay's back to all of the jacks you frequently plug and unplug on your gear. This way, you just need to plug into the front of the patchbay—no more reaching behind a piece of gear in the dark, or holding up a mirror and the flashlight to see what you're doing.

A patchbay consists of pairs of jacks (one top and one bottom), with a corresponding pair on the back. You can use a single jack as an output, perhaps for a favorite synth—just connect the synth to the corresponding rear jack. The front jack becomes a synth-output jack, ready to be sent wherever you need it. Similarly, a single jack can serve as an input, perhaps for an effect. But you can also have a signal flow *behind* a pair of front-panel jacks when nothing is connected through the front. To do this, plug a signal source into a top-rear jack, and connect its destination to the rear jack immediately under it (see Fig. 7a). Since the two jacks are connected inside the patchbay, this creates a default situation, which you can alter merely by plugging a cable into a front jack. For example, let's say you want a synthesizer to be "hard-wired" (permanently hooked up) to mixer input channel 1. Running the signal through a patchbay along the way would create convenient options. Plug a cable into the top jack on the patchbay's front and the cable effectively becomes a synth output (Fig. 7b); the signal will stop flowing out of the patchbay to the mixer. You can then run the synth through an effect and plug the effect's output into the bottom patchbay jack (Fig. 7c), completing the circuit and sending an effected synth signal to the board. If your effects are also prewired to the patchbay's back, connections become even more convenient.

A couple of patchbay terms: If plugging a cable into a patchbay pair interrupts the circuit (similar to a mixer's channel insert), the patchbay connection is said to be *normalled.* If it doesn't interrupt the signal but instead splits the signal into two identical paths, the connection is said to be *half-normalled* (Fig. 7d). Both types of routing are useful for various tasks.

A basic patchbay costs around $100, plus the cost of cables to wire the back. If you find yourself frustrated by a lot of clumsy plugging and unplugging in dark or difficult-to-access locations, consider adding a patchbay to your studio.

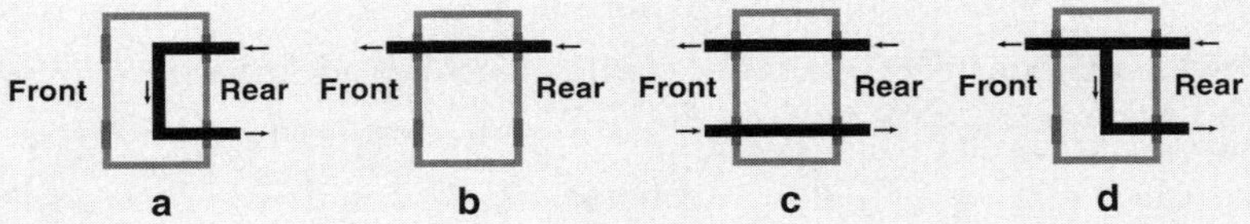

Fig. 7a–d Schematic cross-section of a normalled patchbay pair with no front-panel connections (Fig. 7a). Inserting a plug into the top jack (Fig. 7b) breaks into the signal chain, shunting the signal elsewhere. Inserting another plug into the bottom jack (Fig. 7c) allows the returning signal to continue along the same path that it was traveling in Fig. 7a. Fig. 7d is the same as Fig. 7b, only with a half-normalled patchbay.

Not Enough Inputs!

Since converting to digital, I've been spoiled by being able to work with as many as eight input channels unoccupied. But I remember the days of running an 8-track analog machine into only a 6-channel board. How did I do it? In Chapter 1 I mentioned an ancient mixer that I bought for $50. It had six ins and two outs, all RCA jacks. I used two tracks for drums and two for returning reverb, and I fed its stereo output into the main board's SUB IN jacks, which allowed me to blend a stereo signal straight into the board's outputs. I don't think there was a level control, but it wasn't necessary—I could just set the drums' and reverb's levels on the second mixer.

In this arrangement, the second mixer is known as a *submixer*. (On my 6-channel board, SUB IN stood for "submixer in.") Submixing is a great way to add additional channels to your setup without buying a whole new board (see Fig. 8). If your board doesn't have SUB IN jacks—perhaps it calls them something else, like AUX IN—you can use a stereo effect return, or as a last resort you can sacrifice two of its input channels. Then again, if you buy a submixer that's nicer and more flexible than your main mixer, consider using your new board as the main mixer and relegate the old one to submixing duties.

You may have to be a little creative getting all of your signals to come together, but do whatever it takes. It doesn't have to look pretty—as long as it sounds okay, who cares what it took to get the job done?

Multitrack Recording Media

Let's continue on with our signal-chain tour. We've finally left the mixing board, let's say out of one of the bus output jacks. Our next stop is the multitrack. This part of the studio can come in various forms. On the low end of the scale is the cassette 4-track. Years ago, all home recordists started out on one of these; Bruce Springsteen recorded his classic 1982 album *Nebraska* on one, and Ween made its 1991 breakthrough CD, *Pure Guava*, on one as well. You can get a decent, reasonably quiet sound on a cassette 4-track if you know what you're doing. But cassette 4-tracks are all but extinct now. They've been replaced by . . .

Standalone digital multitracks. Similar to the original 4-tracks in overall design, these record four, eight, or 16 tracks to either an internal hard drive or to removable media. They often have their own limited mixing boards built in, which vary in quality from manufacturer to manufacturer.

Standalones, particularly those that record to removable media, often employ data compression schemes to cram a maximum of track-minutes onto a disc or card. On many machines, you can select the type of compression used. But when data compression is involved, you compromise the sound somewhat. The higher rates are fine

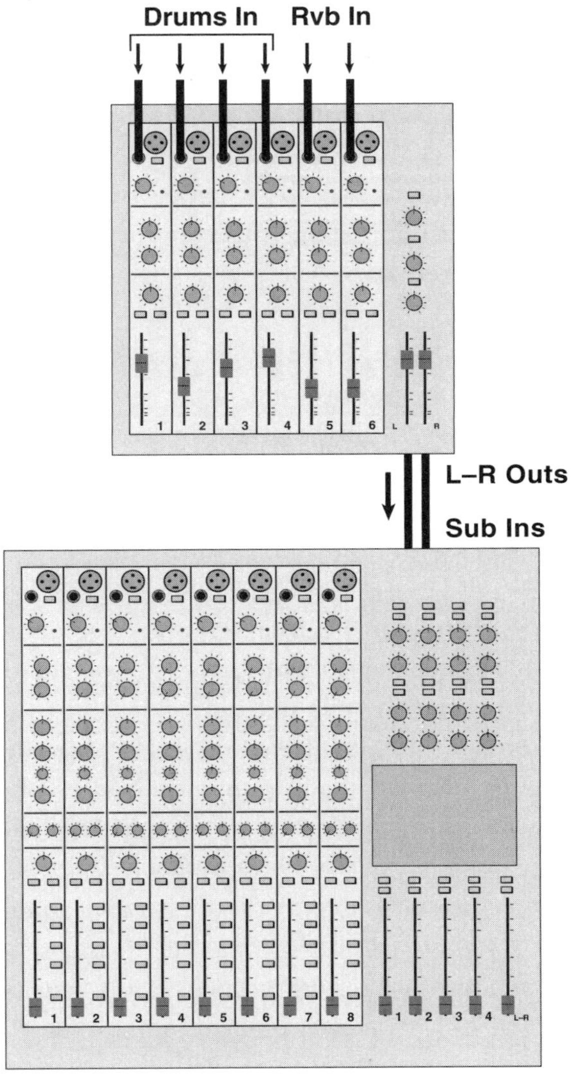

Fig. 8 Using a second mixing board (top) as a submixer for drums and reverb.

if you're using the machine as an audio sketchpad. As your ears improve, you'll begin hearing that the sound files recorded with data compression don't quite make it to CD quality. If you're shopping around, consider going with a unit that has the ability to record without data compression, as well as one with an internal hard drive—preferably with a USB or FireWire port, because you will need a way to back up the data as the drive fills up. For those aiming for a pro sound, zero-compression recording is the way to go.

Analog reel-to-reel tape. This is still the standard in many pro studios: the 2" 24-track machine. Analog Guerrilla recordists, though, are more likely to be using ¼" or ½" 8- or 16-track machines. These produce a much quieter, cleaner signal than a cassette 4-track, particularly if used with a good-quality noise-reduction system. For years, I recorded on a Tascam 38 ½" 8-track machine with a dbx noise-reduction system made specifically for the 38. The dbx scheme works by broadly compressing the audio on recording and expanding it an equal amount on playback; tape hiss, which was not part of the original signal, is thereby expanded away to near-silence. It worked very well and sounded great. You should be skeptical, though, of noise-reduction circuits built into more inexpensive recorders, because like built-in mixers, the circuits tend to be cheap and may compromise your sound quality.

Reel-to-reel is a great way to get immersed in recording, particularly if you want to chase after that analog-sound mojo. But analog tape is expensive and bulky, the sound may degrade over time (both with repeated playbacks and in storage), and threading the machine is a bit of a chore. Maintenance is also higher, as you're supposed to keep the tape heads clean and demagnetized.

Modular digital multitrack. This format exploded on the scene in the early '90s with the Alesis ADAT and the Tascam DA-88, opening the world of digital recording to the masses. MDMs record digitized audio onto videotape cassettes; a single machine can record eight tracks, and multiple machines can be cabled together to record 24 or more synchronized tracks. MDMs have become somewhat obsolete, since hard-disk recording has come down so much in price, but many people still use them. The signal on MDMs is much quieter than on comparable analog systems, but it's kind of a drag waiting for multiple machines to sync up when you're doing repeated rewinds and playbacks. Also, since it's a linear recording approach (a song goes down onto the tape in a contiguous manner, from beginning to end), editing capabilities are limited, and you have to hit the REWIND button each time you want to do another take. That's not exactly a hardship, but it seems archaic when you've been spoiled by . . .

Desktop hard-disk recording. This refers to recording digitally on a computer, and hands down, it offers the best combination of sound, convenience, and cost to the Guerrilla recordist. You may be able to record digitally using the computer's internal sound card, but for more track capability and flexibility, you may need an *A/D/A interface.* (A/D/A stands for analog-to-digital-to-analog.) The interface is an external device that does all of the digital encoding and decoding. Here's how it works: A signal enters one channel of the A/D/A interface, it's converted to a digital data stream, and that stream is ported to the computer, which writes the data onto the hard drive. During playback, the process happens in reverse, turning a hard-drive data file into an analog signal. The number of channels on the interface determines how many discrete tracks can be recorded or played back simultaneously, although many more tracks can exist separately on the computer and mixed within it during playback. On the computer, the whole process of recording and playing back tracks is managed with a MIDI-and-audio sequencing program that's set up to work with the interface.

A complete discussion of available sequencer programs and interfaces is beyond the scope of this book—but wherever you are in your journey toward pro-quality recording, I encourage you to look into what's available. Take it from someone who has recorded on every one of the various recording formats: Desktop hard-disk recording rocks. It's just so flexible and user-friendly, to name just a few of its advantages, I would never go back to any other recording method. However, I understand that many of you are recording on other types of systems—so throughout the rest of this book I'll treat the multitrack recorder simply as a generic "black box" that records and plays back a number of tracks. That way, you can adapt most of what I say to your own system, no matter what you're using. Certain techniques, though, will be geared toward specific system types.

The Mixing Signal Chain

Let's say you have recorded eight tracks of audio and you're ready to mix them into a song. Let's look at how you would bring the various signals together, along with effects, on a standard mixing board.

During mixdown, the board's input channels (or at least some of them) accept signals only from the multitrack rather than a mic, direct box, synth, etc.—that is, unless you're employing virtual tracks (see Chapter 1), in which case synthesizers, samplers, and/or drum machines may be in the mix as well. You may need to flip some of your input channels' switches to TAPE to get the multitrack signals to come into the board. Mixing then becomes a matter of setting the faders in order to balance the various tracks' levels, setting the EQs and pan pots appropriately, adding effects with the send and return circuits, and changing all of these variables in real time as the tracks play back and you record the mix to some stereo medium.

If your board has two output channels and no busses, it's pretty much as simple as that. If your board has busses, though, you may opt to use them to help you mix. You can set up the busses to be an intermediate stage between the input channels and the master stereo output: Assign your input-channel signals to various busses, and then combine the busses' signals to produce the master stereo output. For example, you could mix six drum channels to one pair of busses in stereo, four channels of vocals to another pair, and everything else to a third pair. This would allow you to turn all of the drums (or vocals, or everything else) up or down by moving just two faders. This technique is essential for doing things like having everything but the vocals gradually fade out until the song is *a cappella* (vocals only).

Mix Recorder

So the multitrack machine is ready to roll and you have all of your mixer moves ready. What stereo medium do you mix to? It could be anything: a cassette deck (not a good choice), a 2-track reel-to-reel machine, a DAT (digital audio tape) deck, a standalone CD burner (blank CD-Rs are cheaper than DAT tape), or—on a digital system—two more tracks recorded to the same hard drive. One benefit of mixing to digital is that your mix will be ready to master onto a CD, especially if the file is at a 44.1kHz and 16-bit resolution. (Most digital audio sequencers that record at higher resolutions have a function to perform this conversion.) If you mix to analog, you'll have to digitize the file somehow and get it onto your computer's hard drive to burn it to CD.

Compact Disc

As I mentioned in Chapter 2, audio CDs and CD players use sound files recorded at 44.1kHz and 16-bit resolution. If your digital recording system uses something else, you'll need to convert the file first. To be burned to CD, the mix must be in the form of a single *interleaved stereo AIFF file*: This means it's one digital file in which the two stereo channels are woven together, in something called Audio Interchange File Format. Your digital recording program will have settings to determine how the file is saved onto your hard drive. Be sure not to save your mix as two mono files; you won't be able to burn a stereo CD from these.

To burn a CD, just import the file into a CD-burning program—that's it. The program will allow you to set the order of songs on the CD and probably the amount of space between them. This is great for throwing together a test CD of rough mixes. For final projects, though, you may want to use a more powerful program. (For more on that, see Chapter 10.)

Power Amp, Speakers & Headphones

We're finally at the end of the signal chain—the place where electricity is turned back into the sound of a mixed song. Whether you're listening to a CD or a mix in progress coming off the multitrack machine, you need to run the line-level stereo signal either to a pair of headphones, to a power amplifier feeding a pair of loudspeakers, or to a pair of powered loudspeakers (which are speakers with built-in power amps). In true Guerrilla Home Recording form, I've never used a dedicated power amplifier; I've always just run my mixer's master stereo output to a home-stereo receiver, a setup that works fine. I use the same home stereo when I'm listening to burned CDs.

As for speakers, I don't recommend using a pair bought from a stereo store unless that's all you have. You'd benefit from owning a pair of good *close-field studio monitors*. Manufactured specifically for small recording studios, these are designed to be listened to at close range, so that almost all of what you're hearing is what's coming out of the speakers themselves, not a combination of that plus whatever is bouncing off the walls and other surfaces around you. Professional studio control rooms have monstrous speakers and perfect acoustics that allow for a near-flawless listening situation in locations all around the control room—but a Guerrilla studio doesn't. We need to listen carefully on close-fields and headphones, and we need to augment this monitoring setup by listening to rough mixes on other speaker systems, in other listening environments. For example, it's always a good idea to burn a CD of a mix and listen to it in the studio, in the living room, on computer speakers, and in the car. Such variety will tell you much more than hearing a mix on just one set of speakers will. Even pros do this; I recently read of a studio that ran a snake cable out to the owner's truck so people could go out and listen in the vehicle as the mix came off the multitrack. You never know what kind of system people will play your CD on, so it makes sense to check it out on as many systems as you can. I'll go into more detail about mixing in Chapter 10.

Three Efficient Board Setups For Tracking

The way you use your mixing board during tracking sessions (the recording of individual tracks to be mixed later) depends on the size and flexibility of the board with regard to your multitrack setup. In all cases, more mixing channels is better—basically, you can never have too many channels, because more inputs equals more flexibility and options for getting sounds. Let's look at three sample board setups for a studio with a generic 8-track system: one with a smaller, cramped-for-space 8x2 board (eight ins, two outs), one with a 16x4x2 board (16 ins, four busses, and two main outs), and one where much of the mixing is done digitally within a computer.

Small-board setup. With an 8-track recorder and only eight input channels on the board, you've run out of channels before you've even begun recording. Each of the multitrack's outputs needs an input channel (assuming you'll be recording on all eight tracks), leaving no channels open for tracking sources like microphone or direct-recorded bass. It's not impossible to record on a setup like this, but you need to conserve your channels and make creative use of every input you have.

In a channel-challenged situation like this, it helps to use a consistent tracking strategy from song to song that's conducive to your particular board setup. For example, when I was recording on 8-track with an 8-channel board, I got into the habit of recording all of my drum sounds in stereo on tracks 7 and 8, and I always had those tracks' outputs feeding into my board's SUB IN jacks. That way, no matter what song I was tracking or mixing, I knew the drums would be coming into the submixer inputs (you could say the drums had already been submixed). I sent tracks 1–6 into channels 1–6 on the board, leaving channels 7 and 8 available for tracking or (during mixdown) effects. In this setup, channels 1–6 were perpetually switched to TAPE input, so that I could always monitor what had been recorded on the corresponding tracks. During tracking I might have a microphone feeding channel 7, with the return from a delay feeding channel 8, and a reverb running into a stereo effect return (see Fig. 9). If I wanted to "print" reverb—record some mono reverb along with the signal—I would probably disconnect the reverb-carrying cables going into the effect return and plug one of them into channel 8, which would allow me to EQ the reverb separately.

That's fine for getting signals *from* the multitrack—but what about sending signals *to* it? That can be tricky on a board with no busses. Most boards offer a DIRECT OUT jack (or something similar) on each input channel. Assuming that this jack is situated post-fader and post-EQ in the signal chain (which it normally is), you can just plug in a cable here and connect the other end to the appropriate input jack on the multitrack. A downside to this arrangement is that each time you want to record a new track, you'll have to unplug the cable from the old track's input and plug it into the next track's input. Using a patchbay (see page 69) can be a big help here.

If you don't have DIRECT OUT jacks, you could use an effect send to get a single mono signal out of the board and into the appropriate track input. Or, as a last resort, you could split the master stereo output into a monitoring side and a bus to the multitrack: Pan all of the already-recorded channels to one side, and pan your new signal(s) to the other side. In this case, one master output would go to your monitoring amplifier, and one would go to the multitrack. This is hardly ideal, but the point is you can get it done. You just have to be resourceful, look at your options, and plan a course of action. If the situation is this dire, consider upgrading your mixer or converting to a digital system (see below)—such extreme limitations get old fast!

Large-board setup. It's much more convenient to record using a board with busses as well as more input channels than your multitrack has tracks. If you're recording on 8-track and you have a 12x4x2 board, you can set channels 1–8 to permanently monitor tracks 1–8, and devote the other four channels to source inputs or anything else you might need. You can use the four busses to feed the eight tracks by doubling them up: Bus 1 feeds tracks 1 and 5, bus 2 feeds tracks 2 and 6, and so on. This kind of arrangement is called *double bussing*, and many boards have two or even three identical output jacks per bus for just this purpose (see Fig. 10).

Having extra channels opens up your options for using virtual tracks, discussed in Chapter 1. In this 12-channel example, you could reserve channels 11 and 12 for a drum machine or sampler, leaving tracks 9 and 10 available for tracking sources like microphone or bass. Then again, if you're using virtual tracks with analog tape, you'll have one or two additional mixer channels available: One tape track will be devoted to sync tone, and you may be employing a guard track as well. So you could use these inputs for additional virtual-track sources, such as two synthesizers.

Mixing with a digital system. Among the many advantages of recording digitally, most recording programs allow you to set up "virtual" mixing consoles with dozens of channels to route and blend signals *before* they leave your computer. Just like on a mixing board, the program allows you to assign each channel to a single output in mono, or a pair of outputs in stereo, with a "virtual pan pot" determining where in the stereo pair it goes. As a result, even if your digital system offers eight discrete outputs, you may use only four of them, thereby requiring only four mixer channels for monitoring (see Fig. 11). For instance, for quick-and-dirty recording projects I usually mix everything on the computer to four outputs: Two channels in stereo for all instruments that will be mixed "dry" (with no reverb), and two that will be mixed "wet" (with reverb). Having kept these two stereo pairs separate, I can apply reverb to only one pair using the board's effect sends. I often break out the bass onto channel 5 so I can EQ it on the board separately, and sometimes I break out a lead vocal on channel 6, or I use that channel for other purposes. I don't think I've ever used outputs 7 and 8, but they're there if I ever need them.

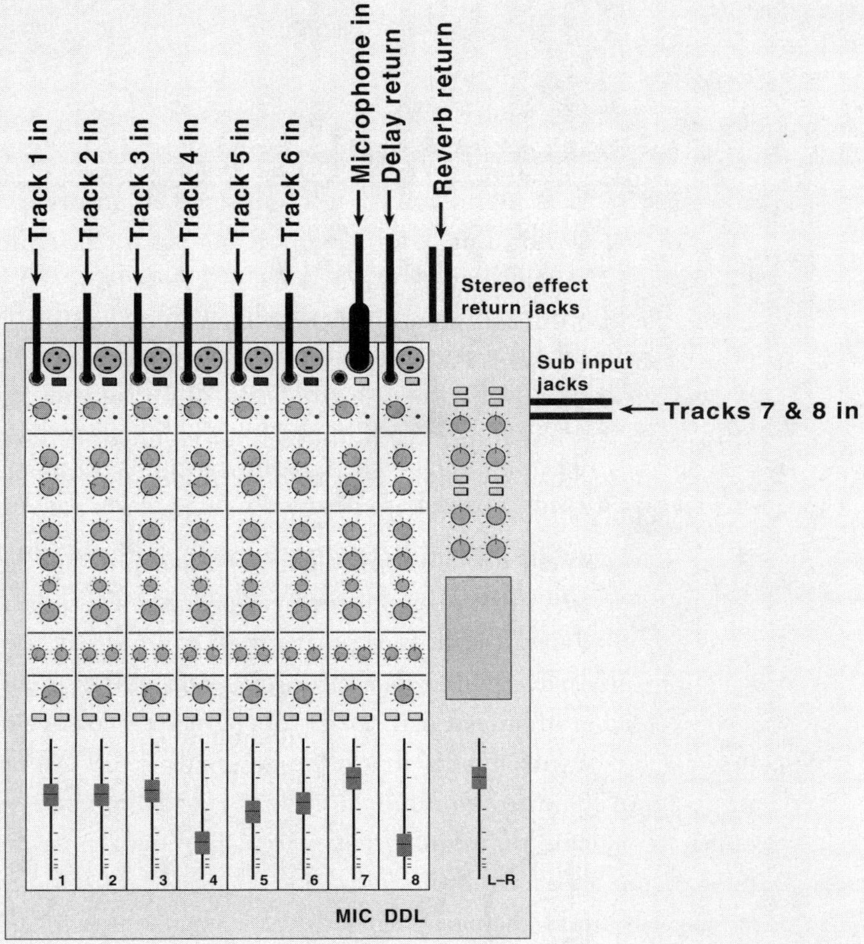

Fig. 9 Getting the most out of eight mixer channels and eight tracks. Faced with a shortage of inputs, we can use the board's SUB IN jacks for tracks 7 & 8, and a stereo effect return for the reverb. Two of the board's channels can be used for overdubbing onto tracks 1–6, and six channels can be used for monitoring tracks 1–6.

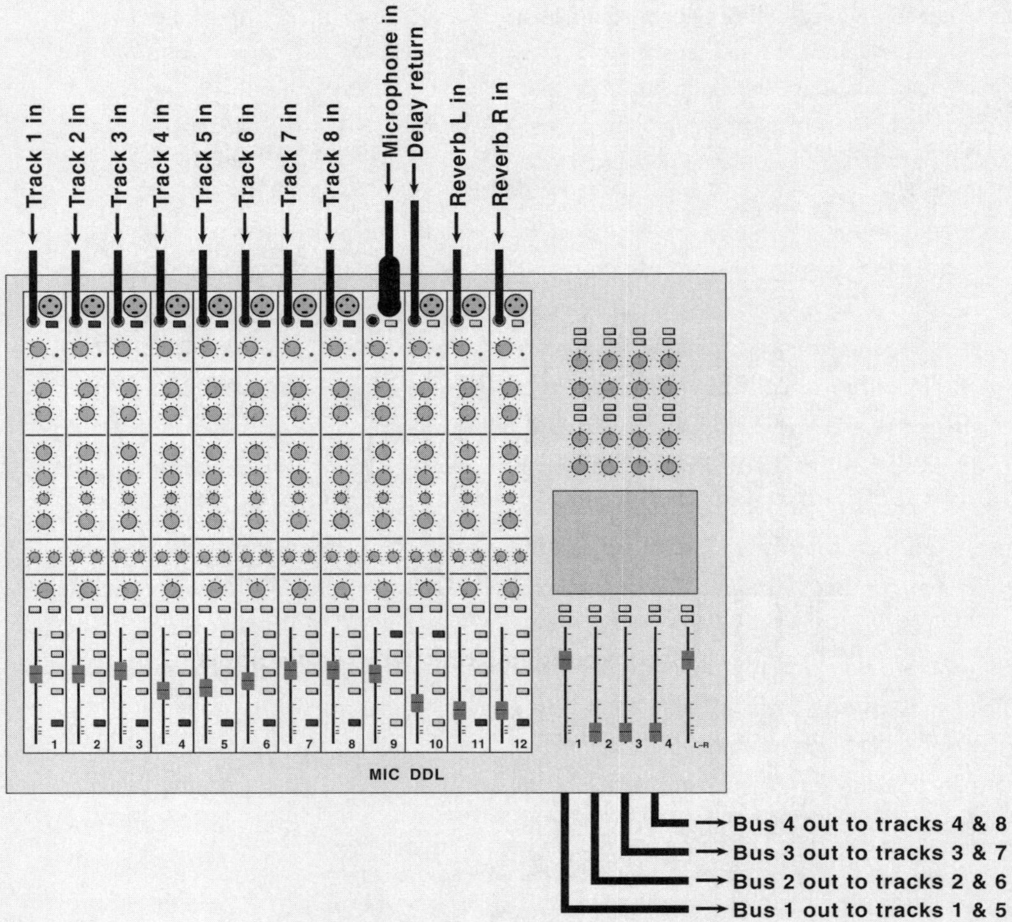

Fig. 10 There's considerably more elbow room—and flexibility—when your board has busses as well as more input channels than your recorder has tracks. From this 12x4x2 board, each of the four busses is feeding two tracks on the 8-track recorder; each track gets its own board channel for monitoring, and the reverb gets its own channel pair as well. In this case, a mic and a delay are being sent to bus 1, which is feeding tracks 1 & 5. Probably only one of these tracks would be record-enabled on the 8-track.

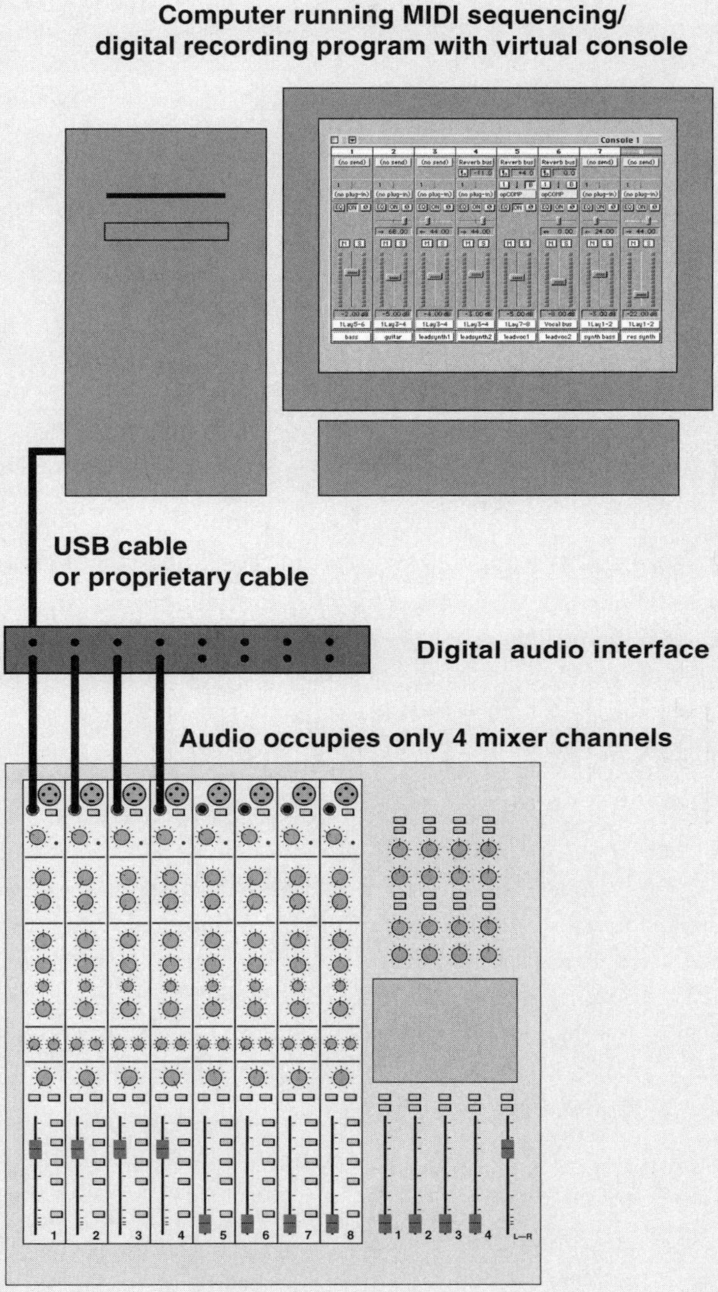

Fig. 11 Recording with a computer program allows the computer to do much of the mixing, freeing up "real" mixer channels.

CHAPTER 4

Controlling Dynamics

In Chapter 2 I introduced the concepts of dynamics (variations in signal level between loud and soft) and dynamic range. Even with today's inexpensive recording systems, it's possible to achieve a dynamic range of over 90dB—in other words, the loudest sounds you record can be over 90 decibels louder than the background noise. Managing all of the "area" between these two extremes, for each and every sound you record, is a skill that's critical to making a good-sounding recording. Fortunately there are devices called expanders, compressors, and limiters (collectively called dynamics processors) that help in this task. In this chapter I'll explain how to use them.

Using An Expander

Of the three types of dynamics processors, compressors are probably the most familiar—but let's begin with expanders, because they're a bit easier to understand. A lot of people record without using an expander in the signal chain, and I think that's a shame, because effective use of an expander can do an awful lot in cleaning up the tracks that you record.

Expansion refers to the process of increasing the dynamic range—making it bigger. Isn't 90dB a large enough dynamic range, you ask? For most purposes, absolutely—but that refers to a system's ideal dynamic range, not necessarily the range you'll get if you plug a mic into a mixer and start recording. An expander is important in optimizing the actual dynamic range you get out of a system.

An expander operates at the low end of the dynamic range, where signals are at their quietest, or perhaps nonexistent. In other words, when audio is coming through the signal chain, the expander may be doing nothing at all. But when that audio stops coming through, the expander goes to work by lowering the signal further, expanding the background noise floor downward so that there's a larger dynamic range overall (see Fig. 1). Not surprisingly, this is called *downward expansion*. There is such thing as upward expansion, but you don't really need to know about it.

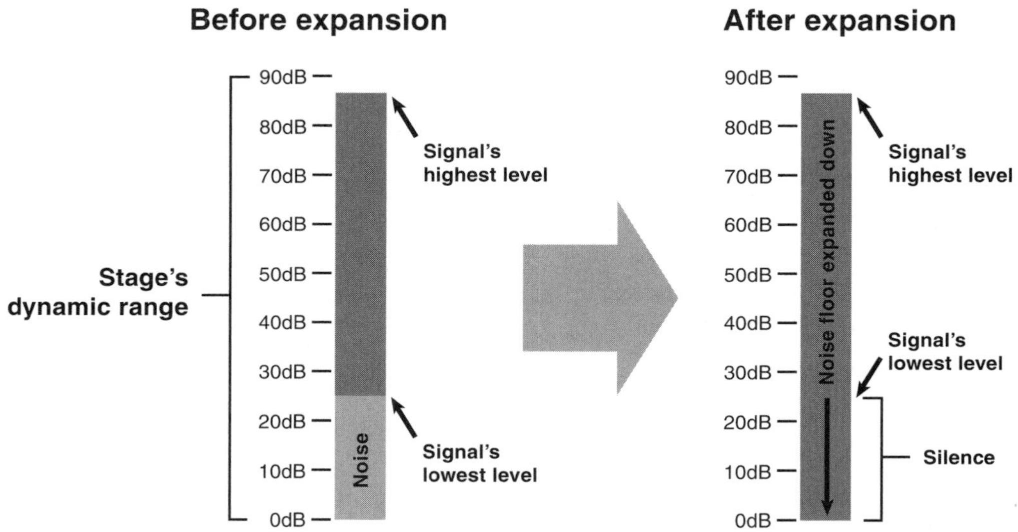

Fig. 1 Without expansion (left), the noise level in the signal chain can far exceed a stage's background noise. With expansion (right), the noise is brought down to the stage's noise floor without affecting the signal itself.

To understand this better, consider what happens when you plug a microphone into a mixing board and crank up the gain. If you sing into the mic, you'll hear yourself coming through the headphones loudly (and you might even get a shriek of feedback if it's too loud). But if you stop singing, odds are you won't hear silence—especially in a bedroom or den Guerrilla studio. You'll hear the heating or air-conditioning system, planes going overhead, street traffic, or your kid brother's video game down the hall. This is all stuff that doesn't belong on your recording! Sure, domestic sounds are charming—if it's 1970 and you happen to be Paul McCartney recording your first solo album. We Guerrilla recordists are going after a slick, clean sound, and part of "clean" means not having anything on your tracks that you don't want there.

Here's where expansion comes in. You may have encountered something called a *noise gate*, which is a crude form of an expander. In a noise gate, once the signal falls below a certain threshold, the electronic gate closes and no sound is allowed to pass through (noise or otherwise). However, when the signal begins to rise above that same threshold again, the gate opens up, allowing the signal to pass through once more. Naturally this also allows unwanted noise to pass through along with the signal, but the idea is that noise is less troublesome when a signal is present to mask it. Like faint starlight in the night sky, noise is most noticeable when it's by itself. Mix in a little signal (or sunlight in this analogy) and you're less likely to notice the faint background stuff. An expander works on the same principle as a noise gate, but an expander is a bit more subtle: It's not as obvious to the ear when it's doing its thing.

Here are the parameters that you're likely to find on an expander, or the expander component of a compressor/expander:

Threshold. This control sets the level at which the expansion effect begins to set in. Imagine a cymbal crash that begins at 0dB (the top of the dynamic range) and slowly decays to –∞dB. At a certain point in its decay, the sound of the cymbal will get so quiet that you'll hear background noise mixed in with the cymbal, and at a still-later point you'll hear only background noise, as the noise masks what's left of the crash. If you were miking this cymbal, you might want an expander to kick in toward the tail end of the decay in order to take the background noise out of the sonic picture (see Fig. 2). The THRESHOLD control determines when this would happen. If it's a loud, busy song arrangement, you could get away with setting the threshold higher. If it's set to –30dB, the expander will begin to kick in and shut down the signal when the cymbal decays 30dB below its initial peak. In this case you could get away with a lot more noise happening in or outside your studio without worrying about these sounds making it onto your track. On the other hand, if you're working on a quiet song with a sparse arrangement, you'd probably want to set the control lower (perhaps –60dB) and record it at a time when your studio is at its quietest, such as late at night. Since the expander is set to a low threshold, the signal chain will be more susceptible to noise coming into the mic or created by the mic preamp.

To learn how to set the threshold control, here's an exercise. Pretend you're about to record a fairly loud electric-guitar part using a miked amp. Set up your signal chain, with your mic in front of the amp, and gain-stage the chain (explained in Chapter 3) so you're exploiting the full dynamic range of all the stages without unwanted distortion. Next, put the expander into the signal chain by way of the mixer channel's insert jack. If the expander has compressor or limiter sections, bypass them by pressing the

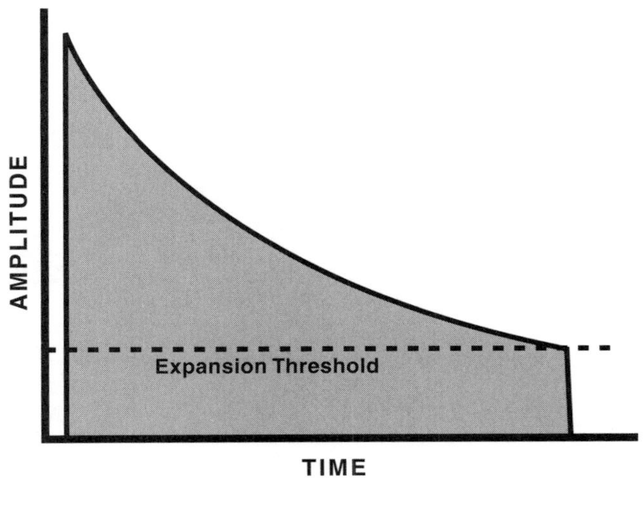

Fig. 2 When a real crash cymbal is miked and run through an expander, the threshold level determines how much of the cymbal's decay makes it through before the expander closes down.

appropriate bypass switches or turning those sections' threshold controls all the way up. Turn the expander's ratio knob (which I'll discuss in a moment) all the way up, turn the threshold knob all the way down, and let your guitar sit on a stand with the amp running and the mic picking up the amp's background noise. Now put on the headphones, slowly turn up the expander's threshold knob, and listen to what happens. At a certain point in the knob's travel, the sound of the idling guitar amp will cut out—this is the point you're looking for. Set the threshold slightly above this point. Now, if you so much as touch the guitar's strings, you should hear the gate open up, with the amp sound (and perhaps some string noise) coming through. That's what you want—the expander is gating out the noise, unless some signal is present as well (you touching the strings), at which point the gate opens to let both signal and noise pass through. The expander's threshold is properly set, at least for now.

Ratio. In the exercise above, you probably noticed that when the expander's gate closes, no sound is let through—the gate closes completely. That's okay, but it isn't ideal. Setting an expander's RATIO control properly allows the circuit to close more gradually as a sound decays, and it allows the expander to stay slightly open after the sound has decayed below the noise floor. It's a little like leaving a bedroom door open a little when you sleep: Doing this lets in some of the light from the hall (analogous to the background noise). Depending on the recording situation, setting up an expander to work like a noise gate—where it slams shut, resulting in sudden silence—can sound unnatural. This is particularly true with a gently decaying sound such as a crash cymbal, which would be abruptly cut off by noise-gate-like expander action (see Fig. 3). A hard-closing gate can mess with the sound in even worse ways, for instance

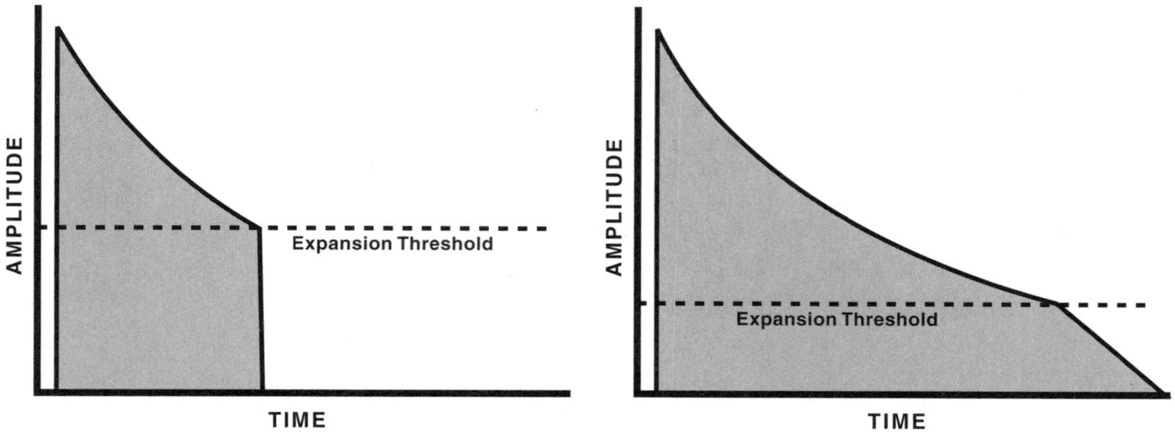

Fig. 3 Recording a crash cymbal through an expander set to a high threshold and high ratio (left) can cut off the cymbal's natural decay. Lowering the ratio and threshold (right) can result in a more natural sound.

> LOOK ■ OUT!
>
> ### Dynamics-Processing Plug-Ins
>
> If you're recording on a computer, you may have compressor and/or expander plug-ins available to use within your system. These can be useful in some situations—but unless you have a lot of experience working with compressors and expanders, I absolutely recommend that you use hardware versions of these effects instead: You know, the kind with real knobs and buttons. When you're setting up a signal chain, you need to be able to hear what a dynamics processor is doing in real time, so that you can tweak the unit's parameters before you start recording, and without your recording system in the signal chain. Depending on your computer system, you may not be able to do this with a plug-in. Plus, some of these plug-ins offer so many variables, you may find yourself confused by them, unsure exactly which parameters are having what effect on the signal. Don't get me wrong—digital plug-ins are great for a lot of things. But learning how to apply compression and expansion isn't one of them.

chopping off consonants at the ends of vocal phrases. We need to set the ratio control to avoid these problems, while still allowing the expander to clean up the sound.

With the guitar from the previous exercise still in its stand and the threshold control set, start turning the ratio control down and listen to what happens. At a certain point, you'll start to hear the sound of the idling guitar amp coming through—that's the gate opening up slightly. When the ratio control is all the way down, the amp noise should be exactly as loud as if the expander weren't in the signal chain at all; in other words, the gate is all the way open. When you record a track, look for a happy medium between these points: When the signal chain is idling, the gate should be closed enough to quiet the track significantly, but not closed so much that passages with no playing sound unnaturally silent next to played passages. You also shouldn't be able to hear the gate noticeably opening or closing when you start or stop playing.

The trick to using an expander effectively is to find suitable threshold and ratio settings based on the sound you're about to record, as well as the song you're recording. You want the expander to be responsive to anything you play during the performance—in other words, to anything that you actually want recorded on your track—but not necessarily anything else. Play lightly and let some notes or chords decay. Think about the performance you're about to record: Will you be playing full-out through the whole track? Is there a point where you'll need to hold a chord for several seconds? Will you be playing any passages very quietly? Test out any such critical performance moments and listen to how the expander reacts. If the expander seems to be too sensitive to what you're doing, turn up the threshold control a little. Adjust the controls one at a time until the expander is doing its job cleaning up your signal chain, without calling attention to itself. You may need to compromise—one pair of settings may be good for one part of the song while another is good for a different passage. Try to find settings that work as well as possible across the whole performance. If necessary, you can always punch in (see Chapter 9) certain sections that require very different expander settings.

Attack & decay. Most (if not all) expanders have these controls. You'll recognize these terms if you have experience programming synthesizers: Attack specifies how fast something rises, and decay specifies how fast it falls afterward. In the case of an expander, attack determines how fast the gate opens when its threshold is suddenly exceeded, and decay determines how fast it closes again when the signal goes away. In the Guerrilla studio, you can usually set these knobs and forget them. Normally you want a very quick attack (so as not to cut off the beginnings of sounds) and a medium decay—perhaps around 200 milliseconds—to make sure the ends of sounds don't get truncated. The two sections of a compressor/expander unit may have only one set of attack and decay controls but separate ratio and threshold; that's okay. Having the same settings for both sides usually works fine.

Indicator LED. This is a handy visual element that you can use in conjunction with your ears. One LED, or a series of LEDs indicating a range of levels, may light to show that the device is actively expanding the noise downward. When the gate begins opening, the LED may go dark, or a series of LEDs may progressively turn off as the gate opens wider. Indicator LEDs aren't really that necessary on the expander side—they're much more useful in compression—but they're nice to have anyway.

Compression

Unlike an expander, which increases dynamic range, a compressor reduces dynamic range. In recording, running signals through both a compressor and an expander can be very effective. Why would you want to reduce and enlarge the dynamic range at the same time? Actually, they don't both come into play at the same time; an expander does its thing when signals are at their quietest (or nonexistent), and a compressor does its thing in the louder part of the dynamic range. So if you're recording a cymbal crash through both a compressor and an expander, the expander will be working before the sound begins; then the expander's gate opens up immediately when the cymbal is struck, and the compressor takes over. The compressor works perhaps for a few seconds while the cymbal decays (with the expander doing nothing, since the signal is over the expander's threshold). Then the signal enters a kind of no-man's-land between the compressor's and the expander's active ranges, where neither circuit does anything to the signal. Finally, when the expander senses that the crash is decaying below its threshold, its gate begins to close again (see Fig. 4). This process accomplishes two things: The expander cleans up the noise before and after the crash, and

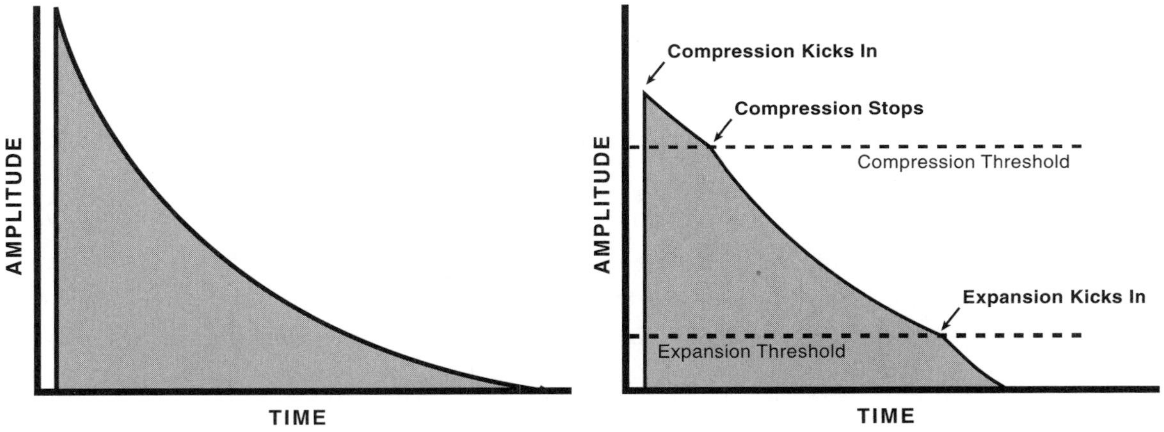

Fig. 4 A crash cymbal (left), and the same crash cymbal through a compressor/expander (right). The compressor and the expander come into play at different points of the cymbal's decay.

the compressor tames the initial peak and thereby allows the whole signal to be brought up in volume, allowing it to have more punch and presence in the mix. If you were recording a bunch of "real" (not sampled) cymbal crashes one after another, the compressor would be even more beneficial: It would tend to even out the crashes in volume, which would make the quieter crashes less likely to get buried in the mix and the louder ones less likely to overwhelm the mix. As an added bonus, compression makes a sound less likely to overload a stage in the signal chain—which is particularly important if you're recording digitally.

Here's a look at a compressor's typical parameters and how to use them:

Threshold. This should sound familiar. You kind of have to think of downward expansion upside down to imagine how compression works. When a signal *rises* past the compressor's threshold, the compression circuit begins to kick in, and when a signal falls below this threshold, the compressor stops working. So compression happens only when the signal is above the threshold—just as expansion happens only when the signal is *below* the expander's threshold. Given a gradually rising signal, compression can kick in suddenly, which is called *hard-knee* compression, or the circuit can come into play gradually as the signal rises, which is called *soft-knee* compression. Some compressors allow you to specify which kind it performs; soft-knee compression is generally more transparent and natural-sounding.

Ratio. This term is a little easier to understand regarding compression. In an ordinary signal-chain stage, such as a mixing board's channel fader, the gain is linear: Any increase in level at the circuit's input will be matched by an identical level increase at the output, regardless of whether the signal is at the bottom or top of the dynamic range. If it's a unity-gain stage (meaning that no amplification is occurring), three more decibels going into the circuit will result in 3dB coming out. This is a 1:1 ratio: What you pump in is the same as what the circuit pumps out. A compressor changes this ratio in the dynamic-range region that's above the compression threshold. If the compressor is set for a 2:1 ratio, that means that above the threshold, increasing the level going into the circuit by 2dB will result in only 1dB more amplitude at the output. Likewise, pumping in an extra 10dB will result in only 5dB of output. But if the signal is below the compression threshold, pumping in an extra 10dB will result in a 10dB increase at the output—the compressor is unity-gain (1:1 ratio) below the threshold. Fig. 5 shows how this works in graph form. It should be easy to see that if you set the compression ratio higher, you need to pump even more signal into the circuit to get the same rise in output: With a 10:1 ratio, a whopping 20dB of extra signal level will cause the compressor's output to rise by only 2dB. With an infinite compression ratio, you can't get the output to rise over the threshold no matter how much signal you pump into the circuit. Any compression stronger than about 20:1 is considered *limiting*. A limiter is like the flipside of a noise gate—it's kind of black-or-white, either doing its thing or doing nothing (depending on the signal level at the moment), without much subtlety.

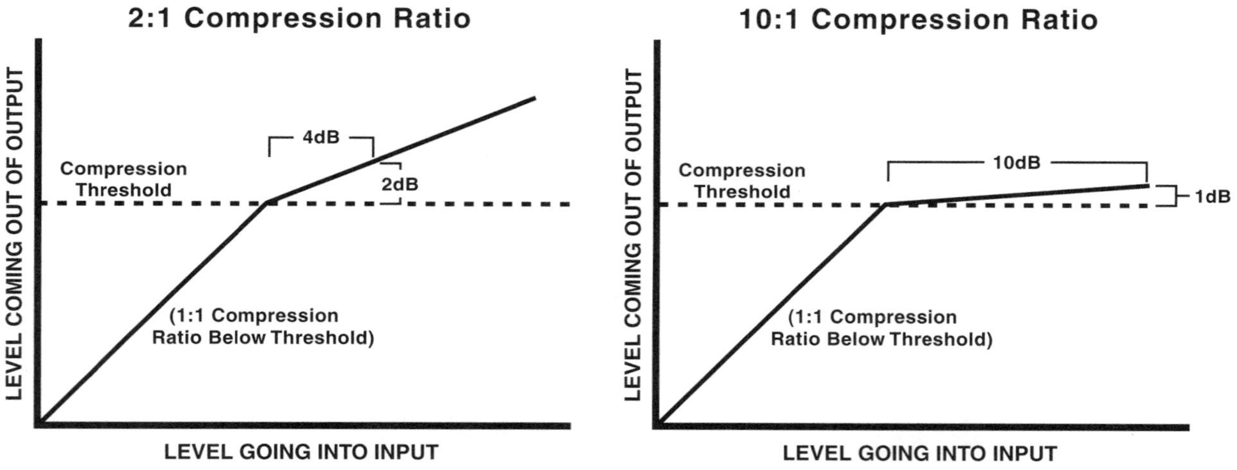

Fig. 5 Above the compression threshold, at a 2:1 compression ratio (left), a level increase of 4dB at the input results in a level increase of only 2dB at the output. With a high compression ratio of 10:1 (right), you need to put 10dB more signal into the input to get 1dB more signal at the output.

Attack & decay. These parameters are essentially the same as in an expander. Attack specifies how fast the compressor gets to work when presented with a signal that's above its threshold, and decay specifies how fast it returns to a 1:1 ratio when the signal falls below the threshold. With a soft-knee compressor and a signal that slowly rises and falls in level, attack and decay may not come into play at all—but when presented with things like sudden transients, they can have a definite effect on a sound. As I mentioned, in a combined compressor/expander unit there may be just one set of attack and decay knobs; I tend to leave mine set to a very fast attack and a medium-length decay, which to my ears works just fine for most sounds.

Indicator LEDs. For Guerrilla recordists, a "compressor active" LED is a critical feature on a compressor. Since you can't always hear when compression is kicking in, particularly with a low ratio, it really helps to have an LED that lights immediately when the compressor's threshold has been exceeded. It provides great visual feedback as to how the compressor is operating with regard to the dynamic range of the performance you're recording. A compressor without this LED is much harder to use effectively, requiring more guesswork and listening skill. Some compressors have additional "gain reduction" LEDs or a gain-reduction VU meter; these are nice to have, but they aren't as important. If you're shopping for a compressor, by all means get one with at least a compressor-active indicator LED.

For the following exercise I'll assume you're using a compressor with ratio and threshold controls as well as a compressor-active LED.

Using A Compressor

Set up a condenser microphone for vocals and run it into an input channel on your board. Put the signal through your compressor by way of the channel insert jack, and put on a pair of headphones. If you have a compressor/expander, set up the expander section as described above—get it to clean up all of the background noise in your studio, but don't let it chop off any final consonants or slowly decaying vowel sounds. If you find that the expander's gate is fluttering open and closed (which can happen if the threshold is right around the background noise level), try raising the threshold a bit, increasing the decay time a bit, or both. Now you can go to work setting up the compressor section.

Set the compressor's ratio knob to about 3:1 and stand in front of the mic, about where you'd be when you're singing. While you watch the indicator LED, make vowel sounds that start soft and increase in volume, and notice when the LED comes on. (If it doesn't come on at all, turn down the compressor's threshold knob and try again.) A good starting position for the threshold is the point where your vocal starts to get loud—in musical terms, somewhere in the mezzo-forte range. If your compressor has a gain-reduction meter or LEDs as well, watch as your vocal sound gets louder above the threshold. When the meter says that 6dB of gain reduction is occurring, it means that at that particular moment the output would be 6dB hotter if the compressor weren't there.

Now try turning the compressor's ratio knob up or down and repeat the exercise, and try to hear a difference. You may notice that with a higher ratio setting (like 6:1), as you sing louder and louder above the threshold, the sound of your voice in the headphones may seem to get quieter. What's actually happening is that the sound of your vocal cords being conducted through the bones of your skull is overtaking the headphone sound, because the latter is being compressed while the former isn't. That's okay. If you want to hear what the compression really sounds like, record yourself. Record your vocals getting louder and louder first at 2:1, then 4:1, and then 8:1, and listen to the difference.

The best compression—and this applies pretty much to every instrument—should do its thing without calling any attention to itself. If you recorded yourself in the above exercise, you may have noticed that the sound can start to get "squashed" near the top of the dynamic range, particularly with lower compression thresholds and higher ratios. How much "squashing" you can get away with depends largely on the context of the track you're recording. If it's a loud, rocking song with loud, rocking vocals, you can get away with a more "squashed" sound—in fact, audible, noticeable compression might even be a cool effect in certain cases. On the other hand, if you're recording a Norah Jones–like tune with an intimate vocal, you need to be more careful about how the compression is sounding. Audible compression in this kind of setting can flat-out ruin a performance; it sounds unnatural and detracts from the performance's intimacy. Try to make the compression as transparent as possible—it should sound like it's not even there. If you can hear the compression kick in during playback, try using a lower ratio as well as a slightly lower threshold. The lower ratio will make the compression less audible, while the lower threshold will bring down the hottest peaks' levels to about where they were with the previous settings. If you end up being the only person in the world who knows that a track was compressed, then you know you've done a good job applying compression.

Why Compression Is So Important

In the Guerrilla studio, you should consider compressing just about every track you record, before you record it. An exception is sampled drums—first, because drum samples are often already compressed somewhat; second, because you may be bringing these into the mix by way of virtual tracks (see Chapter 1) and therefore aren't actually recording them during the tracking phase; and third, because sampled drums

"Manual Compression": Proper Mic Technique

If you watch skilled singers like Christina Aguilera perform live, you'll notice that they constantly vary the position of the microphone relative to their mouth. During loud notes the singer may pull the mic away quite a bit, and during quieter passages the mic may be much closer. This way, the singer can "track" the mic's distance according to the level of the note being sung at that exact moment. This is an important element of mic technique, and because it tends to even out the notes' levels somewhat, it's a way of adding "compression" without actually using a compressor. The more of this "manual compression" you can supply while you're recording a vocal track, the less electronic compression you'll need to get the same sound in the end. In a studio with a mic on a stand, it may involve simply backing up a foot or so for a particularly spirited phrase, or turning your head slightly away from the mic when you hit a loud note. I wouldn't say you could ever perfect your mic technique to the point where you don't need *any* compression; an electronic circuit is just better at tracking and adjusting levels than your ears and muscles are. But a little mic technique can go a long way toward reducing your dependence on compression, thereby allowing you to use compression in a more subtle and transparent manner.

have more even, predictable dynamics than live drums. For everything else, adding compression while tracking just makes everything much easier.

Here's why: Acoustic sounds, as well as many electronic sounds, tend to vary quite a bit in level. If you're recording a shaker percussion part without any compression, the loudest shakes may be a good 9dB louder than the softer shakes. Meanwhile, on your uncompressed rhythm-guitar track, some chords may be right up near the top of your system's dynamic range (0dB), while others are at –4dB. This kind of variation could be occurring on most of your song's tracks, including the all-important lead vocal, throughout the whole song. It's extremely difficult, if not impossible, to create a good mix of a song under these circumstances. Even if you could get the mix perfect for one moment in time, when the instruments' levels are fluctuating wildly, a half-second later the mix will be totally different—the rhythm guitar could suddenly get much louder and suffocate the lead vocal for a moment, which may have gotten suddenly quiet at that moment anyway, making matters worse. It would be like trying to cook a dish while someone was standing over you randomly adding more of certain ingredients while taking others away. You'd have no control over the blend, and the end result would probably be a culinary disaster.

Compression solves this by getting levels under a certain amount of control. If the levels of each instrument vary by only 2dB or 3dB, you can achieve a much smoother mix than if each instrument is varying by 9dB. From the song's beginning to its end, the mix will be much more consistent than a similar mix of uncompressed tracks.

Simply stated, it makes things easier in the studio. And since we Guerrilla recordists mix as we go, we need to have the tracks compressed as they go down. Million-dollar facilities may be able to compress each track separately during the mix; we can't.

De-essing

The process known as "de-essing" is a type of compression. If you record a vocal track very bright, adding some top-end EQ between the microphone and the multitrack, you'll get a very present, airy sound—two good qualities to have on a vocal track. However, moments where words have "s" sounds can cause an explosion of nasty, noisy *sibilance*. Sibilance refers to excessive high end associated with the sound of the consonants *s*, *z*, etc. Sibilance can destroy an otherwise well-recorded track, and if you have an effective way to tame a track's sibilance, you should use it.

The most common way to do this is by de-essing the track (see Fig. 6). De-essing refers to compression based only on the signal's high-end frequency content. Here's how it works: An audio track is split into two parts, and one of the parts goes through a highpass filter, which removes everything but the highs—say, everything below 8kHz. This signal is then fed into a compressor's *side-chain input*. This is an input that allows the compressor to react to a signal different from the one it's actually compressing. Meanwhile, the non-filtered portion of the signal goes into the compressor's normal input. When there's a burst of high frequencies from an excessive "s" sound, it easily passes through the highpass filter, goes into the side-chain input, and causes the compressor to attenuate the full-bandwidth signal going into the input jack. The result: The track is compressed slightly at the moment where the excessive sibilance

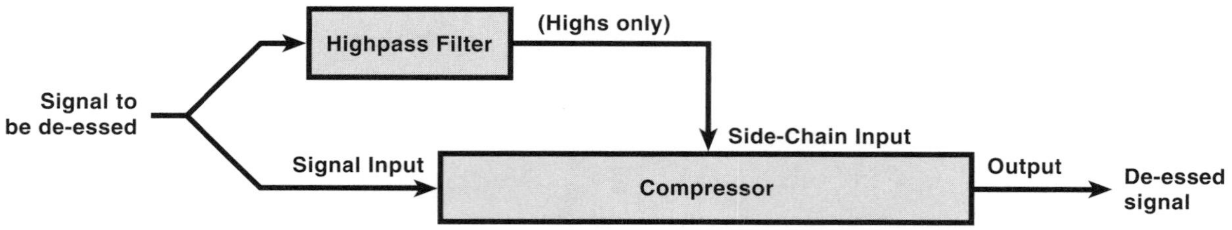

Fig. 6 In de-essing, the signal is split, and high-frequency-dependent compression is applied to one side by sending a highpass-filtered signal into the compressor's side-chain input.

occurred, thereby taming the sibilance. You could theoretically achieve the same result by manually pulling down the fader whenever the harsh "s" sounds occurred, and immediately returning the fader to its original position when the sibilance is over for the moment—but this would be difficult or impossible (particularly if you're singing at the same time!). De-essing, like ordinary compression, makes this process automatic, so you don't have to worry about it.

The main difficulty with de-essing is that it requires its own compressor or compression stage, meaning that if you have only one compressor, it won't be available for ordinary compression while you're performing de-essing. One solution is to do ordinary compression while tracking, and then run the track through a de-essing circuit during mixdown. Or, if you're recording digitally, you could apply a de-essing plug-in to the track after you've recorded it; this is a simple and often effective approach. Or you could always buy a second compressor. Some compressors have a built-in "de-ess" button which, when pressed, turns the compressor into a de-esser (mid- and low-frequency dynamics remain unaffected). If you use this type of compressor in a de-essing role, be sure to experiment with various threshold, ratio, attack, and release settings to see what sounds best.

Of course, it's better to avoid excessive sibilance on a track in the first place. With many condenser mics, singing too closely to the mic or too directly into the mic can enhance sibilance in an unnatural way. I've found that by backing off the mic and singing a little off-axis—meaning you're kind of singing *past* the mic rather than directly into it—you can achieve a more natural sound with fewer sibilance problems.

LOOK OUT!

Watch That De-esser!

A good de-essing stage allows you to brighten up a vocal track considerably without making the "s" sounds harsh or spitty. The object of de-essing should be to return the performance to natural-sounding sibilance—nothing more, nothing less. After applying de-essing, listen carefully to the track and make sure it simply sounds natural. If you overdo or incorrectly set up the de-essing, you'll hear the vocal track "duck" or "breathe" every time there's an "s" sound: The track will seem to collapse in an unnatural way for a moment. Another possible by-product of de-essing is a lisping sound; "th" sounds are similar to "s" sounds, only with much less high frequencies. If de-essing is causing either of these side effects, it's doing more harm than good. De-essing, like good full-bandwidth compression, should not call any attention to itself. Experiment with the de-essing compressor's parameters until you achieve a natural-sounding sibilance while leaving the rest of the track untouched.

P-Pops

"P-pops" aren't really related to controlling dynamics, but in terms of the frequency spectrum they are the polar opposite of sibilance, so I'll mention them here. A P-pop results when *plosive* consonants—the sounds of the letters *p* and *b*—produce a puff of air that hits the mic diaphragm, causing a low-frequency thump on the track. At worst, this thump can have so much energy it causes the signal to distort one of the downstream stages—but often it just sounds annoying and unprofessional, and it often causes a compressor to make the signal "duck" for a moment, which sounds unnatural. The simplest way to prevent P-pops is to install a pop filter in front of the microphone. These are available commercially, either as a cover that slips over the mic itself, or as a two-layer fine-mesh screen stretched over a ring, which attaches to the mic stand and can be positioned with a flexible assembly. For a while I used a piece of silkscreen stretched on a wooden frame with good results. And as with taming sibilance, you can go a long way toward preventing P-pops just by singing a little off-axis. There's really no reason you need to sing directly and closely into a mic, unless you're recording background vocals consisting of pure vowel sounds and you want to make them sound as airy and intimate as possible. (More on recording vocals in Chapter 7.) You'll get a more natural, balanced sound if you back off the mic a bit and sing over it or past it a little.

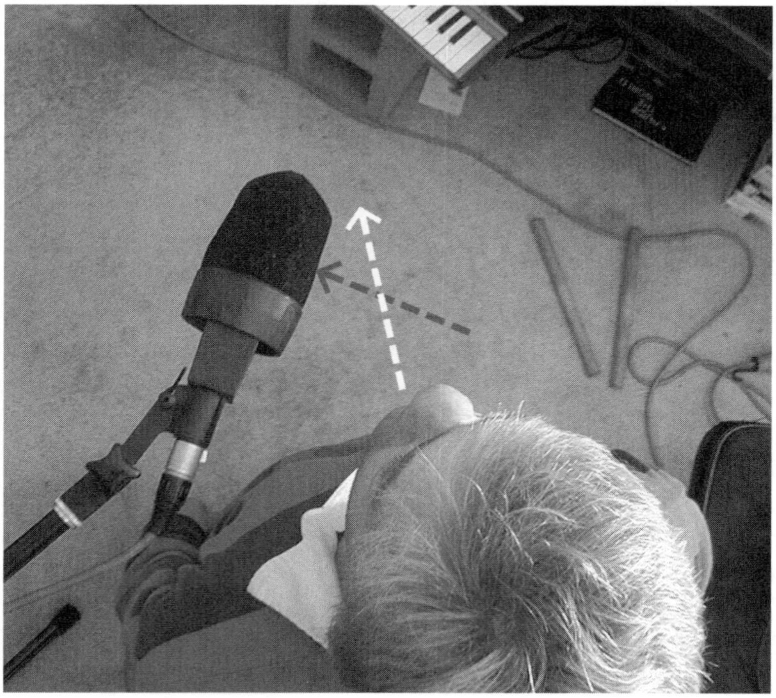

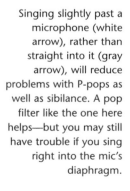

Singing slightly past a microphone (white arrow), rather than straight into it (gray arrow), will reduce problems with P-pops as well as sibilance. A pop filter like the one here helps—but you may still have trouble if you sing right into the mic's diaphragm.

CHAPTER 5

Separation

One characteristic common to all good recordings is *separation.* In a recording with good separation, you can hear each individual instrument, or perhaps even each particular performance in the case of double-tracked instruments. The result—assuming the recording is also free of excessive noise and unwanted distortion—is a sound that many people describe as "clean." If, on the other hand, the recording was made with poor separation, the instruments tend to blend into a kind of ambiguous blur of sound. In some cases, this may be what you want. But in most cases, recording musicians want a clean-sounding, clear mix where the instruments have good presence, and this means the separation needs to be good.

Separation Fundamentals

What contributes to good separation? Actually, all three of the "dimensions of sound" that I've been mentioning: dynamics, frequency content, and pan position.

Dynamics. If the instruments' dynamics are uncontrolled and are fluctuating all over the place, the sound can disappear for a moment while it's masked by other instruments; then it may reappear and mask other instruments, causing them to disappear for the moment. Even if the instruments are otherwise well separated, the mix will be uneven, and you'll have trouble picking out one instrument in the mix for any length of time. The solution, of course, is controlling the dynamics through compression (see Chapter 4). If you give each instrument its place in the mix by settling down its dynamic fluctuations, you lay a solid foundation to achieve good separation via the other two "dimensions of sound."

Frequency content. One way to make an instrument fall back in a mix is to cut its high-frequency content. Highs and upper-mids make things sound more up-front, so cutting these frequencies tends to make an instrument less "present"—and in a dense mix, that can mean the instrument practically disappears. This may be what you want; by no means does every instrument need to be at the forefront of the mix. Some sounds work well as "ear candy," contributing to the mix almost subliminally. But if it's an important part, like a funky rhythm guitar, it should be up where it can be heard—and that means it may need a high-end boost. However, many inexperienced recordists pile the highs onto every instrument, causing all of them to wash out equally and causing the mix to fatigue the ear. It's a matter of balance and taste. A large part of learning to record and mix involves learning how much upper-frequency content is appropriate for each part—as well as learning when you've gone too far, like a cook with a jar of curry powder and a heavy hand.

Actually, the *entire* frequency spectrum is important in achieving separation, not just the highs. A huge factor in getting instruments to separate is a concept called *frequency slotting*. Frequency slotting means making sure each instrument has a "niche" in the frequency spectrum, and making sure that the instruments don't conflict with each other in this way. More on how to achieve this in a moment.

Pan position. In terms of separation, this is the simplest "dimension" to understand. On a monophonic recording, all of the instruments are bunched up together in the middle of the (non-) stereo image. Panning the instruments in various ways from left to right is a simple way to almost physically separate them from each other. If a recording consists of piano and guitar, even if their dynamics are all over the map and they occupy the same zone of the frequency spectrum, all you have to do is pan them left and right somewhat and they'll separate from each other. It might still be an ugly recording, but at least the two instruments will be clearly distinct, coming differently out of the left and right sides.

Determining pan positions is a matter of personal taste and artistry. I'll discuss pan position as it relates to individual sounds in Chapter 7.

Frequency Slotting

Frequency slotting is an important part of the process of creating a clean, balanced, and crisp-sounding recording. Even among those who put slotting into practice, some think about it only when it's time to mix. But Guerrilla recordists—who likely don't have mountains of outboard gear at their disposal for mixdown—need to be a bit more ahead of the game. You should think about frequencies *before* the instruments go down on tape in the first place.

Think of a painter creating a still life of a bowl of fruit. If he uses only one color for all of the fruit, the table, and the background, it will be pretty hard to distinguish the various elements depicted in the painting. They'll all kind of blur together, and you might have to squint or look closely to tell them apart. But if each element has a distinctive hue and shade, there will be contrast and a heightened sense of drama. The composition's strengths will be enhanced, too. These hues and shades are not unlike the tone "colors" on an audio recording: They create a more detailed, more interesting, less homogenous sound-image of all of its various elements.

The Peek-A-Boo Principle: Arranging Comes First

This book is about recording songs, not writing or arranging them. But when your goal is instrument separation, it really helps to put some thought into the song's arrangement before you start recording. There's probably no better way to separate two instruments sonically than by separating them *temporally*—making their relationship vary as a function of time. If you have a piano and a guitar in a mix, and the piano is playing on the downbeats and the guitar is on the upbeats, they're separated, in time—before you even consider how they sound. Even if they're panned together and occupy the same frequency space, you'll be able to hear both instruments well.

A whole book could be written on this topic, so it's something to keep in mind either when you're arranging a song or laying down a track. If you're recording a bass line, for instance, don't put that slick upper-register fill during the lead vocal's climactic moment or even during the triplet-16ths drum fill. No one will hear it, and it'll probably just make that moment of the song unnecessarily busy. Instead, *pick your spot*—listen for a place, perhaps between vocal phrases, where something is needed. That way, when you mix your song, you won't need to reach for an EQ knob or something to make sure the listener catches your slick fill. It'll be the focus of attention at that moment—and a song that shifts around its focal points in this way is more interesting than one that doesn't.

If your mix consists of ten different instruments, spreading them out across the frequency spectrum will allow each one to be more present or audible in the final mix, because the instruments won't have to compete against each other for space in the frequency spectrum. But what if you don't want the instruments separated out? What if you want a "wall of sound," like the kind producer Phil Spector made famous in the 1960s? Then you can employ a kind of anti-frequency slotting: Just bunch all of the instruments together in a similar frequency range through your choice of tones, EQs, etc. You'll get more of a unified, sonically amorphous texture than a blend of distinct instruments.

Here's another objection you may have: Maybe, you argue, you don't really want the instruments to separate out in the mix. After all, on a good record, the instruments sound tight and together, like they're a unified whole, right? Absolutely. But *before* you get them to blend into a unified whole, each sound needs to be separate and pure. It's like a recipe: Imagine if you had to bake chocolate-chip cookies but there was a lot of salt in your brown sugar, eggs in the flour, and flour in the butter. The cookies might still turn out all right, but you'd have less control over the final product than if all of the ingredients were originally pure and high-quality. Mix good ingredients together in the right proportions and you'll get good cookies. It's similar with recording music: Get clean, good-sounding recordings of your instruments first, and then blend them together just right. More about how to get the perfect blend in Chapter 10.

Frequencies & Their Roles

Again using the cookies example, each ingredient serves a different function in the final product. The flour gives the cookie body; sugar makes it sweet (the blend of brown sugar and white sugar imparting a certain type of sweetness as well as color); and chocolate chips and walnuts add texture and diversify the taste, making the cookie more interesting. Similarly, each region of the frequency spectrum has a function in music. All of the frequencies, at least in the audible 20Hz–20kHz range, are important—and they should all be represented, in some way, in your mix. Even if your recording is a solo acoustic guitar performance, you want to capture the sound with a mic that reproduces a broad range of frequencies, from the very bottom to the very top. If you were recording solo didgeridoo (a low-sounding aboriginal wind instrument from Australia), you certainly should get some of that airy breath in the top end as well as the bellowing fundamental on the bottom. If you recorded the didgeridoo's lows only and cut off everything over 1kHz, the recording would be dull. The upper half of the frequency spectrum has a function—in this case, to add life and excitement to the performance. Then again, sometimes the low end has the function of supplying excitement; it depends on the instrumentation, the musical style, the tempo—lots of things.

When you're recording an instrument, take a moment to think about how it should sit in the frequency spectrum. For example, a fingerpicked acoustic guitar (see Fig. 1) has a lower region that represents the "body" or "fullness" of the sound; a middle that covers the fundamentals of the upper, more melodic notes; an upper region that makes up the picking sounds and the "zing" of the strings; and finally a high region for that hard-to-describe "air" or "openness." To hear what I mean, record a simple fingerpicked acoustic-guitar part with a condenser mic and flat EQ. Then, as

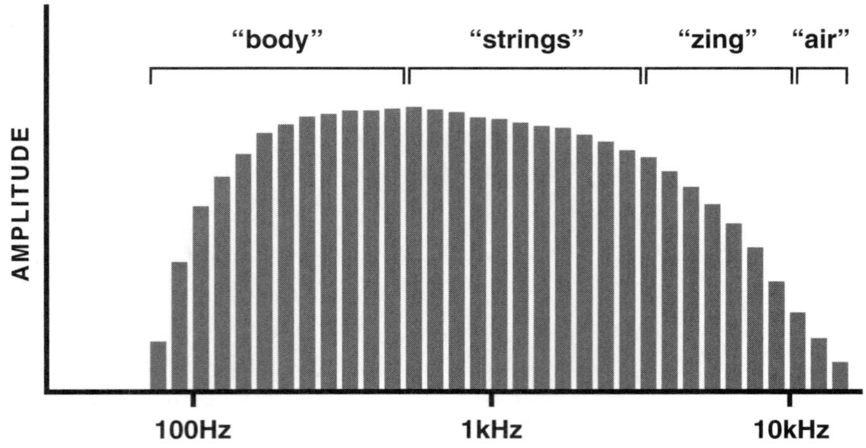

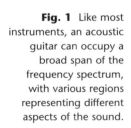

Fig. 1 Like most instruments, an acoustic guitar can occupy a broad span of the frequency spectrum, with various regions representing different aspects of the sound.

the track is playing back through a mixing-board channel, turn up the channel's mid EQ knob to about 3:00, and slowly sweep through the frequencies using the mid-frequency knob. Listen to how different aspects of the sound are enhanced as you sweep, and notice where, in terms of hertz and kilohertz, these aspects reside. (If your mid-EQ doesn't cover a broad-enough frequency range, use a graphic EQ or outboard parametric EQ instead.) Achieving this kind of familiarity with sounds is an important step in learning to record, because if you're mixing a song and you decide the acoustic guitar should have more "body," you'll need to know how to get it.

That said, it's important that you learn how to record instruments "flat," with as little EQ as possible, as well. Don't fall into the habit of recording a track haphazardly, thinking you can always "fix it in the mix" later. For example, recording an acoustic guitar with the mic too close to the soundhole may yield an overly boomy sound with insufficient note definition and highs. If you subsequently try to balance out the sound by cutting the lows and cranking up the highs, the lows may be tamed but may sound thinner or less natural than they should—and while the highs may be enhanced somewhat, they won't sound as natural as "real" highs. (Of course, boosting the highs means there will be more noise as well.) You'd be better off playing around with the mic's positioning before you record the track: Record a short segment with the mic in one place, then listen back, move the mic a bit, and repeat until you get something that sounds, to your ears, like a real acoustic guitar. Of course, this ability to judge what sounds natural will develop over time, but you should at least approach the situation with the proper mindset.

Bottom line: If you can record a solid-sounding track without using EQ during the tracking process, by all means do. As much as possible, reserve the EQing for the mixing process.

Separating A Simple Mix

Let's consider how you would go about enhancing separation on a simple recording: just acoustic guitar, recorded with one condenser mic, and a male lead vocal recorded (in a separate performance) with the same mic. The two performances exist in mono on separate tracks. The vocal has been compressed somewhat, so that the louder part of its dynamic range is even and present and its softer moments are more audible, and the guitar has been compressed just a bit to bring down its loudest moments, allowing the instrument to be more present in the mix overall. Depending on the music's style, you could have excellent results simply by blending the two tracks: If the vocal and guitar play off each other rhythmically so that each gives the other space, then you may not even have to think about frequency slotting or panning. If, however, the vocal and guitar often crash into each other (particularly at key lyrical moments), then the mix

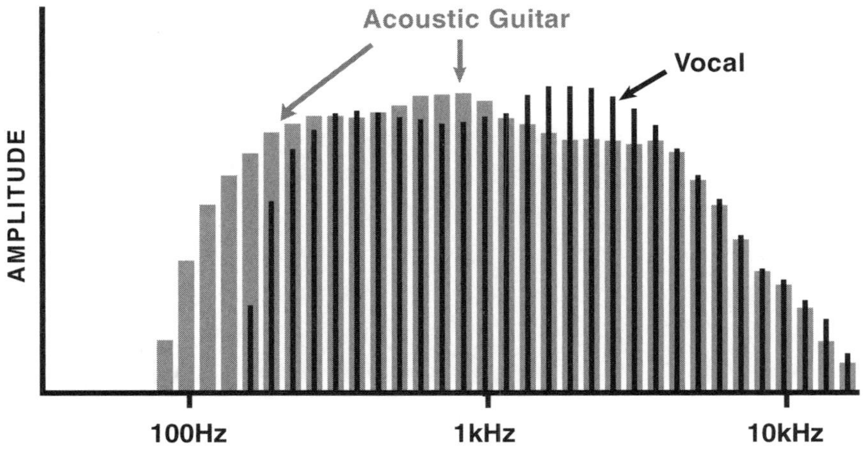

Fig. 2 The frequency profiles of an acoustic guitar and vocal can each be gently shaped to give each sound more "room" in the frequency spectrum—and therefore better separation.

would probably benefit from some slotting. Here's how to proceed if you like the levels of the vocal and guitar against each other but some of the words aren't as intelligible as you'd like, or if the vocal just seems a bit sonically "crowded" by the guitar.

Let's think about the goals of the recording. Is the song a showcase for the guitarist, with the vocal serving merely an atmospheric or embellishing function? If not, you'll probably want to think "vocals first." You can assume the audience will be listening to vocals closest; typically, a vocal is what most listeners' ears latch onto. Therefore, craft the mix so as to feature the vocal, without necessarily burying the guitar.

Vocals—particularly male vocals—have a broad frequency range, with fundamentals in the low-mids and breath sounds and sibilants ("s" sounds) extending well past 10kHz. But vocals tend to be "centered" somewhere around 2kHz. This is the area that gives vocals presence; it's where you'll find most of the voice's formants—the harmonics, as resonated and enhanced by the singer's anatomical features. You can think of this frequency region as the track's "signature" frequency band. Simply put, boosting this area will give the track more presence and make it more up-front. Boosting other frequency bands will have different effects, but they won't necessarily enhance the vocal's presence.

Acoustic guitar, on the other hand, has a somewhat lower "signature" frequency region—let's say somewhere around 800Hz. That's one of the reasons why vocals and acoustic guitar go well together: Their frequency characteristics tend to naturally separate from each other somewhat. Recorded, the guitar needs to provide the song's foundation frequency-wise. There needs to be some bottom end to anchor the recording; the vocal doesn't "live" down in that region enough, so the guitar should provide that function. Also, the sound of vibrating acoustic guitar strings contains plenty of harmonics, but they're subordinate to the fundamentals. A guitar doesn't have the resonating chambers that a human head and chest do, so it has ordinary harmonics rather than formants.

So now we have figured out roughly where both sounds' "signature" regions exist: around 2kHz for the vocal and 800Hz for the guitar (see Fig. 2). I would begin slotting this mix by giving the vocal a gentle, somewhat broad boost at 2kHz, and I'd give a similar cut to the guitar at the same frequency. Then I might try enhancing the guitar's 800Hz region. Since the guitar needs to be supplying a solid bottom end, I'd listen to hear if the vocal's low notes are muddying up the mix as they coincide with the guitar's frequencies in that region (let's say 400Hz); if so, I may gently cut the vocal's low mids. You don't want to cut a vocal's lows too much, though, as that can remove its "body"—almost literally—and make it sound detached and less warm.

By now, the guitar and vocal are living in their "homes" and are conflicting less with each other, frequency-wise, than they were when we began. In terms of frequency, they're separated. But what about pan position? We have two tracks—if we pan both to the center, then the recording will be monophonic, except perhaps for some reverb we might add into the mix. Can we pan the tracks somewhat left and right? Sure—but this is kind of unconventional, because the all-important lead vocal is normally panned to the center, and listening to a mix like this won't exactly conjure the feeling of sitting in front of a singer while he's playing a guitar. How about panning the vocal to the center while the guitar is off to the left or right? Okay, but now

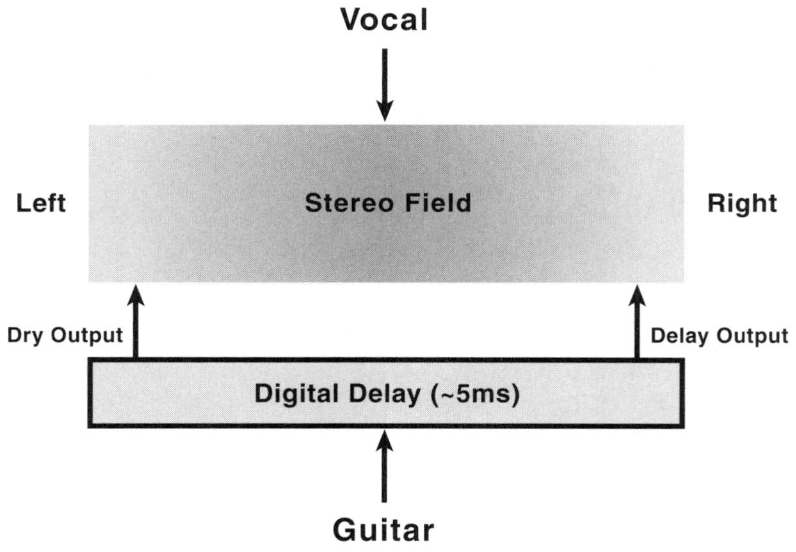

Fig. 3 To separate a vocal and a guitar in the stereo field, one approach would be to set up a very short delay on the guitar and pan the original and delayed guitar around the center-panned vocal.

the mix will be lopsided in the stereo field—one channel will have a higher level than the other—and correcting this in the mastering stage (see Chapter 10) will only tilt the vocal off to one side again.

What to do? If you had recorded the guitar with two mics on two tracks, you could pan them left and right somewhat, with the vocal in the center. But using multiple mics opens up a Pandora's box of potential problems that are best left to pro engineers. In Guerrilla Home Recording you probably would have been better off recording a mic track plus a signal from a magnetic or piezoelectric pickup, on its own track; these would be easier to mix together, and you could pan the mic and pickup sounds apart somewhat to give the guitar its own space in the stereo field on either side of the vocal. With only one guitar track, though, you have a couple of options. You could pan the guitar a little to one side, use its channel's effect send to feed a delay, set the delay to something short—maybe 20 milliseconds—and then blend in the delayed signal panned to the other side (see Fig. 3). Or, as long as it didn't sound cheesy or inappropriate, you could use the same effect send to give the guitar a slight chorusing sound, panning the chorused guitar hard left and hard right. Effects such as chorusing offer many opportunities to alter the stereo-field placements of sounds. I'll cover them in detail in the next chapter.

CHAPTER 6

Effects—The Recording Spices

Many home recordists think effects are a bit like the frosting on a cake: They're kind of an afterthought, slopped on top after the cake is finished cooking, perhaps to help mask inadequacies in the cake itself. But I recommend thinking of effects more as spices—intrinsically important parts of the whole, to be added with care and good taste. If you think of effects this way, you'll be less afraid to add an effect to a track during the tracking process (i.e., "printing" the effect), a technique that can serve the Guerrilla recordist very well.

Let's take a close look at all of the effects you're likely to need at your disposal: what they are, how to get them, and how and why to apply them.

Reverb Effects

Reverb is the king of recording effects. It refers to the smooth, gradually decaying sonic texture that occurs after a sound is made in an acoustically reflective space. If you go into an empty concert hall and yell "Hey!" you'll hear reverb for a few seconds. People sometimes refer to this as "echo," but in the recording world we distinguish echo from reverb. Echo refers to discrete, repeating reflections of a sound, similar to what you'd hear if you yelled "Hey!" at a not-too-distant cliffside. In a concert hall, however, there are so many reflective surfaces that the individual random echoes almost immediately blend into a smooth sound that's pleasing to the ear. That's reverb.

Types of reverbs. Decades ago, the only way a recording engineer could add reverb in the studio was to use either a real acoustical space (popularly called an "echo chamber") or a mechanical device to simulate real acoustical reverb. In the first method, a sound was fed into a loudspeaker situated in a room with highly reflective surfaces. On the other side of the room was a microphone, which fed a reverb signal back to the studio's control room. The invention of the *plate reverb* (and to a lesser degree the *spring reverb*) provided an alternative to the actual reverb chamber. A plate reverb—still used in many studios—consists of a suspended sheet of metal with a transducer at either end. One transducer causes the source signal to create vibrations in the metal; myriad reverb-like reflections then bounce back and forth across the sheet, and another transducer picks up these reflections and turns them back into an electrical signal. (Two receiving transducers can generate a stereo reverb signal.) A spring reverb is similar but uses a set of metal springs. Spring reverb doesn't sound as authentic as plate reverb, but spring reverbs can be small and cheap to manufacture, which is why spring reverb "tanks" are still found in many guitar amplifiers. Spring reverbs also don't respond very well to quick transients like drums or handclaps; the result is an otherworldly, shooting *ping* that reminds me of the sound I heard as a kid when I'd toss rocks onto a newly frozen lake. Pump a very percussive sound into a guitar amp with spring reverb and you'll hear what I mean. It's a cool effect with a unique sound that can be useful sometimes, but it's nothing like authentic reverb.

Of course now we have digital reverbs, which have made mechanical reverbs pretty much obsolete. While pro engineers still often get real room reverb by putting mics around the performance space, in Guerrilla Home Recording this is unfeasible—so this is where digital reverbs save the day. A digital reverb digitizes a source signal and runs it through a reverb algorithm, which generates many reflections of the sound (and reflections of the reflections) and blends them together. The great thing about digital reverbs is they're small, inexpensive (compared to plates), and highly versatile. Even some downright cheap reverbs sound pretty good. A digital reverb often has algorithms to simulate acoustic hall reverb, small-room reverb, and plate reverbs, plus other specialty algorithms.

Choosing a digital reverb. In Chapter 1 I mentioned that there are awful digital reverbs and there are great ones. Simply put, a bad reverb is one that doesn't sound real, and a good reverb is one that does. This isn't something you can tell from a magazine ad or even the price tag; you've got to listen to a reverb to judge it. You can choose a reverb based on recommendations, or you can use your ears. My own reverb, a first-generation Yamaha SPX90 circa 1986, is also the first one I bought—I got lucky. As it turns out, this classic piece of gear is still found in many pro studios. I knew I had something good when I read that Peter Gabriel had two of them in his own super-high-tech studio.

Poor reverbs don't create as smooth a sound as a good reverb. A simple way to check for this is to run a finger-snap sound through the effect. A finger-snap is an extremely short sound—it's basically a sharp transient and nothing else—so it will help expose where on the cheesy-to-complex continuum the reverb's functioning falls. A good reverb will do an okay job generating a smooth, realistic-sounding reverb "tail" from a finger-snap. A poor reverb will not; it will be gritty and digital-sounding, especially as the reverb tail fades to silence. Longer sounds like strings might sound pretty good through a reverb like this, but they'll sound better through a good reverb—and a good reverb will be able to perform well with more percussive sounds like drums and handclaps (and maybe even finger-snaps).

> LOOK ■ OUT!
>
> ### *Blend At The Board—Not In The Box*
>
> Many effect devices such as digital reverbs allow you to specify the output mix of "wet" and "dry" components. But if you're feeding the effect by way of an effect send, this "feature" can only cause trouble. You don't want the effect to output any "dry" signal at all, because the "dry" signal already exists at the board, pure and unadulterated. Therefore, make sure the effect is outputting 100 percent "wet" signal all the time, and blend in however much of it you want at the board.
>
> Yes, you could send 100 percent of your source to the effect and determine the mix there—but why? Doing so only introduces another stage where the source signal can be corrupted by distortion and noise. You'll get a cleaner sound by keeping the source within the board's channels, taking a feed from an effect send, and then blending in a small amount of the effect (or a large amount, as the case may be) with an effect return or a separate pair of channels. Any noise created by the effect will be attenuated at the point where you bring in the returning effect. Bringing back a blend of "wet" and "dry" signals, however, may introduce more noise into your mix than you need to.

Another thing to check is the reverb's high-frequency response. Some reverbs are designed with a hyped-up high end in order to provide a crisper, more dazzling sound, but this can create a sizzling, unnatural-sounding response to bright source signals. Try feeding quick "s" sounds into a reverb from a condenser mic and listen to how the unit reacts. Does it sound like an "s" sound in a room or concert hall, or does it sound like someone started frying a huge pan of bacon? There are a lot of "s" sounds on any lead vocal track, and if your reverb reacts to each one with a little explosion of sizzle, it's not going to make the track sound very much like a live performance in a real space.

Applying reverb. Don't make the mistake of thinking that reverb's function is to cover up flaws in a track. Going back to the spices analogy, that's like using hot sauce to cover up the taste of rotting meat—the end result will likely be even worse. Except in special cases where the reverb is a track's featured component, avoid mixing it so heavy that the reverb level begins to approach the source's level. In most cases, reverb sounds best when it provides just a tasty "aura" or "glow" around a sound—to cushion it and give the sound a subtle spatial context, but in no way to overwhelm it.

Then again, there are times when you want a track to be mostly reverb, or even all reverb. For a lush, pillowy texture on a sustained sound like strings, crank up that reverb. By "crank up" I don't mean send more source to the reverb box; as always, observe proper gain-staging (see Chapter 2). That means the reverb should always be receiving a near-maximum level of source, and you should be controlling the reverb level with the board's effect-return or reverb-channel level control. In other words, control the reverb level *after* it's generated by the effect, not before. One of my favorite sounds is a vocal with no "dry" signal, consisting of reverb only. Perhaps slowly panned around a mix, it can create an ethereal, detached sound that seems to be coming from another dimension. A good way to achieve this sound is to set the vocal channel's effect send to pre-fader and then mute the channel. The "dry" signal will therefore be muted, but the reverb unit will still receive a source signal. Blend the resulting reverb into the mix with an effect return or a pair of input channels dedicated to the reverb.

Generally, the proportion of reverb to "dry" signal determines a sound's perceived distance in the mix. If you want to make a sound seem to fade off into the distance, slowly fade out the source while increasing the reverb send level, or switch the send to pre-fader and then fade out the source. If the whole mix is fading out at the end of the song, you can make the fade-out a bit more "organic" by turning up the master effect-send level knob(s) to boost the reverb while you're bringing down the master fader; this will make the song seem to go off into the sunset rather than simply get quieter and quieter.

How about no reverb at all? That can be a great effect (or non-effect). Reverb-free lead vocals create an aggressive, in-your-face sound; think the Red Hot Chili Peppers' or Alanis Morissette's more aggro songs. Bass, unless the song is slow and/or sparsely arranged, usually sounds best with no reverb, because reverb tends to reduce its tightness and make it muddier (neither is good for a bass line). By all means, don't feel you need to apply reverb to all of your tracks, or even to most of them. A mix is more interesting when it has an artful combination of "wet" and "dry" tracks.

Inexperienced recordists often apply too much reverb, simply because it's easy and because reverb "sounds good." But avoid drenching a mix in reverb, the same way you'd avoid drenching a salad with dressing. Also, avoid using the same amount of the same reverb on several instruments at once. Putting the same reverb on a lead vocal, guitar, and drums tends to make the reverb flat and uninteresting. Your mix will be better served if certain tracks get some reverb (say, the lead vocals), certain tracks get just a hint (maybe the guitar and snare drum), while other tracks get none at all (the bass and hi-hat, for instance). And if you can tastefully bring in a second or third reverb, either by "printing" reverb onto tracks or using additional reverb units during mixdown, you can really enhance the spatial influence that this effect adds to a mix.

Also keep in mind that reverb channels need not be panned hard left and right. For instance, you can get interesting stereo-image effects by bunching a background vocal's reverb more toward the center while the lead vocal's reverb spreads across the whole stereo field (see Fig. 1), or vice versa. Another great trick is to pan a "dry" track to one side and all of its reverb (or maybe just one reverb channel) to the other side. This can create the impression of having a large acoustical space way off on the opposite side of the stereo field from an instrument. It's similar to a surround-sound effect you might hear in a film: The sound seems nearby (from one direction), yet distant

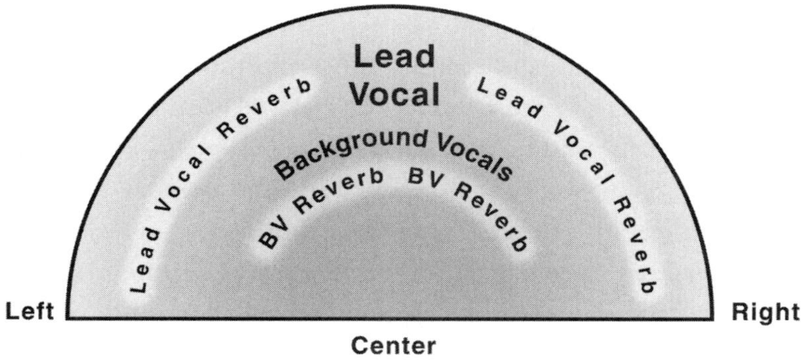

Fig. 1 This kind of diagram illustrates a way to think about the panning of sounds and effects. Here, the lead vocal is panned to center with its reverb spread across the stereo field; the background vocals are spread across the central region, with their own reverb spread slightly wider.

(from the other direction) at the same time. So much can be done with reverb; it offers a ton of potential for artistically creative techniques.

Reverb parameters. The primary variable in a digital reverb sound is the *decay time*. This represents the time, in seconds, for the reverb to drop to 60dB below its starting point. Two to three seconds is about right for a lead vocal; four seconds can be useful for a more lush, expansive effect, although be careful—the longer a reverb lasts, the more it tends to pile up in the mix, leading to clutter and mud. Rolling off some of the lows or low mids can remedy this somewhat. I've found that in general, the faster and busier a song is, the "tighter" (shorter and less muddy) the reverbs need to be. A fast ska song is no place for a languorous five-second reverb! But in a sparse, ambient type of recording, the same reverb may be perfect.

Below two seconds, a reverb can begin sounding metallic or "hard." This is where other parameters, such as "liveness," "diffusion," and "lowpass filter," can help give the reverb a more natural sound. A reverb shorter than one second can create interesting special effects—try it and see what you come up with.

Other than delay time, reverb parameters are not standard and therefore vary quite a bit from unit to unit. For example, some advanced reverbs allow you to specify the dimensions and materials of the room being simulated. With a unit like this, it's a blast to "build" a concrete room that's ten feet square and several hundred feet tall and hear what it might sound like. But as with many effects, I recommend not getting caught up in the meaning of all the various parameters. It's helpful to know how to get sounds that you're imagining, but too much knowledge can also bog down your creativity. Just run your sound through the thing, tweak the numbers in real time, and listen to the results. Eventually you'll hit upon something that works well—and that's really all that matters.

Early reflections. Many reverb units have programs for *early reflections*, kind of a cross between reverb and delay. Early reflections represent reverb's first-occurring component: the direct echoes from the walls of a concert hall, for instance, before the echoes become so many and so diffuse that they blend into a smooth reverb sound. It's a dense, stuttering delay; the number of echoes and the spacing between them can be specified with the effect's parameters. You can use early reflections to create a robotic, gated-reverb-like sound on a snare drum, and I've also laid it on thick with a vocal to spoof an aggressive radio commercial for a monster-truck rally. Used more delicately, it creates nice atmosphere behind a strummed acoustic or electric guitar. Because it's a wide stereo effect, it could work well on anything that needs broad ambience where reverb might sound too simple, obvious, or cluttered.

Gated reverb. This effect, which combines reverb and noise-gating, is generally attributed to engineer Hugh Padgham in his work on Peter Gabriel's 1980 self-titled "Melting Face" album. It subsequently became the effect that essentially defined '80s drum sounds, and it's still often used today. By following a reverb with a high-threshold noise gate, you get a reverb that abruptly cuts off after it has decayed slightly (see Fig. 2). Applied to drums (or perhaps only the snare), this allows you to use a "big room" reverb time of two or three seconds—but the gating cleans up all of the reverb between each drum hit, allowing the drums to remain tight-sounding. Basically, a drum hit with gated reverb results in an explosion of reverb for a moment, followed by silence. It's an effective way to create a big drum sound without drowning the drums in reverb. Listen to any dance hit from the mid '80s and you'll likely hear gated reverb in action.

Many digital reverbs have gated-reverb programs built in, which is obviously more convenient than following a reverb unit with a separate noise gate. These programs often allow you to specify the reverb time as well as a "hold" time (the duration that

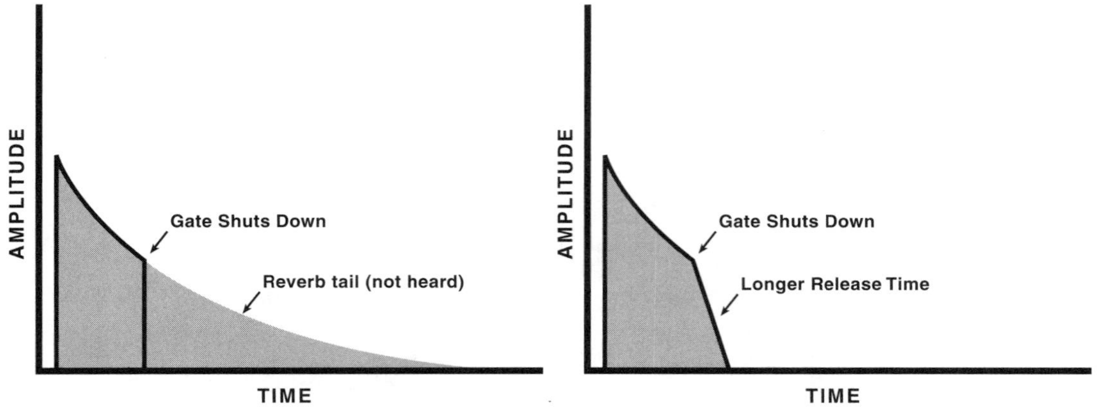

Fig. 2 Gated reverb cuts off soon after the reverb has begun to decay. The cutoff can be made to sound less abrupt by increasing the "release" parameter.

GUERRILLA TACTIC

Sampling Gated Reverb

Paul Simon's song "You Can Call Me Al" (from *Graceland*) features gated reverb tastefully applied to each tom-tom drum. When I first heard that tune, I wanted to create a similar sound using sampled drums. Putting one gated reverb on all of the toms didn't work out the way I wanted; the toms had individual pan positions, but the gated reverb's panning remained static—it didn't follow the toms through a fill. My solution was to resample each mono tom sample in stereo, along with its own gated reverb. In order to create the impression that each tom had its own reverb, I tightened up the reverb's panning so that it "surrounded" the tom. For instance, if a high-medium tom was panned to 2:00, I panned the left and right reverb channels to around 12:00 and 4:00. This way, when all of the toms sounded in succession, their respective reverbs "followed" along, creating a large, spacious sound with a complex stereo image. That's much more interesting than what you'd get with just one reverb panned hard left and right.

the gate is held open after a sound exceeds the gate's threshold). A "release" time parameter slows down the gate-closing speed, which makes the gate's cutoff a little less artificial sounding.

If you have only one reverb and want to use gated reverb on the drum track as well as conventional reverb on the vocals and other instruments, you have a couple of options. If you're recording sampled drums onto the multitrack (rather than having the drums come in by way of virtual tracking), just "print" the gated reverb with the drums. As long as you're using a sync tone or other synchronization method, you can always redo the drums later if you don't like the reverb or anything else about the drums; if you're not syncing, you'll just have to live with what you've recorded or else start the song over from scratch. Another option is to build the gated reverb into the drum sample (see the sidebar Sampling Gated Reverb, above).

Reverse reverb. Sometimes called "preverb," this sound was made famous in the 1982 film *Poltergeist*. By running a tape backward, recording reverb from a track onto the backward-running tape, and then playing the tape forward, you get reverb that *builds up* to a sound rather than trailing off after it. The effect can be startling, but use it tastefully—reverse reverb gets old fast. (An effective use can be heard on Pearl Jam's "Evenflow," where it appears in just a few select spots.) Some digital reverbs offer "reverse" reverb programs, but since even the most expensive box can't predict the future, the reverse reverb doesn't begin until *after* the sound occurs. As a result, you hear your source sound, then a swell of reverb that builds to a peak, but the source sound doesn't occur at the peak. If you're recording digitally, you can use reverse reverb to create true preverb: Print the reverse reverb, and then shift the reverb track earlier so that it builds to the source sound rather than to nothing (see Fig. 3).

Delay-Based Effects

Along with reverb, delay is one of the most useful effects. The basic idea is simple: A sound is recorded digitally by a delay unit, a.k.a. digital delay line or DDL; it's held in its memory for a predetermined time, and then played back. The first studio effect I bought (even before I had a cassette 4-track) was an Ibanez digital delay, and I still use it often—unlike reverbs, all digital delays sound pretty much equally good, so I've never felt the need to upgrade.

Delay effects come in many forms, which is what makes a DDL one of the most powerful outboard devices in a studio. The factors that determine what a delay does are the delay time, *feedback* or *regeneration*, and *modulation*. Feedback or regeneration refers to adding some delayed signal back into the input stage, which causes an echo to repeat again and again, softer each time. Modulation refers to altering the digital playback speed, which can do various things to a delay effect, as we'll see.

Basic echo. With a DDL set to a delay time of, say, 300ms (milliseconds) and feedback to zero, you'll get a single repeat of everything the DDL "hears" at its input. Turning up the feedback will result in multiple echoes; the higher you set this parameter, the more echoes you'll get and the closer in volume they'll be to each other. On some delays, cranking up the feedback all the way will cause more sound to feed back to the input than what you started with, causing the echoes to "run away" into distortion.

Medium to long echoes are usually best applied as "spot" effects. A good way to do this is to keep the DDL's effect-send knob all the way down for most of a vocal and turn it up only just before the last word or syllable of a phrase. This way, only that word or phrase is sent to the DDL, and its echo or echoes occur when the vocal track

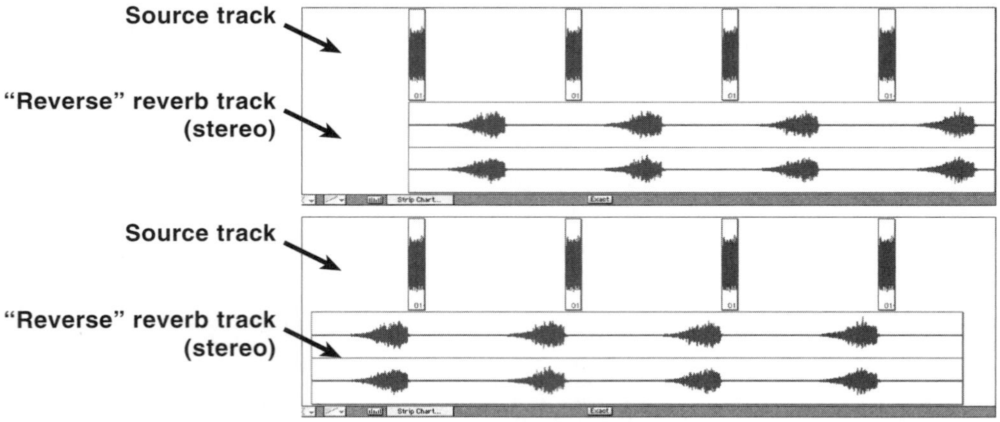

Fig. 3 Using a reverse reverb sound to create "preverb": Record the reverse reverb on a separate track (top), and then shift it backwards in time so that it peaks immediately before the source sound (bottom).

is otherwise silent—the delay doesn't obscure the lyrics. If you do run a delay through an entire vocal, keep it much lower in level than the source, unless you want a psychedelic effect with an obscured vocal melody and lyric. If you do apply a "spot" echo, choose your spots at the effect-send knob, not at the effect-return knob—particularly if you're using feedback. This will give you more control over the result. If you're sending the whole track to the delay and selectively turning up the effect-return knob, you kind of need to guess where the echoes will fall. Also, if there's feedback on the echo, the word or syllable you want to repeat could be contaminated by previous sounds on the track. Working that effect-send knob instead will send what you need delayed to the delay, and nothing else.

Down around 100ms is where you get what I call the "John Lennon delay." On many of Lennon's early-'70s solo recordings, producer Phil Spector used a tape-echo device (the precursor to the digital delay) to add a short single echo to Lennon's vocal. Shorter than 100ms, you get a *slapback* echo that kind of blends in with the source; the two sounds are close enough in time that the delay doesn't obscure the lyrics as much, so you can use it at a high level through a whole track. The amount of delay you use in the mix determines the effect's intensity.

Shorter than about 50ms, and with a good amount of feedback, you get what's called a *hard reverb* sound—it's similar to reverb in the way it decays, but you don't get the random-like blending together of a real reverb. It's the sound you might get if you were standing between two large, parallel concrete walls. Hard reverb is a distinctive vibrating, metallic effect that can be cool (if used tastefully) on the snare drum and other sounds.

When you're using a delay line, pan positioning can make a big difference in the results you get. With longer echoes it's often effective to pan the echo away from the source—a vocal snippet can appear at left and echo to the right, for instance. With shorter echoes, though, it's usually better to pan the "dry" and "wet" signals together. If you're doing a 100ms "John Lennon" delay, panning the "dry" signal center and the delay off to the side may result in what sounds like just a tight performance in the center and a lagging-behind performance off to the side. That's because the stereo separation allows the listener to hear the delay as a distinct sound; it doesn't blend in with the "dry" sound. But maybe that's what you want—try each approach and see which works best for your song.

Multi-tap delay. With a simple delay line, you get an echo that may or may not repeat, depending on the feedback setting. A *multi-tap delay*, though, is like having several delays in one box: You could tell it to provide an echo at 100ms, another at 150ms, a third at 350ms, and finally a fourth echo at 600ms. Often these delays are entirely independent, each with its own parameters for feedback and perhaps EQ. A stereo multi-tap usually lets you assign a different pan position for each delay, so you can have echoes appearing all over the stereo field. (The term *ping-pong delay* refers to a multi-tap in which the echoes are programmed to bounce back and forth across the stereo field.) This effect is so cool it's easy to overuse; unless your mix is sparse or even *a cappella*, your song will be best served if you use a multi-tap only subtly, or in a few carefully selected spots. Otherwise your mix can clutter up fast with seemingly random echoes everywhere. Remember, just because you have an effect doesn't mean you need to use it!

Doubling. When a delay is short and by itself (no feedback), it tends to blend into the source sound and disappear somewhat. This is where modulation can make things happen. When the delay is modulated, its playback speeds up and slows down in a cyclical fashion, like an off-center vinyl record. This makes the delay's pitch go up and down. By applying a small amount of slow modulation to a delay of around 20ms, you get a "doubling" effect that old-school engineers called ADT, or automatic double-tracking. It approximates what you'd get if you recorded the performance a second time on a different track: The timing and pitch might not be exactly the same. Doubling with a delay is a pretty good way to thicken a track, but it never sounds as good as actual double-tracking. You can increase the thickening effect by adding a little feedback, but not too much—the repeats will accentuate the pitch-shifting effect, so just a few low-level repeats can smear the performance's pitch and timing into ugly-zone.

Modulation's character is controlled by two parameters: width (or intensity) and speed (or rate). Width controls how far from normal the delay's playback speed varies; a low width results in a subtle pitch variation, while a high width causes more extreme pitch fluctuations. The amount of width you can get depends on the delay time parameter; longer delays allow for broader modulation. The speed parameter determines how fast the modulation occurs; like sound itself, it's often measured in hertz (cycles per second), only using much lower numbers. A moderately fast modulation rate of 2Hz means the circuit will go through two speed-up-slow-down cycles every second; a 0.1Hz rate means it takes ten seconds for the cycle to repeat, which is a very slow modulation. Anytime you're working with a modulation delay effect, spend a little time tweaking these two parameters, as they often have a huge influence on the sound you get.

Chorusing. Similar to delay doubling, this effect attempts to simulate the sound of a group of singers or instrumentalists performing in unison. Really, though, it usually just adds some movement and interest to an otherwise static sound. Compared to doubling, chorusing delay times are usually a bit shorter (maybe 10ms or 15ms), the modulation is wider and perhaps faster, and there may be some feedback to thicken the sound. Chorusing is popular on synth pads, clean electric guitar, and bass (particularly fretless). On bass, though, chorusing can have a "blurring" effect on the pitch, particularly if the part is played in a low register; with bass you normally want the low end to be tight and solid. One way to get around this is to split the signal into two, roll off the lows on one of the sides, and chorus the high-frequency side only. When you blend together the two halves again, the bottom will be tight and solid, while the top will have some motion and animation.

Chorusing and other modulation-based effects with short delay times (see below) can be produced in stereo by an effect box with stereo outputs. An effect box achieves stereo chorusing by splitting the signal into two channels and flipping one channel's waveform over so that it's a mirror image of the first. (An engineer would say it's "180 degrees out of phase.") Both sides are then delayed by the specified time. When the "dry" sound is blended back in with the two-channel delayed signal, frequency cancellations occur in the out-of-phase side, causing the frequency makeup of the two stereo channels to be different at any given moment. The ears therefore perceive a subtle difference between the two sides, creating the impression of a "wider" sound. That's why stereo chorusing is a popular way to "widen out" sounds that might otherwise seem thin and one-dimensional, such as clean electric guitar.

Although chorusing is useful, it doesn't sound particularly authentic. So, for background vocals and other applications where you need a more symphonic, layered texture, you're usually better off just piling up multiple takes if you have enough tracks. Alternatively, you can use bouncing or sound-on-sound (see Chapter 1).

Flanging. When delay times get into the single-digit-millisecond range, an effect called *flanging* occurs. Flanging is commonly described as a "whooshing" or "jet airplane" sound; it creates a kind of filtering or resonance that audibly moves up or down in frequency depending on what's happening with the modulation. If a sound is delayed by five milliseconds or so and then combined with the source sound (particularly if feedback is added), certain frequencies cancel out, resulting in a peaks-and-valleys pattern across the frequency spectrum. With modulation applied, the delay time either shortens or lengthens, causing this peaks-and-valleys pattern to shift up or down. This shifting is what you perceive when you hear flanging: As the delay times shorten the flanging appears to go "up," and as they lengthen the flanging seems to go "down."

Flanging got its name in the 1960s, when engineers learned that if they recorded the same sound on two tape machines and played them simultaneously—one slightly delayed relative to the other—the two recordings would react with each other by causing frequency cancellations between them. By touching the flange of one of the machines' tape reels, that machine would slow down, causing the delay to change in one direction or the other, also changing the way the sounds reacted to one another. This is considered *true flanging*, because it allows the two sounds to cross in time: If the machine that's ahead is slowed down, eventually the other machine's recording will pass it by, like runners in a race. At the moment where they cross, the delay time separating them gets infinitesimally short, causing the flanging to sound like it's shooting through the roof. Effect-box flanging can never achieve this state of "flange nirvana," however, because it relies on one source sound and one delayed sound; the two can come close to each other in time but never actually cross. That's why many engineers still prefer true flanging. A famous example of this sound, expertly applied to a whole mix, can be heard at the climactic point in the middle of the Doobie Brothers' "Listen to the Music."

Flanging is kind of a special effect; it has such a distinctive sound, and the sound is so bold, it's easy to overuse. If I were recording a CD of 15 songs, I might use flanging on only one or two tracks.

Phasing. *Phasing* occurs with even shorter delay times than flanging—from 2ms down below 1ms. Essentially, phasing is the high-in-the-stratosphere component of flanging—pretty much only the highest frequencies are involved in the frequency cancellation. It results in a "liquidy" sound; that's truly the best way to describe it. Phasing isn't of much use unless a lot of modulation is applied, and often the modulation is quite fast. But because the delay times are so short, to get good phasing the delay unit needs to be very precise. Interestingly, dedicated analog effect-box phasers usually produce a better phase sound than most all-in-one digital delays. In fact, the Small Stone phaser, manufactured by Electro-Harmonix in the 1970s, might have the best phase sound ever made. A good example of phasing can be heard on the main guitar riff of the Rolling Stones' "Shattered." (Keith Richards may well have used a Small Stone phaser on that cut.)

Phasing is good as an ear-catching special effect or a subtle texture, but it also works well as a first stage on lead guitar. Not surprisingly, the phasing doesn't sound much the same after it's gone through several distortion stages—but the phasing adds a cool extra dimension to the lead tone, with frequencies gently whipping around, that rarely seems out of place.

The Many Faces Of Dirt: Distortion

As any guitarist knows, distortion is one of the most popular effects around. But distortion is like the witches of Oz: There are good kinds and bad kinds. There's distortion that you intentionally apply because you want it, and there's the kind that happens by accident because you've done something wrong—improper gain-staging is the most common cause.

Strictly speaking, distortion refers to any change of a waveform; usually this means there's an addition or subtraction of frequency components. The technical specification known as THD, or total harmonic distortion, refers to this broad definition: It

GUERRILLA TACTIC

True Flanging With A Sampler

You don't really need two analog tape machines to get the sound of true flanging. All you need is a sampler. Sample a sound that has already been recorded—either a portion of a track or a portion of a whole mix—and then duplicate the sample in the sampler's memory, or sample it again the exact same way. Detune one of the versions by just a few cents so that it plays a bit faster or slower than the other, and experiment with starting both samples at *almost* the same time—offset them by the tiniest amount, so that the slower sample starts first and the faster one starts immediately afterward. If you do it right, as the two samples play in unison you'll hear the samples crash together and flange, with the flanging sound going "up." At the moment where the faster sample catches up exactly, you'll hear that "flange nirvana" moment where the frequencies go through the ceiling—a sound unattainable with delay-box-based flanging. Analog purists will argue that "true flanging" is strictly achievable only with two analog tape machines, but sampler-based flanging can still produce a cool sound.

specifies how different a wave is when it leaves a circuit compared to when it entered. For our purposes, though, we can think of distortion as the electronic addition of harmonically related frequencies due to some stage being overdriven. In this sense, distortion is kind of like pornography: You know it when you hear it.

If you pump a sine wave into a basic amplifying circuit, ideally the same sine wave will come out of the circuit, only larger. But if the incoming wave is too strong for the circuit to handle, or if the circuit is told to amplify the wave beyond what it's designed to do, the wave's tops and bottoms will start to get cut off (see Fig. 4). This is called *clipping*—the wave is being horizontally clipped off, as with a pair of scissors. When this happens, the wave's shape changes; if it happens to a great degree, the sine wave essentially becomes a *square wave*—one with flat tops and bottoms and nearly vertical sides (see Fig. 5). A sine wave by definition has no harmonics, but a square wave has plenty; therefore, the process of distortion has actually added harmonics—specifically, odd-numbered harmonics—to the sound. Where a sine wave sounds somewhat like a muted whistling tone, a square wave sounds more like a clarinet. Distortion has changed the tone.

In a different kind of distortion, a raspy, gritty, or buzzing quality is imparted to the signal. This is generally not the kind of distortion you want in a recording. But you also may not want the strictly square-wave kind, either—unless you're going for something like the ultra-smooth sound of the lead guitar on the Guess Who's "American Woman." In most cases, guitar distortion consists of a more complex wave than one simple circuit can provide. Most good distorted guitar tones contain both even and odd harmonics; the proportion in which they occur, and the ways in which they're added, largely determine the distortion's effect on the original tone.

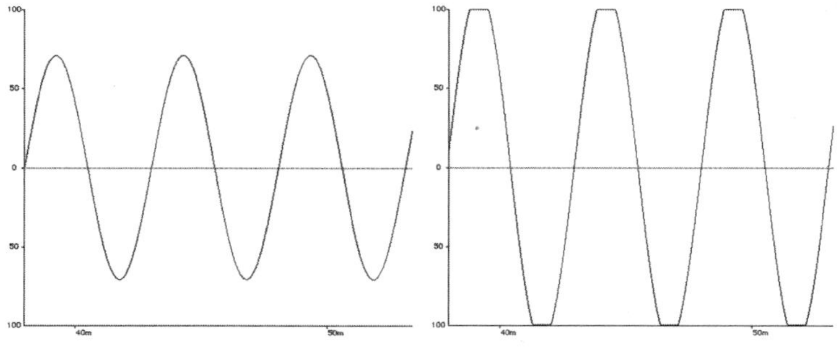

Fig. 4 If a sine wave (left) is amplified beyond a circuit's dynamic limits, the tops and bottoms of waves are "clipped" off (right), which is a form of distortion.

A complete treatise on guitar distortion is beyond the scope of this book. So I'll just offer a few observations about generating and capturing distortion in the Guerrilla studio.

Distortion sources. Before the mid '90s, you could get distortion in one of two ways: with a tube circuit, and with a solid-state circuit. Most guitarists feel that tube amps produce distortion that's more pleasing to the ear. Solid-state circuits use transistors instead of vacuum tubes; for decades electronic designers have tried to emulate the tube-distortion sound with solid-state circuits, with mixed success. (The famous Ibanez Tube Screamer pedal is one of the better such circuits.)

Even an all-tube amp, though, can produce fairly bad-sounding distortion if used wrong. If you overdrive only the preamp tubes, for instance, you may get a buzzy, electronic-sounding grit that doesn't sound much like anything you hear on records. Better-sounding distortion often happens only when you overdrive the amp's big power tubes. This means you need to crank up the amp *loud*. That may or may not be possible in your Guerrilla studio—if not, a device called a *power soak* allows you to replace

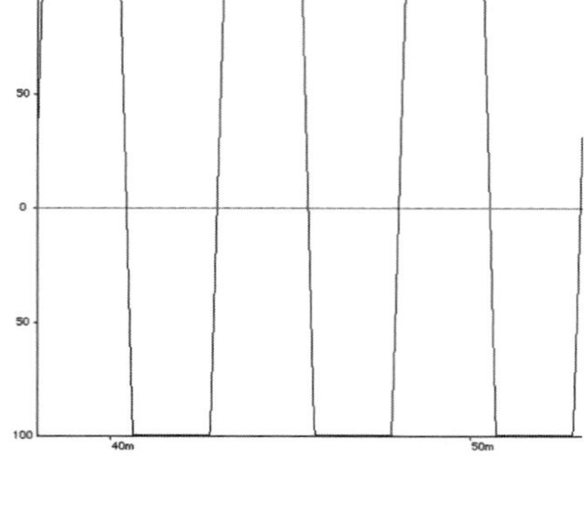

Fig. 5 A single extreme distortion stage can turn a sine wave into a square wave, with flat tops and bottoms and nearly flat "sides."

> **GUERRILLA TACTIC** ***Digital Distortion?***
>
> You often hear that "digital distortion" is horrible and unmusical—something to be avoided at all costs. Actually, that's only partially true. I've gotten useful distortion from a sampling keyboard by intentionally boosting and resampling a sound—in other words, applying a destructive edit that overwrites the original sample with one, say, 40dB hotter than the original. On that particular keyboard (a long-obsolete E-mu Emax II), the result was a completely blown-out sound, but without any of the harsh, grating brittleness often associated with digital distortion. In fact, it sounded great in drum-n-bass and other electronic genres. If you have a sampler that allows this function, give it a whirl and see what you get—digital distortion just might end up playing a prominent role on your next recording.

the speaker with a circuit that acts (electronically speaking) like a speaker but produces a direct, balanced signal rather than acoustic loudness that must be captured with a mic. A power soak allows even apartment-dwelling Guerrilla recordists to crank up a 100-watt Marshall stack and put the tones to tape.

In the mid '90s the first *modeling* circuits came along. These use digital technology to shape waves based on the analysis of real sound waves from specific sources. The Line 6 POD was the first portable modeling device, and right off the assembly line, it blew away all other strictly solid-state circuits, both in terms of mimicking actual tube sound and sheer versatility. The POD included models of not only real vintage tube amps but also speaker cabinets and effects, allowing you to mix and match them at will. Since then other manufacturers have joined the modeling fray, and some of these products sound so authentic it's scary. It should come as no surprise that modeling circuits are extremely Guerrilla-friendly: They allow you to build big-studio sounds even in a small, low-budget studio—particularly if you employ some special techniques, which I'll discuss in Chapter 7.

Getting good distortion is tricky; I've always relied on trial and error to determine what combination of effect-box, modeling-unit, and amp settings result in a tone that's useful for the situation. In other words, I tweak, listen, tweak, listen, and so on, until I'm satisfied with a sound. I've noticed that perhaps more than any other sound, distorted guitar requires you to actually record and play back a segment of a track to hear what the tone *really* sounds like. Listening live through headphones or speakers often just doesn't cut it—probably because there's usually a live amp blasting somewhere nearby, interfering with the monitoring process. This makes the trial-and-error process more tedious, but that's the price you pay in the pursuit of great Guerrilla guitar tones.

Bass distortion. This isn't as ubiquitous as guitar distortion in rock & roll, but it's still quite popular. In fact, a bass version of the Line 6 POD came out shortly after the guitar version, offering models of classic overdriven bass rigs like the Ampeg SVT. The trick with bass distortion is to make sure you don't lose that critical low end. Run bass through most guitar-distortion circuits and you'll hear a noticeable thinning out of the tone—almost never a good thing when recording a bass track. One solution is to split the bass signal into two; you can then add distortion to only one side, and when you recombine them, the clean side holds up the low end. Another slightly more complicated approach involves splitting the signal coming out of the bass, running one side to a cranked-up and miked bass amp, and running the other side to a DI box. Pro studios commonly use this approach, although they usually record the clean and dirty sides as two separate tracks, so the blend between them can be altered later at mixdown. If this isn't feasible in your Guerrilla studio, obviously you'll need to commit to a blend on one track. Recording the bass late in the tracking process and using the "mix as you go" approach (see Chapter 1), or employing the technique of re-amping (see Chapter 9), may make it easier for you to get this blend right.

Distorting other instruments. Especially in the last ten years or so, we've heard more and more instruments being subjected to distortion. A Hammond B-3 organ run through a Marshall stack (or a modeled equivalent) can result in a massive, monolithic sound. You can give a drum loop (see Chapter 7) more aggression, and also make it sound less generic, with some distortion. Vocals can sound very cool when given a crunchy edge, although bear in mind the lyrics will likely be made completely unintelligible, which may or may not be a good thing. As long as it works artistically, distortion can be applied to pretty much any instrument or track—give it a try and see what happens.

In most cases, though, you don't want to put two sounds through the same distortion at the same time. Doing so will mash and mush them together, and things can get ugly really fast. Of course, maybe that's what you want. But if you want to maintain separation and keep the sounds distinct—messed up though they may be—give each instrument or track its own particular distortion, and either apply distortion to one instrument/track at a time, or use different distortion units to grunge up two or more sounds at once.

Pitch-Change Effects

One of the greatest by-products of digital signal-processing technology is the ability to change a sound's pitch without altering its speed or tempo. On analog equipment (as well as on digital), you can easily slow down or speed up playback, and the pitch will change in exact proportion. If you record something on tape at 15 inches per second (IPS) and play it back at 30 IPS, it will naturally be twice as fast, and the pitch will be exactly an octave higher. But when digital technology came along, people began to realize the usefulness of being able to change pitch without changing playback

> **GUERRILLA TACTIC**
> ### *How To Shred Like Yngwie*
>
> I've never been a fast guitar player—but there have been a few occasions when I needed to *sound* fast. Here's how I once doubled my apparent playing speed using only analog technology and no drugs: I had 16 bars to fill with a guitar solo and already knew what I wanted to play (I just couldn't play it anywhere near up to speed). I recorded a rough mix to a ¼" tape machine running at 30 inches per second. I played back the mix with the machine set to 15 IPS, and recorded the half-speed version onto a cassette. I then set up my board so I could monitor the cassette mix in headphones while I recorded only my half-speed guitar solo (which I played down an octave) back onto the reel-to-reel, still running at 15 IPS. Finally, I played back my solo at 30 IPS and recorded it onto the multitrack, using trial and error until I got it synchronized to the rest of the song. Instant Yngwie!
>
> Obviously, this kind of maneuver is a lot easier on a digital system that allows for things like digital time-scaling, or even with a basic sampler, which would simplify the speeding-up and slowing-down as well as synchronizing processes.
>
> Tip: When playing a solo that you know will be sped up, you'll get a more authentic sound if you think "slow": Slow down your vibrato, slides, etc., to about half-speed, trying to make your solo sound like one that's been slowed down by half. That way, when it's sped up, it will have less of a "sped-up" sound.

speed—or being able to alter pitch in real time, while the performance is happening. Several useful effects are based on changing a signal's pitch in this way.

Octave division. *Octave divider* or *octaver* effects, which often come in pedal form, generate a note or notes that are one and/or two octaves below the input signal's pitch, and they output a blend of source, one-octave, and two-octave tones. A bit of a backtrack, though: The first octave dividers were not digital but analog. They produced rather crude, synthesized square waves for the octave tones; the waveforms weren't based on any of the source wave's characteristics other than its fundamental frequency. (This approach has made a comeback in the form of "synth" effect pedals.) Today's digital octave boxes are a lot better, and there are even pedals and rackmount units that can generate diatonic harmonies of single-note (non-chord) lines based on a specific key center. Some octaver boxes sound better than others, and some *track* better than others, meaning they follow the source signal's fundamental pitch more faithfully. (Octavers with poor tracking tend to glitch and produce unstable gurgling sounds, particularly in certain pitch registers.)

Octave dividers are great for beefing up sounds that might otherwise be too thin. For instance, putting a bit of octave underneath a guitar solo—even an amount so small you can't hear distinct octave notes—can do wonders to fatten up the tone. Piling on a more noticeable amount of octave can give a guitar a distinctive quality that sets it apart from most lead tones. Octave is great on bass, too—but you'll want to play the bass line an octave higher than normal; otherwise the unit might track poorly, and the octave notes may be too low to be useful (or even audible). Octave effects sound especially good on fretless bass. If you don't want to commit to how much of the octave you're blending in, either record the line "dry" first and print the octave to another track afterward, or apply the octave during mixdown. Either way, this approach will give you more options, and it also allows you to pan the source and octave sounds away from each other if you want. (As long as you don't blend the dry and octave sounds onto one track, you won't need to decide on a final balance between the two until mixdown time, which is a good thing.)

Digital pitch shift. An extension of the octaver idea is a unit that allows you to shift an incoming signal's pitch anywhere within a ±1- or 2-octave range, often with a precision down to one cent (a cent is 1/100th of a semitone). These devices work with any sound: single-note lines, chords, and even drums and cymbals. Also, many units allow you to generate two independent pitch shifts at once, with separate pan positions and perhaps also a delay parameter for each shift. Depending on the unit you're using, the sound isn't always great (particularly when performing large shifts), but tracking isn't an issue. This effect was popularized in the early '80s by Laurie Anderson, who developed a trademark sound with her masculinized but somehow alien down-shifted spoken-word vocals. It's also often heard on news programs and documentary films where it's necessary to disguise an interviewee's voice.

The ability to digitally pitch-shift a source with precision is an extremely useful effect. Chorusing effects (see page 112) sound a lot more authentic if, instead of using a simple delay, you shift the source both up and down by about five cents. Where a simple modulated delay results in a pitch that's wavering slightly (and often crossing with the source's pitch), a pitch-shift chorus produces two sounds that remain exactly parallel with the source pitch, resulting in a more uniform, solid texture. I never use a simple delay chorus on background vocals, but I use pitch-shift chorusing quite often, because it just sounds better.

You can also get cool special effects by performing a small pitch shift with a little delay and adding feedback (i.e., adding some of the pitch-shifted and delayed signal back into the input). For instance, applying a 20-cent downward pitch shift and a 20ms delay to a snare drum, with some feedback, will give the snare a hard reverb (see page 107) that pitch-bends downward, kind of like an early electronic drum-machine sound. Similar downward or upward shifts applied to a vocal can produce bizarre futuristic or "alien" effects. Try it with a longer delay and a shift of a whole-step—notes will climb up or down the whole-tone scale as they fade out, a very distinctive sound. Doing the same with a minor-3rd shift will send notes cascading up or down the diminished scale, and using a major-3rd shift will do the same over the augmented scale.

GUERRILLA TACTIC *Party Of Five*

I always reach for digital pitch-shifting when I want to make crowd noises or perform any kind of non-pitch-specific layering. For instance, if I want a song to depict the sound of a party with people shouting a word or phrase, I run my mic signal through the pitch shifter set to two semitones up and two semitones down, and I blend the "dry" signal and the two "wet" signals at the same level. When I shout the word or phrase, it kind of sounds like three different people shouting. I then do this on several more tracks, each time shouting at a different pitch, and if necessary I bounce them together. If I record five tracks this way, the result sounds quite convincingly like 15 different people in a room shouting—and in my opinion, that qualifies as a party!

Auto-tune. Auto-tuning, often performed with a digital-recording plug-in these days, is popular in some genres. Basically, it tracks the pitch of a signal and applies a constantly changing pitch shift in order to round off the pitch to the nearest semitone. It's kind of like a pitch version of quantization on drum machines and sequencers. Depending on the parameters you set, this effect can be anywhere from subtle to "computerized" and artificial—think of Cher's mega-hit "Believe" as well as numerous subsequent imitators. Sometimes, though, it's useful to apply a small pitch shift to correct pitch across an entire performance. For instance, I'm often about ten cents sharp when I sing while wearing headphones; to correct this, sometimes I have run entire vocal tracks through my Yamaha SPX90, re-recording the corrected performance on another track, to bring down the pitch by that amount. The results sound fine—I can't hear a difference, except that the performance is more in tune overall. More recently I've used a pitch-shifting edit option in my digital recording program, which works even better (and is a lot faster and more convenient). If you do pitch-correct something, why tell anyone? What your listeners don't know won't hurt them. Keep it your little secret!

Enhancer Effects

These barely qualify as effects, any more than Accent flavor enhancer (monosodium glutamate) qualifies as a cooking spice. Enhancers usually come as rackmount devices, and they're also sometimes available as digital plug-ins or even built into instrument amplifiers. In terms of physics and electronics, there are numerous approaches, but they all aim to enhance certain areas of the frequency spectrum in an EQ-like way but without actually using equalization. In other words, frequencies are rendered more audible without actually being boosted in level. Most of these circuits work on the high end of the spectrum; Aphex's pioneering Aural Exciter and BBE's Sonic Maximizer are two examples of these circuits. Newer circuit designs such as the Aphex Big

Bottom and the Waves MaxxBass enhance the low end—amazingly without eating up power or headroom, as normally happens when boosting the bass.

I used to love enhancer circuits in my earlier recording days; everything just sounded shinier and more alive with lots of enhancement added, and vocals tended to sound more crisp and intelligible. But after a while they started to strike me as artificial sounding. I've also tried the bottom-end enhancers, and while they work to a certain degree, they don't knock me over. I figure there's only so much enhancing, exciting, and maxxing you can do before the music's natural qualities get completely stripped away and replaced with something that may be big, bold, and bright but just overly synthetic. I prefer to try getting crisp, shiny highs in the first place without heaping on the enhancement, kind of like the way a recovering drug addict seeks natural highs rather than artificial ones. I still occasionally use some enhancement on background vocals when I want them to be super-glossy and breathy, but that's about it. (I keep on hand a couple of insert sub-chains with enhancement, so I can do this in stereo whenever needed.)

Other Effects

Tremolo & vibrato. *Tremolo* refers to a regular up/down fluctuation in signal level, an effect built into some vintage guitar amps. It's often confused with *vibrato*, which is a regular fluctuation of pitch. Fast, subtle tremolo adds a shimmering quality to a track. A deeper tremolo (meaning one with greater level fluctuation) is more of a specialized ear-catching effect, most effectively applied when the fluctuations are in time with the song; think of the Smiths' "How Soon Is Now?" Vibrato, on the other hand, is rarely applied as an effect—usually it's just a feature of the performance itself—but if need be, you can get vibrato by using a short delay with a medium-fast modulation. Adding vibrato to an instrument that normally doesn't "do" vibrato, such as piano, can give it a curious quality. A more obscure variant on these effects, *filtrato*, is a rapid fluctuation in upper-frequency filtering; say "yayayayaya" and you'll get an idea of what filtrato sounds like. Filtrato is easy to get on a programmable synth, but adding it as an effect requires a specific type of auto-wah (see below).

Auto-pan. This is one of my favorite effects, particularly with keyboards. If you have a sound that seems "stuck" in its pan position, and you want to give it some life and movement as well as stereo-image breadth, try auto-pan. This effect automatically varies a sound's position in the stereo field, usually back and forth around its original pan position. (There's also a "triggering" auto-pan that causes individual sounds to move from one starting pan position to a destination position, but this type of auto-pan is more difficult to set up and get to work properly.) A width or depth parameter controls how far the auto-pan moves the sound from the original pan position. Some

Effect Plug-Ins

As I mentioned in Chapter 4, plug-ins for digital systems offer an alternative to hardware or outboard effects. You just load one into a channel on your onscreen "virtual mixing console," and away you go. This is great for speeding up the creative process, particularly with simple effects like delay, which can be thrown onto a track in a matter of seconds. Even better, some plug-ins for effects like delay or tremolo allow you to synchronize the effect with the song's tempo; for instance, you might tell a tremolo to cycle once per 16th-note in time with the music—something that wouldn't be easy to achieve with an outboard effect. Plug-ins are also a godsend when a track just needs *something,* but you're not sure what it is; just cycle through a bunch of plug-ins one after another and you're bound to hit on something that inspires your creativity. At that point, you can tweak the effect to get it just right for that track and that song. I've found, though, that the more complex or demanding an effect's sound, the more wary you should be about grabbing a plug-in for that sound simply because it's quick and convenient; sometimes the plug-in version just doesn't sound that good. So I'd say unless you've purchased a really good bundle of plug-ins and you know you're happy with the way they sound, reserve plug-ins for basic grunt-work effects like delay, auto-pan, and tremolo, and get your higher-tech effects (such as reverb) in a more conventional way.

units allow you to specify the wave shape that drives the auto-pan: A sine wave makes the sound move in a round, pendulum-like fashion; a triangle wave makes it shuttle back and forth at a constant rate without stopping; and a square wave makes the sound stutter between two pan positions. (To me, a sine wave usually sounds most natural.)

Leslie. Named after the classic Leslie rotating speaker, which is traditionally used with Hammond organs, Leslie effects (sometimes generically called "rotary" effects) combine elements of tremolo, vibrato, and auto-pan. A real Leslie speaker spins like a washing machine at a rate controlled by the player, throwing the sound around the room; rotary effects simulate this sound electronically. Naturally, they're great on organ sounds, but they can be used tastefully on just about any instrument, including vocals. The high guitar line on Soundgarden's "Black Hole Sun" is a great example of an unorthodox Leslie effect, with a very memorable sound.

Auto-wah. A *wah-wah pedal* is a guitar effect that's essentially a semi-parametric equalizer with a sharp boost and a pedal-controlled frequency sweep. An auto-wah automates the pedaling process, based either on a fixed, tremolo-like back-and-forth rate, or (more commonly) based on the signal's amplitude. The latter type of auto-wah is commonly called an *envelope follower* or *envelope filter,* because the filter "follows" the sound's *envelope,* or its shape (in terms of level) over time. You might put an auto-wah on a guitar track, for example, and set it to be fully open at the start of the note and close as the note decays. This would give each note a "yowwwww" sound, with the filter boosting progressively lower frequencies over each note's duration. Most auto-wahs allow you to specify the filter's direction (downward vs. upward). Auto-wah is a fairly extreme, wacky effect, so it's best reserved for super-funky or bizarre situations. The bass line on the Red Hot Chili Peppers' "Sir Psycho Sexy" is a classic auto-wah application—it really pours on that Bootsy Collins/P-Funk vibe.

Ring modulation. Talk about wacky effects—this is a really strange one. Invented by synthesizer pioneers, ring modulation works a kind of frequency-multiplying electronic magic on a signal, giving it non-harmonic characteristics and an extremely off-beat sound. Ring mod is great when you just need to mess up a sound beyond recognition. I used it recently on a guitar solo that just wasn't happening—it was too polite, too conventional, for the whacked-out feel I wanted the song to have. I tried a bunch of effects with no luck. Then I hit on ring mod, and it was perfect—suddenly the solo became evil and demonic, and my lame playing was disguised behind the twisted frequencies that the effect added. No other effect could have created this monster of a sound, and it was perfect for the song.

A Final Word On Effects

I can't stress enough the importance of using effects with good taste. Too many different effects happening at once in a mix is like someone wearing a striped jacket, plaid vest, polka-dot pants, and argyle socks; it's just a bad choice, or rather, a bunch of bad choices. A rule of thumb is: Don't use an effect simply because you have it. You won't impress anyone. Everyone has heard all the effects in the world on pro recordings. Listeners—even non-musicians—are more likely to respond negatively to choices that artistically fail or are made in poor taste, even if it's subliminal or subconscious. Strive to add an effect only where the song truly calls for it. Effects are useful to help cure emptiness in places you don't want to be empty, and provide prettiness in places that aren't pretty enough or ugliness in places that are too banal. You get the idea: Each effect should serve the song. Unless you discover a sound that nobody has heard before, don't try to use the song as a vehicle for an effect.

CHAPTER 7

How To Record Almost Everything

It's time to get specific with regard to what this book is all about: recording sounds. I've offered a lot of general observations, but now let's look closer at the Guerrilla Home Recording tracking process, sound by sound. By the end of this chapter, you should have all the information you need to record great-sounding tracks for all of the instruments in a conventional popular-music mix. Let's get to it!

Sampled Drums

As I explained in Chapter 1, the primary Guerrilla Home Recording approach to putting drums on a song is to use sampled drums. That can mean using a drum machine with samples of real drums, a sampling keyboard/rackmount device, a groove-building software program like Propellerhead Reason, or a sample-player card within a computer. As long as you do it well, you can get good results with any of the four methods. But bear in mind that "doing it well" means more than just plugging a drum machine into the board and pressing PLAY. It means spending some time programming the drums, including building lots of the expressive, non-metronomic human element into it. This is best done by a real drummer—but non-drummers can learn to program real-sounding sampled drums as well. I'll cover techniques for creating superior drum tracks in this chapter as well as in Chapter 8.

I realize it may not be the most popular stance to say you can't record live drums at home. You most certainly can. But unless you have a good drum room, a good mic collection, exceptional ears, and some serious experience recording live drums, your results will be inferior. Believe me—I've been there, as have many home-recording musicians. An approach using sampled drums just sounds better and is much easier to achieve, given limited resources and experience. And since the drum sound is arguably the most important sonic element of a mix—rarely does a song sound good if the drums don't—I believe this is the way for most home recordists to go.

The sounds. Assuming you aren't starting with poor drum samples (there are plenty of places to get good ones), you have an immediate advantage over a live-drum recordist: The drums have been professionally miked and sound good right away,

> LOOK ■ OUT!
>
> ### Ix-Nay On The Everb-Ray!
>
> Good drum samples often sound even better with reverb added—which is why you'll find reverb actually *on* many drum samples. Often, though, these are samples to avoid. The reverb may have been added just because a manufacturer's R&D department decided a drum machine or sample set would sound sexier (and therefore more attractive to consumers) with some slick, high-priced reverb slapped on. But nine times out of ten, the reverb pre-recorded onto a sample is not going to be appropriate—let alone perfect—for the song you use it on. Worse, pre-sampled reverb often gives drum tracks a prefab, right-out-of-the-box sound, one that typically lays on the reverb too heavily. Even though it's a bit more work, you're better off building a custom sound tailored to the tune you're using it on. While building your own custom reverb into a sample (see page 109) can be a useful technique sometimes, in most cases, start with dry drum samples and apply reverb to taste, or apply none at all. You can add whatever effects you want to a drum sample at any point in the recording process—but if it's plastered on there from the beginning, it's not coming off.

before you've lifted a finger. Still, some drum samples sound a lot better than others, and, of course, a snare or kick-drum sound that's perfect for one song may be totally wrong for another. But guess what? As long as you're using virtual tracks (see Chapter 1) or some kind of synchronization, using sampled drums allows you to completely change the drum sounds right up to mixdown time. Try doing that with a live-drum recording—you simply can't.

The following are some guidelines for choosing drum samples in order to create the sound of a live drum kit. Of course, if your music is more electronic (techno, drum-n-bass, etc.), these guidelines don't necessarily apply.

Kick drum. A good kick-drum sample has lots of low-end *thud*, plus the crisp attack of the beater hitting the head. One of the best kick samples ever recorded was built into the world's first digital drum machine, the LinnDrum. I once heard someone say that if you put a candle in front of a speaker, the LinnDrum kick sounds like it would blow the candle out. That's a good thing for a kick sound—but at the same time, the low-end aspects are balanced by that sharp *snap* at the beginning: The attack defines the kick drum's timing, and the *thud* imbues the sound with power. There are so many kick samples available it's overwhelming, but whatever your situation, keep both the *snap* and the *thud* in mind when you're choosing a kick sample. Even in a drum machine with ten kick sounds, some of them will be far superior to others.

Snare drum. Snare sounds are more diverse than kicks, and trickier to choose. You might not worry about using the same kick sound on every song on a CD, because the kick drum is kind of under most listeners' radar—but the snare is a more audible, characteristic element of a song. Remember the highly synthetic, gated-reverb

GUERRILLA TACTIC

Layering Drum Samples

You can build new drum sounds, and make drum sounds bigger, by layering samples of individual drums. For instance, when I was working with an Alesis HR-16 drum machine, I learned that I could increase the "crack" of another snare sound by layering every snare event with the HR-16's "brush" snare sound. Even though the sample was of a snare drum being hit with a brush, it had a sharp attack that could work well to give other sounds more impact. I also found that I could make a kick drum broader by duplicating a kick sample, panning the two versions left and right somewhat, and detuning one of them by a semitone. The kick overall ended up sounding more or less the same, but the subtle tuning difference between the two sides gave it a wider stereo image—particularly if I added a little gated reverb. Later, I learned that I could take a kick sample with lots of "snap" attack, truncate the sample down to just the first few milliseconds, and layer that on top of *any* kick to provide a more pronounced attack. If you use these techniques, though, make sure the attacks of the various samples are exactly simultaneous and not fighting each other, and also listen to the combined drum sound in mono to ensure that frequencies in the various samples aren't canceling each other and thinning out the blended sound.

snare on the Fine Young Cannibals' "She Drives Me Crazy"? It sounded kind of like a cork popping with a blast of steam. Now, can you imagine that snare on Norah Jones's "Don't Know Why"? Don't think so! But I bet you can't remember the kick sound on either song. So, choose wisely with snare samples; you wouldn't want to use a slamming thrash-rock snare on a ballad, or a gunshot-style dance snare on an acoustic country tune, for example. Like a good effect, your snare must be appropriate for the song. I usually start with a basic *forte* dry snare sound and then replace it with something more customized once the recording process is further along—in fact, I do that with all of the drum sounds, but the snare is the one most likely to be replaced.

A few of the characteristics that determine a snare sound: The drum's tuning (loose vs. tight), how hard it was hit, how much of a "crack" it has at the attack, and where it's hit (center, off-center, or rimshot). On a ballad you'd probably want to go with a looser snare that's hit somewhat softly and without a lot of "crack." On a hard-rocking number you might want to go with a tighter snare that's hit harder, with a lot of "crack." And on a fast punk-rock song, you'd probably want a snare that just slams. Think about songs that are similar to the one you're making, and check out the snare sounds that were used—this should give you ideas for what direction to head in.

Hi-hat. The hi-hat is a crucial element in a drum part, and one that's often neglected. Great sampled hi-hat sounds are bright and a little noisy: They have tons of high end, but with a clear attack. I have a few hi-hat samples in my collection that sound like variations on this theme, and that's about all I use. Even though there are millions of hi-hat sounds out there, you don't need many to cover just about any recording need. If you want to create the impression of real drums, stay away from hi-hats that sound the least bit electronic, or which sound dark; the hi-hat is there to provide pretty much only a high-end pulse, and any darkness in the sound will just detract from that. A closed hi-hat sound should have a bit of duration; an instantaneous "tick" tends to sound more artificial in the context of a full drum program. A good hi-hat sample sounds like the cymbals are bright, shiny, thin discs of polished brass—not an engine part, a whistle, or a three-ring binder being snapped shut.

Naturally, if you use closed and open hi-hat sounds together, they should sound like they're from the same hi-hat (even if they aren't). Their levels and pan positions should sound the same, and you should make it so the closed hi-hat immediately cuts off any open hi-hat that may be sounding. (Some drum machines do this automatically, which is helpful.) If you have two closed hi-hat sounds that are almost identical—preferably, two samples of the same hi-hat being struck—by all means use both, and have your pattern alternate between them. Even if you can't distinctly tell them apart, this can have an amazing effect on making the pattern sound more natural and less "drum-machine-like." Human ears, like eyes, are incredibly good at discerning patterns of repetition, so anything you can do to break up repetition will help your cause.

Toms & cymbals. Tom-toms should sound natural and acoustic (not electronic), and their attack should have a strong, punchy impact. High toms should have good "pop," and low toms and floor toms should have lots of what I call "dooge": plenty of low-mid *oomph*, but with a biting attack.

Ride and crash cymbals are the toughest challenge in sampled drums—but they also represent an opportunity to make your sampled drums sound *really* real. Cymbals are by far the longest drum samples, and since long samples eat up memory and disk space, this is where drum-machine manufacturers and sample collections usually cut corners. Crashes in particular are often cut miserably short. On real recordings, of course, crashes and rides decay into silence over many seconds, and this is one of the elements that subliminally tell the listener, "These are real drums." That's why whenever I need a good, long crash, I reach for a CD-ROM collection of drum sounds only, all very well recorded. The durations of the crashes and rides are all in the seven-second range, which is plenty. (A drum machine's crash might last for two seconds or less.) Along with a sample-player card that has enough memory to handle several of these cymbals, believe me, using long, high-quality samples makes a difference. There's nothing like a crash decaying over the course of half a verse to make people say, "You mean those *aren't* real drums? No way!"

Bear in mind that for any application, you need to consider the dynamic of each drum sample you're using in terms of how it will work with a song. You can't get the sound of a softly struck crash just by turning down a crash that was slammed—they're

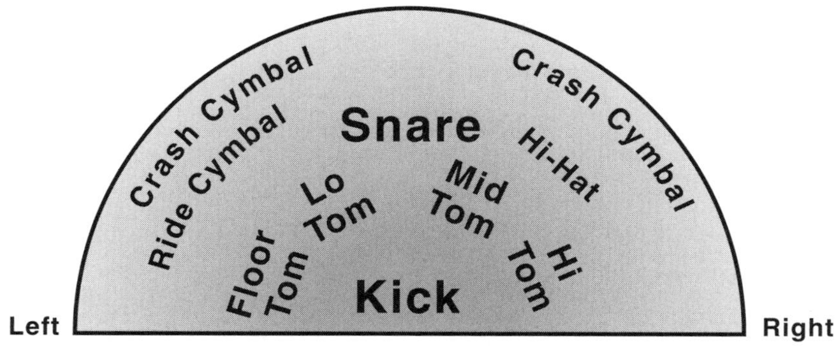

Fig. 1 Typically, drum sounds are panned to simulate the way a live drum kit sounds, with high toms on the right and low toms on the left, and the kick and snare more or less straight-up center.

entirely different sounds, and it's not going to fool anyone. Therefore, it's useful for your collection to include not only a variety of drum sounds, but also a variety of dynamics for each. It gets tedious to set up a song that combines drum events with different dynamics (a hard-hit crash as well as a soft-hit one, for example), but you can go a long way with your production simply by making each sound appropriate to the song. If you have the patience to tweak the sounds further by adding dynamic variations, great—but if possible, do it after you're well into or done with the tracking process. I recommend having two or three (or even just one) standard "drum kits"—preassembled collections of samples—at the ready so that when you have a musical idea, you can start working on it right away. If step one always involves looking for a kick-drum sound, recording becomes a tiresome chore, and you'll likely get bogged down in the tedium of it all. Certainly, your creativity will suffer.

The panning. Traditionally, a recorded drum kit is panned to represent what listeners might hear if the drums were positioned right in front of them. The kick is usually straight up (12:00 noon on a mixer's pan pot), and the snare may be straight up or a bit to the right (perhaps 1:00). The hi-hat is quite a bit to the right (maybe 3:00), and the toms are panned differently by pitch, from the highest tom far to the right (maybe 4:00) to the lowest tom on the left (about 8:00). Crash cymbals might be panned at 10:00 and 2:00, with a ride cymbal around 9:00. Fig. 1 shows a typical arrangement of drum sounds within the stereo image.

You'll notice that in this example, with the exception of the kick and a straight-up snare, no two drums share the same exact pan position. This takes advantage of the pan-position element of separation (see Chapter 5): Each individual drum will tend to be more audible if it has its own pan position in the mix. Also, if the drums occupy the entire stereo field from left to right, they won't sound like they're bunched into only a few clumps, which tends to make them sound more drum-machine-like.

Pink Floyd tended to pan the drums as above but backwards, from the drummer's listening position (perhaps because they produced their own records). You could put the snare hard-left and the kick hard-right if you wanted to—hey, in the right song, it might be bitchin'. But if you want your drums to sound like conventionally recorded live drums, this is the way to go.

Levels & dynamics. The kick often needs to be the loudest of the drum samples, because the ear is less sensitive to its low frequencies. So, set a kick level and base everything off that. There's no strict formula, because different musical styles call for different drum mixes—but I often find myself giving the snare around 70 percent of the kick's level, the hi-hat around 55, and the cymbals around 60. I tend to set toms pretty loud—90 percent or more. They don't occur as often as the kick, snare, and hi-hat, and they're not as long as cymbals, so you can afford to crank them up a little for maximum punch.

The elements of a drum track have different individual dynamic ranges—the difference in level between their softest and loudest hits. In terms of MIDI programming, this is expressed in *velocity*, which represents the relative speed of a finger coming down on a keyboard, or of a drumstick striking a MIDI drum pad, for example. If you're hitting hard, the MIDI velocity values are high (maximum: 127 units); if you're barely hitting it, velocity will be low (minimum: 1). Snare events on the *two* and *four* backbeats should be within only a few velocity units of each other; otherwise it will sound like the drummer or programmer is wildly inconsistent. Other snare events, like the lighter-hit ghost-notes in a New Orleans–style drum pattern, can go down to around the velocity halfway point (64). The same is true of the kick drum: The strong beats (like *one* and *three*) tend to be high-velocity, with other events going down to about halfway. Hi-hat events can vary in a more fluid fashion, from high-velocity to about two-thirds; hi-hat events on beats tend to be stronger than those on the subdivisions. Toms should be fairly high-velocity throughout (although some tom fills may dictate exceptions). Crashes, because they happen only occasionally and usually one at a time, are usually all around the same velocity; ride patterns vary dynamically similar to the way hi-hat patterns do.

Programming all of a sound's events at the same dynamic/velocity level tends to sound robotic and mind-numbing. This is especially true with a hi-hat part: Even if you program the pattern with a great rhythmic feel, if all of the events are at the same velocity the result will tend to sound mechanical. You'll get the best results by allowing both human timing variations *and* human dynamic variations to be part of your drum programs.

Live hi-hat & ride. If you're a drummer or you know one, by all means try putting a live hi-hat track on some of your songs. More than any other component of a drum part, the hi-hat is responsible for the human feel element. There are also a million things you can do on a hi-hat with regard to tightness, playing location, little rolls, etc., that breathe life into a part—most of which just can't be reproduced with

Recording Live Drums

If you want to shoot for a sound that's competitive with pro recordings, don't bother trying to record live drums in a Guerrilla-type home studio. That's not to say you can't give it a shot—you might get lucky and come up with a very workable sound, especially if the rest of the arrangement is unconventional.

If you do want to try recording live drums at home, keep the setup as simple as possible. Remember that the more mics you put up, the more complex things get. Adding a couple more mics does not mean the sound will be that much better—in fact, it may be worse. See if you can get it done using only four mics: one on the kick, one on the snare, and two "overheads"—mics suspended over the kit to catch the toms and cymbals. It helps if you have several mics to choose from. For the kick you're best off with a dynamic mic that can handle the high SPLs (sound pressure levels) that occur there. A classic choice is the AKG D 112, which has a large diaphragm—great for accurately capturing the deep kick-drum sound. Dampen the kick drum's batter head with a blanket from the inside, so it has good *thud* without much over-ringing of the head, and put the mic near the front of the kick drum. (To do this, you'll have to take off the kick drum's front head.) For the snare, a Shure SM57 (or a similar all-purpose dynamic mic) is a fine choice; point it at about a 45-degree angle aimed at the center of the top head. The overheads should be two condenser mics of the same model; place them at least three feet over the kit, angled slightly away from each other.

The key to miking drums is trial and error with mic placement—and *lots* of patience. Even with a simple setup like this, it can take a while to get a usable drum sound. Move each mic a quarter-inch at a time and listen to what happens to the sound. Of course, this is tough to do if you don't have a soundproof control room in which to monitor the mic signals, but do whatever you can. If at all possible, record each mic on its own track; if you need to bounce them to stereo later, do it at the last possible stage. After all, if you find halfway through tracking that the sound wash from the cymbals is blowing away everything else in the mix, there's only so much you can do with global EQ on the drums to get them under control. And it really helps to be able to EQ the kick and snare separately once all (or at least some) of the other instruments have been recorded.

A last word about recording drums: In order for drums to sound good in a full mix, they usually have to sound absolutely incredible by themselves. If you settle for drums that sound only pretty good by themselves, by the time you pile all of the other instruments on top, the drums will probably end up sounding lifeless and dull. Actually, this applies to sampled drums as well—but it's much harder to replace or upgrade live drums after you've added other instruments, so you must get them to sound great at the outset. This is one of the things that make recording live drums very difficult in the Guerrilla studio.

sampled drums. The trickiest aspect is getting the live hi-hat to mesh well with the sampled drums, in terms of playing feel, timing, and sound. Be extra critical about whether the hi-hat and the other drums are sounding detached from each other, and do whatever you can to get them to fuse into a more unified whole that sounds like a real drummer playing a full kit.

Here's how to record a live hi-hat: Set up a click track and program in some kick and snare (you can polish the programming later). Put a condenser mic on a nice, bright hi-hat, pointing straight down at the edge. You might want to roll off all of the lows to keep the track as clean as possible. Then, start recording and do your thing! But beware: Resist the urge to overplay. Since you're playing only the hi-hat, you may be tempted to play every roll, fill, and rudiment in your repertoire. (What am I saying...drummers *never* overplay, right?)

Programming is everything. If you own a drum machine or sequencer, you're probably familiar with the term *quantizing*—it's the automated rounding-off of a performance's timing to a chosen time grid in order to make the performance rhythmically tight. You know what, though? If you want to sound like real drums, *quantizing is evil!* Sure, it's easy to throw together a kick, snare, and hi-hat, and then "select all" and quantize everything to the nearest 16th-note. Home recordists do this all the time, day in and day out—but it's the worst mistake you can make. Not only does it make the performance sound brutally robotic, it just sucks out any human timing nuances that may have been there originally. My advice is simply to play the part in, in real time (unless it's too fast for you to do so). Program the part in sections, and if you screw up, just go back and redo it. You may want to do the kick and snare together first (to a click track), or do the hi-hat first, followed by the kick and snare. Or, you may want to lay down a scratch vocal for reference first; it may inspire you to do more interesting and appropriate things with the drum program.

Programming drums is such a crucial element of Guerrilla Home Recording, I'm devoting all of Chapter 8 to it—that's where I'll go into more detail about humanizing your drum programs or sequences.

Drum Loops

An alternative to using sampled drums (aside from using no drums at all) is to use *drum loops*. First popularized by disco producers in the '70s and refined by hip-hop artists, this technique involves repeating a short segment of a prerecorded live-drum performance, resulting in a seamless, never-ending drum track over which other instruments are layered. Originally this was done with a piece of analog tape, spliced together end-to-end to create a loop. (The famous sound-effects loop that begins Pink Floyd's "Money" is a good example.) Since the mid '80s, samplers have been the primary tool for creating drum loops. So many hit songs have been made with drum loops, there's a whole industry devoted to producing drum-loop CDs and CD-ROMs. Some of these discs include loops taken from old vinyl records (presumably with copyrights cleared); others are made from original performances. Drum-loop collections can come in the form of audio CDs that must be sampled, edited, and looped by the end

Making Loops With A Groove Program

Groove-building software programs, such as Ableton Live and Propellerhead Reason, are excellent tools for creating and customizing drum loops. These programs have a function that allows you to select a loop and export it as an audio file, which you can then bring into a sampler or sample player or import directly into your recording program. When I do this, I like to create several variations on the drum groove and export them separately, and I save the master file so I can go back and tweak the loops if necessary. To transfer loops seamlessly from one program to another in this way, you need to remember the loops' tempos. (Tip: When you export a loop, include the tempo in the filename, such as: **bitchindrums.144.aif**.)

With one of these programs, you can also export other loops besides the drums, including synth bass, keyboard parts, etc.—anything you've created in the groove program. Many of these programs also allow you to record audio and MIDI information directly into them—so more and more people are using them as their primary recording tool.

user, or CD-ROMs made for particular brands of samplers, sample players, or software looping programs. The latter are far more convenient, as they typically come pre-edited and looped and ready to load.

Usually, drum loops that are made from live drum performances not only sound great, they feel great, too. The downsides are that they're obviously repetitive (which can be good or bad), and if you're making your own drum loop from an old record, to use the sample you either must secure permission or risk getting busted for copyright infringement.

Making your own loops. If you want to live dangerously and make your own loops from other artists' music, your safest bet would be to use them on songs you don't intend to release, such as demos for more polished productions. Dig out your old turntable and the record you want to sample. Vinyl turntables produce an extremely weak signal and must be grounded to reduce hum, so you should wire it up to a stereo receiver that has "phono" inputs and a grounding screw for a turntable. Listen to the space between two songs to ensure that the sound you're getting is decent and hum-free. (If you need to buy a new stylus, check with a DJ-supply company—your local Circuit City will probably laugh you out of the store.) Whenever I need a line from a turntable, in true Guerrilla fashion, I just take it from the receiver's headphone jack rather than mess around with the dusty, crowded RCA jacks in back. Hey, it's quick and it works—in Guerrilla Home Recording, that's all that matters. I plug a ¼" "Y" adapter into the headphone jack, and I plug a regular RCA stereo cable into the adapter's male RCA jacks. What you do with this signal depends on your studio. When I was using a sampling keyboard, I had cables semi-permanently wired up to the sampler so I could grab a sample from the receiver anytime; this allowed me to sample off not only vinyl records but CDs, cassettes, videotapes—anything that could feed sound into the receiver. Since I do all of my sampling within my computer now, I run the line into two input channels of my mixer, using two more adapters and the line-input option. Either way, I control the level going to the sampler/mixer with the receiver's VOLUME knob. Remember, to minimize added noise in the sample, you want to get plenty of signal to the sampler/mixer—but not so much as to light OVERLOAD LEDs or max out the sampler's headroom. Check your sampler's owner's manual to learn how to monitor the levels of incoming signals.

Next, sample the segment you want. You don't need to be exact—you'll need to edit the sample later, anyway. When you're done, listen to the sample on headphones to make sure you've got both channels and that the sound is good. Still using headphones, find the *exact* starting point of your loop, which is normally the first downbeat of a bar. By moving the sample's starting point ahead in time, slice off piece after piece of the sample, retriggering it each time, until you hear the downbeat's attack soften—that's when you know you've gone too far. Back off the start point just enough until all of the downbeat's attack is there; when you trigger the sample, it should then start *immediately* at the downbeat.

Most samplers allow you to edit a sample's end point so that it loops within the sampler (i.e., when you hold down a key, the loop repeats indefinitely). You may or may not want to set up your loop this way. If you aren't using a sequencer and you're recording in a "free-run" fashion—for instance, you're recording to analog tape with no synchronization—then go ahead and make the loop within the sampler. Listen on headphones to ensure that the loop point—where it ends and then begins again—is smooth, with no clicks. (A click occurs if the position of the wave is different at the beginning and end of the sample.) You want the end of the wave shape to flow smoothly back into the beginning, like one continuous wave (see Fig. 2). Also make sure the timing is the way you want it. A popular, funky hip-hop device involves having a drum loop's rhythm "hiccup" a bit at the loop point, but if you don't want this sound, make sure the rhythm is solid and steady through the loop-point transition. If it isn't, or if there's a click, move the loop point until the problem is gone. Samplers usually allow you to move the start and end/loop points with precision.

If you're recording digitally with a sequencer/audio program, or if you're recording to tape with a sync track and somehow automating your MIDI gear via "virtual tracks" (see Chapter 1), I advise against letting the sampler do the looping. Why? Because as the loop repeats again and again, the timing of the loop in relation to your virtual tracks will drift over time. After 30 seconds or so, the loop will no longer start at each bar's downbeat. Depending on how fussy you are with your sequences, this can really mess things up. But if you want your loop to be locked to the sequencer's

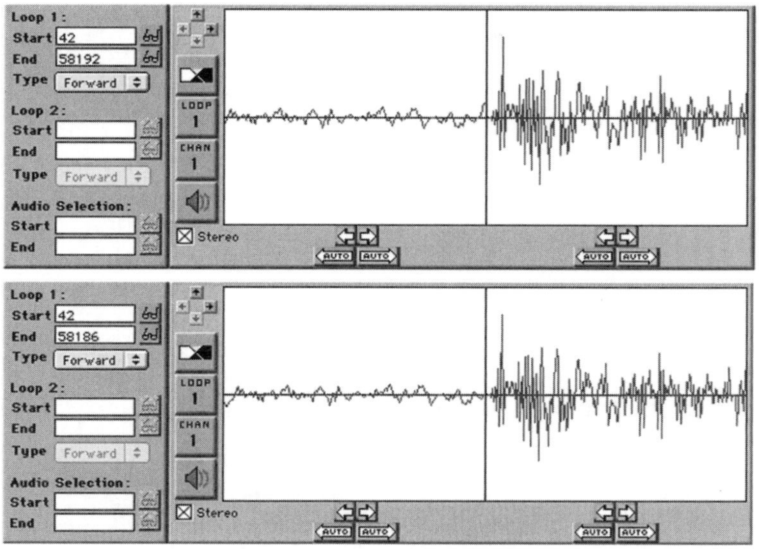

Fig. 2 In a drum loop, if the wave shape is not smooth across the loop point (top), there will be a click in the audio. Moving the loop's end point so that the wave shape is continuous (bottom) eliminates the click, for a seamless-sounding transition between loops.

or synchronizer's time grid, which certainly comes in handy when you're editing the sequence, go at it another way: Tell the sampler *not* to loop the sample (some samplers call this "one-shot" mode). Then, set up your sequence so that the sample is triggered *each time* it needs to repeat—exactly at each bar's downbeat, or the downbeat of every other bar if it's a two-bar loop. This way, no matter how long the song is, the loop will *always* start exactly at the beginning of each bar.

This technique invites a problem, though: The transitions at the loop points might not be as smooth as you want, because the sequence will be sending a MIDI note-off message to the sampler before it sends the next note-on message. Here's how to get around this problem: Turn off the sampler's key tracking, so that the sampler will play the sample at the same speed and pitch regardless of which MIDI note it receives. Then, on the sequencer program, stagger the sample-triggering events so that as the sample is ending on one note, it's beginning on another note (see Fig. 3). Once you've done this, you can tweak the sample's end point on the sampler (or the sampler's release rate—how quickly the sample cuts off when a MIDI note-off command is received) until the loop transitions are perfect. You may have the best success when the sample bleeds over just a bit into the next bar, as this creates a smooth kind of crossfade over the loop point.

Editing loops & adding fills. As I mentioned, drum loops are by their nature endlessly repetitive. But that doesn't mean you can't incorporate fills and variations into the drum pattern—you just have to do a little extra work.

One approach is to duplicate the loop sample and edit the copies to create individual drum samples, which you can then program into a rudimentary kind of fill.

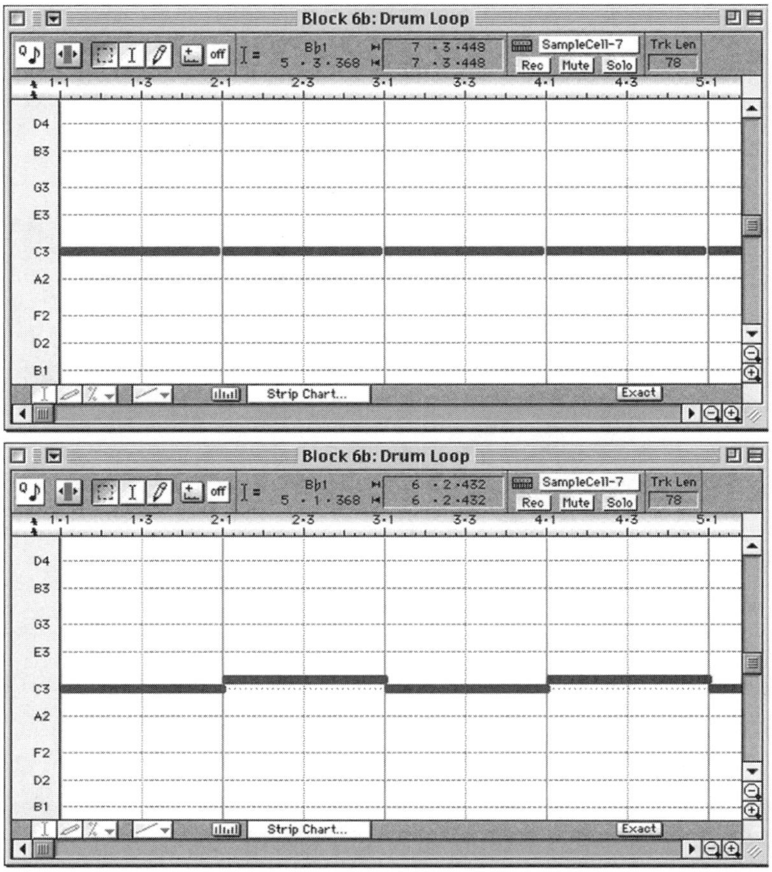

Fig. 3 Triggering a "one-shot" sample at the beginning of each bar with a sequence (top). If the loop transitions aren't sounding smooth, try staggering the events across two MIDI notes (bottom); this allows you to tweak the lengths of the loop samples. Turn off key tracking so the sample plays at the same speed on both notes.

For example, you can make individual kick and snare samples from your loop and, every eighth bar, introduce a syncopated fill made up of the shorter samples. One advantage here is that the fill's sounds will be the same as the loop's sounds, so the drum track won't suddenly change sonic textures at the fill. Alternatively, you can use samples—either your own or from collections—of actual drum fills. The fill will likely sound very different, but that can be a cool way to add variation and interest to a static drum track.

Layering & changing loops. Sometimes, using one stock drum loop for a whole song not only sounds boring, it's cookie-cutter. There's nothing worse than playing a song for someone and hearing him say, "I used that same drum loop on a song yesterday!" It's a lot more creative and interesting (if time-consuming) to *build* a drum loop from several parts and customize it to the song you're doing. It could be a matter of simply changing the playback speed by altering the sample's tuning; this immediately makes the loop less recognizable. Or, you could find two loops that sound different but share the same feel. To give them some separation, pan one sample slightly to the left and the other slightly to the right; if they're stereo samples, pan one sample's channels hard-left and about 2:00, and the other sample about 10:00 and hard-right. You can get some exciting, extremely funky drum loops this way.

If you have the patience, you can also layer and build drum fills in the same fashion. Have the fill start with one sample panned to 3:00, and then finish it with another sample panned to 9:00. Or, create variations of a fill with the sampler's filter parameters. The possibilities with drum loops are endless (no pun intended); get your hands in there and just start having fun with them!

You can also edit loops with software designed to do just this. Propellerhead ReCycle is a program that can isolate the individual events of a loop, allowing you not only to edit the loop but also change its tempo without altering its pitch. This is a brilliant development for anyone who uses loops in recordings.

Electric Bass

The drum track represents one-half of a mix's foundation, and the bass represents the other half. It's often said that if the drum track doesn't sound good, nothing sounds good—and this absolutely goes for the bass track as well.

Fortunately, it's pretty easy to get a good electric bass sound. You need: (1) a bass that produces a good-sounding signal, and (2) a decent direct box. That's about it—there are plenty of other toys you can put into the signal chain, but as long as you have a good-sounding bass and a decent DI, you can record a good-sounding bass track. This assumes, of course, that you can play the instrument well enough!

So what defines a good-sounding bass? That's highly subjective—but here are some things to listen for, either when the bass is amplified or taken direct: Is there plenty of low end or "booty"? You can't create low end with EQ; pumping up the lows from a thin-sounding bass will just sound artificial and "cardboardy," and it may be tough to control those frequencies' dynamics if you need to boost them so much. Second, listen to the notes' definition. Can you clearly hear all of the pitch centers down to the lowest note, or are they all blurry variations on a *woooo* sound? Next, do the mids and upper mids sound nasal and honky, or are they a natural part of the whole sound? Finally, do the highs sound sweet, or are they inappropriately bright, full of clacky string noise and electronic hiss?

You can also consider the instrument's manufacturer, its cost, and its features. If you get a chance, compare a few different instruments and just use your ears. I've heard $400 basses that sounded fantastic, and $1,500 basses that sounded terrible. You're usually pretty safe with long-established favorites like the Fender Precision, Fender Jazz, and Ernie Ball/Music Man StingRay. My own bass, which I use almost

LOOK ■ OUT!

Beware Of Bass Buzz

Many basses (and guitars)—even those with electronics that are thoroughly shielded by foil or graphite paint—electronically "buzz" depending on the instrument's physical orientation. This is especially true if there are fluorescent lights nearby, or if you're recording near a CRT computer monitor. My own bass buzzes in this way—*unless* I point the neck in one particular direction, or 180 degrees from that direction. So, before I record, I sit in my chair, put on the headphones, and play a note while I slowly rotate my position. At the position where there's minimum buzz, I make a mental note of where in the room the bass's headstock is pointing. Then, when I'm actually recording, I try to keep the instrument pointing in that direction for the whole performance. This minimizes the buzz that creeps into the recording, keeping the bass track cleaner overall.

exclusively, is an unusual 4-string made by a Japanese boutique builder you've never heard of. It has a strong, muscular sound with lots of grind and growl and a nice top end that sounds natural, not hyped.

Remember, just because a bass has onboard electronics, that doesn't mean it's better than a passive bass. In fact, some studio vets prefer basses that are not only passive but don't even have volume or tone knobs. This is because onboard controls can slightly "choke" the sound, even when they're turned all the way up; some people like the slightly more open sound of a bass with fewer onboard controls.

Tracking bass direct. The basic signal chain is simple: Just plug the bass into your direct box, and plug the direct box into an input channel on the board using a balanced XLR cable. I always run bass through a compressor/expander/EQ insert subchain (see Chapter 3) before sending it to the multi-track, although I usually bypass the EQ part. Sometimes I add a little low end on the board to beef up the sound, although this isn't always necessary. It just depends on how much low end I envision the bass tone having in the final mix.

Regarding compression, start with about a 3:1 ratio. The compressor's THRESHOLD setting is important: Watch the compressor-active LED (if your compressor has one) as you play notes with different dynamics. I like to see the light coming on with notes that are about halfway between the quietest notes and the loudest notes I plan to play. On headphones, listen closely for "squash"—if you can hear the compressor kicking in and audibly squeezing the note, and you can hear the compression ease up as the note decays, you might be using too much compression. (You can get away with heavier compression on a loud, rocking song with a full mix than on a quieter, more sparsely orchestrated song.) If need be, slowly back off the ratio setting, and/or raise the threshold setting, until the compressed bass sounds more natural.

If you're recording digitally on a computer, you can get an idea of how tight you're locking in with the drums by putting both tracks in one window, one on top of the other (see Fig. 4). Zoom in and see how they line up with each other in time. Then again, if the bass and drums sound fine together, that's all that matters—just let them be. Don't get caught up in "Pro Tools-itis," where you feel you need to make every performance digitally perfect. Over-tweaking can really sap the life out of your music.

Getting gritty. If you want to add a little more grunge or dirt to your bass track, you have a couple of options: You can mic a cranked-up amp, or you can get distortion direct—either from a modeling device (such as the Line 6 Bass POD) or some other distortion box. Keep in mind, though, that a distortion stage can thin out the bottom end. That's why when engineers record distorted bass, they often split the signal into a clean side and a dirty side, so that one side (clean) can hold up the bottom end. So if you want dirt on your bass track, find a way to split the signal—for example, by using an effect send to deliver some of the signal to a modeling device. You could then blend in the distorted signal using an effect return. Even better, record the clean and dirty sides on separate tracks if possible. That way, not only will you be able to pan them apart a little for a broader bass sound, you'll be able to alter their blend right up until mixdown—and you'll be able to EQ them separately, which can really come in handy for getting the bass sound to "sit" just right in the final mix.

If you're miking an amp, use a dynamic microphone. If you have a large-diaphragm type like an AKG D 112, all the better. Miking an amp is tricky, though; you may need to spend some time trying out different mic positions to find one that captures the distortion you're looking for. Also, be sure to pan both the direct and mic sides together and listen to the blend in mono—if frequencies are cancelling, the tone will thin out considerably, which of course is bad. You can usually fix this problem by finding a new mic position.

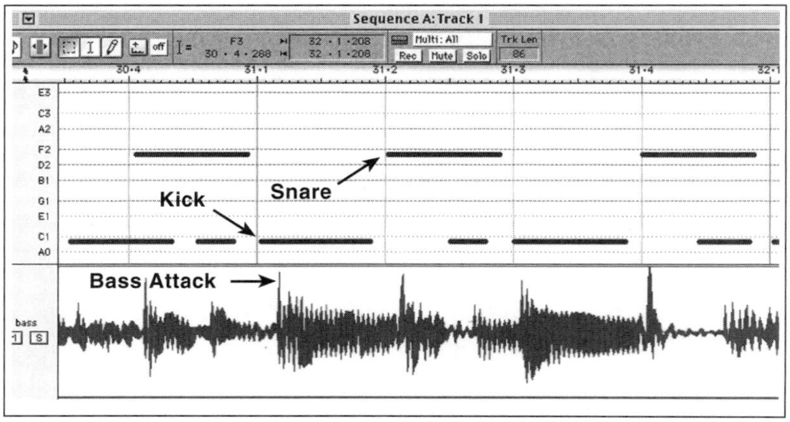

Fig. 4 In a sequencer/digital recording program, putting a bass track directly underneath a MIDI drum track gives you an idea of how tight your bass performance was.

Another alternative is simply to record a compressed clean signal and "re-amp" it later (i.e., send the recorded clean signal out of the multitrack to an amplifier, and mic and record that amplifier). This is often an excellent solution, as it allows you to get the distorted sound just right at a time when you're not also dealing with playing the instrument. Re-amping is discussed further in Chapter 9.

Technique tones: slap & pickstyle. Slap (or thumbstyle) bass isn't nearly as popular now as it was in the 1970s through the '90s, but it's still a great sound. Slap bass is more difficult to record direct than fingerstyle, because of the intense attack of the thumb hitting the strings and the resulting blast of harmonics from the string bouncing off the frets. At the front of every note, there's a sharp dynamic spike that can try the response of a compressor as well as the fidelity of all the signal chain's gain stages. Also, getting the proper balance of bottom and top can be tricky. Set up your signal-chain EQ to "scoop" the sound. Gently but broadly pull down the mid frequencies, from roughly 300Hz to 4kHz, so that the thump on the bottom comes through as well as the most brilliant, zingy highs. A graphic EQ works well when it's placed in the insert sub-chain after a compressor/limiter. Use a smooth "smiley face" curve for the most natural sound. Certain basses produce a much better slap tone than others; the Ernie Ball/Music Man StingRay is a perennial favorite, but there are many other good ones. New strings are a must for slap bass. If you're having trouble getting a sound, consider miking a bright-sounding amp or blending a direct line with a miked amp.

Playing bass with a pick can really accentuate the attack of each note, and it tends to emphasize the "grind" aspect of an instrument's sound, so it works well on harder-rocking tunes. You may need to compensate for the stronger upper-frequency content, though, or else the bottom will get buried. Without EQ, to avoid overwhelming your mix with grinding highs you'd have to keep the bass at a lower level, thereby compromising the track's low end. Another option besides EQ is to mute the strings slightly with the heel of your picking hand. The pick's attack still comes through and gives the bass lots of presence and pitch focus, but the grind during each note's body is greatly tamed, while the lows—which are less affected by your muting technique—power through. This underappreciated sound works well in pop, alternative, and country styles, to name only a few.

Clean Electric Guitar

Clean (undistorted) guitar can be recorded using almost the same signal chain you use for electric bass: guitar into direct box, which feeds a mixer input channel that has a compressor/EQ sub-chain inserted into it. You can ease up on the compression, though; instead of putting the threshold at the halfway dynamic point (as with bass), you can make it more like two-thirds or three-quarters.

Naturally, compared to bass, clean guitar sits much higher in the frequency spectrum. Its function is high-endy, not foundational. Therefore, getting the highs to come through on the track is important. New guitar strings can go a long way toward this goal, as can using a guitar with single-coil pickups rather than humbuckers, which tend to sound darker.

Sometimes a direct-box guitar tone is just too flat and sterile, however. If a direct tone isn't doing it for you, consider miking an amp. A well-chosen amp setting can add considerable bite to a clean tone, and the fact that the guitar signal is going through an acoustic stage between the speaker and the mic, exciting the air and interacting with the environment, can get rid of the flat, somewhat electronic quality of a direct clean signal. Of course, it takes more time and care to mic an amp, but it's often worth it. In fact, often it's the only way to get the clean tone you want.

If you're miking an amp, listen to the amp in the room and find a setting that gets something like the sound you want. Don't be afraid to crank it up a little, as (particularly with a tube amp) this tends to make a guitar amp sound livelier—but play chords and make sure the sound is clean enough for what you want. Since we're looking for quality high frequencies here, use a condenser mic. Position it one to three feet from the speaker; pointing a cardioid-pattern mic (see Chapter 2) directly at the speaker cone's center results in a slightly brighter tone. Bring the mic signal into the board, and compress it as you would a direct clean signal. It won't require a lot of compression, and you don't want to squeeze the tone too much—a little more dynamic "pop" can make a clean guitar track sparkle more than a highly compressed one.

Fattening it up. Perhaps more than any other instrument, clean guitar tends to sound thin in a mix. That's why effects like stereo chorus or flanging are frequently added to fatten it up. Another great approach is to double the performance exactly and pan it to the other side. You can get a really nice clean guitar sound with two identical performances panned to, say, 9:00 and 3:00. For an easier fix, run the guitar track through a DDL with a short delay and a bit of modulation (see page 101) and pan it to the other side from the dry track.

Clean but loud. Sometimes you want a guitar tone that sounds loud but isn't really distorted—for instance, hard-strummed chords on a tune that's big and rockin' but not necessarily heavy or punk-rock. For this sound, you need to mic an amp—direct tones don't cut it. Try to crank up the amp without letting it distort, and play *hard*. Your goal here is to create the sound of the speaker being stressed and breaking up a little. Look for a tone that's muscular; for this job, you need a sound with broader frequencies than the tinkly jangle of a straight clean guitar. Record a little—if the guitar sounds "loud" on a medium-volume playback, you've nailed it. If it sounds thin, wimpy, or weak, try again. You may want to turn up the amp's midrange knob; if the sound is too jangly, turn down the amp's treble (or HIGH) knob. This kind of sound

Isolating A Guitar Amp

If you're miking a guitar amp, it's best to be able to acoustically isolate it in some way from the rest of your studio. Pro studios have soundproof booths (or entire rooms) for this purpose; recording at home, you'll probably have to improvise. I put my guitar amp out in the hall, facing it toward a stairwell, and I shut the door. That's not exactly a soundproof solution, but it's better than having the amp in the same room—plus, the stairwell throws a bit of real acoustic space into the mix. Recording in the same room with an amp, you really have no idea what the tone is that you're sending to the multitrack until you play it back. While this is workable, it takes more time, and you're more likely to settle for just an okay sound because getting a really good one is too much of a hassle.

really needs to be created at the amp. Don't settle for a weaker sound in hopes of making it heavier in the mix; this won't work as well.

Distorted Rhythm Guitar

Perhaps no sound is more fun to record—or play back—than a great distorted electric guitar. It's been keeping rock & roll alive for decades, and it'll make your music rock, too. I covered distortion as an effect in Chapter 6; here are some tips for actually putting together a good "crunch" tone.

A good crunch sounds big and complex. One way to get that is to play into three $2,000 guitar amps at once, each double-miked in its own separate isolation booth, with the six mics recorded to six different tracks. But that's not feasible for us Guerrilla recordists—so we have to improvise. You can get a decent one-guitar sound with just one amp and one mic, but if you really want a sound that's big and powerful, try layering sounds and spreading them around the stereo field a bit.

The key to layering crunch guitar is to put down slightly different tones with each pass, and playing the parts as tightly with each other as possible. A modeling device like the Line 6 POD can really come in handy here. I usually start by recording two passes of direct guitar through one amp-model setting, but I use a different cabinet model for each (perhaps a 4x12 and a 1x12), and I pan these tracks apart—say, 10:00 and 2:00. I might also change the guitar's pickup-selector switch or the pickup-blend knob's setting between passes. When I'm finished with the direct passes, I record two miked-amp passes. Since my guitar amp doesn't have that great a crunch sound (one of these days I'll get myself a real Marshall stack), I again use the modeling device, but this time I bypass the cabinet models. As before, I try to get a slightly different sound with each of these passes, perhaps by changing the guitar's pickup settings/blend *and* changing the amp's settings slightly *and* moving the mic an inch or two. I pan these tracks apart as well, but not to the same exact positions as the direct tracks—perhaps 9:00 and 3:00. If I'm lucky, I'll get an enormous, powerful sound, and if I did a good job in the playing department, it'll sound like one massive performance.

Before I got into modeling devices, I used an approach similar to the one above, only I ran my guitar into a distortion pedal before the amp, and all four passes were miked-amp. (Without using amp-modeling technology, pretty much any direct distorted tone sounds flat and electronic.) I've gotten much better sounds since adding the modeling device to the chain.

Don't forget the chunk. In most applications, distorted guitar needs to be *heavy* and *chunky*. That means you should make sure there's plenty of low end—or at least low mids—getting to the multitrack. You might even need to tame the highs; excessive high end on a crunch tone can be buzzy and annoying, undermining the sound's power. Don't let things get muddy; just make sure you're capturing the sonic equivalent of a brick house. If the tone you're getting isn't heavy enough, try beefing things up on the modeling device or amp—turn up those bass and midrange knobs before you reach for EQ at the board. If you go overboard, you can always bring down the guitar's lows a little with EQ during mixdown.

Lead Guitar

It's not very practical to record lead guitar using the same Guerrilla techniques as with crunch rhythm guitar—there are too many articulation and phrasing subtleties to try layering numerous performances, and if the part is improvised, layering is out of the question. So, you're probably stuck with having to get the sound down in just one miked-amp performance. Since lead guitar is more prone to sounding thin than distorted rhythm guitar (a good crunch sound is a lot ballsier), the key to fattening it up is to mess with the signal quite a bit—both before the guitar amp and after. In addition to using a modeling device (if available), put effects such as distortion, a tone booster, or a phaser in line before the modeling device to give the tone more complexity and sustain, and feed the resulting signal into a guitar amp with the power stage cranked up. Close-mic the amp, compress/expand the signal to clean it up and smooth it out, and perhaps add a widening effect at the board such as light DDL chorus, pitch-shift chorus, or mild flange. Spread out the returning effect signal somewhat in the stereo field, so that it "surrounds" the dry tone. With some careful EQ, not to mention patience tweaking the controls on all of the stages, you'll get a very usable lead guitar tone. If applicable, on mixdown add some reverb that's similar to the lead-vocal reverb; this will put the lead vocal and lead guitar in the same space in the final mix.

Acoustic Guitar

Compared to distorted or even clean electric guitar, acoustic guitar is pretty easy: Just put up a condenser microphone, one to two feet away from the instrument. If you want a bigger, more mix-filling sound, position the mic more toward the guitar's soundhole—this is where the body of the sound comes from. If the guitar is there just to provide texture and rhythm to a denser arrangement, position the mic more toward the end of the neck; this will tighten its frequency profile and make the guitar less likely to muddy up the mix.

Strummed acoustic-guitar parts (particularly hard-strummed parts) can benefit from compression, which makes the guitar more punchy and present in the mix. Fingerpicked parts, particularly a delicate one in a sparse arrangement, call for gentler compression. As for EQ, you many want to gently boost the upper mids and highs to give the sound a bit more sparkle.

Many acoustic guitars come with a built-in pickup, typically of the piezoelectric variety. These are great for live performances, but many people aren't crazy about these in recording; piezos are notorious for sounding "scratchy" and somewhat artificial. But a piezo signal can often be blended with a mic signal to give the sound a bit more dimension. If you're able to record them on separate tracks, you can pan the two signals apart a little to broaden the sound. Magnetic acoustic-guitar pickups—the kind that you fasten inside the soundhole—tend to give a more muscular electric-guitar-like sound, which might be just the thing you need for a song. Again, try blending in a magnetic signal with a mic signal and see what you get. But remember, anytime you blend two different kinds of signals from one performance (like a mic signal and a direct signal), pan them together and listen on headphones, comparing the blended sound with its individual components, to make sure critical frequencies aren't being cancelled and thinning out the sound. If you notice trouble, get the mic either closer or farther away from the guitar and try again—and once you find a good distance, keep it steady while you record. Otherwise the tone will change as you move closer to or farther from the mic.

Like any part, you can double-track acoustic guitar with two identical performances and pan them slightly left and right. The result is a broader sound that fills more space, and the subtle differences between the two performances add excitement and movement in the stereo field. But if the mix is dense and a lot of instruments are competing for space, double-tracking may not be necessary; it may only clutter things up. Double-track only when you think doing so will help the recording, not just because you have an extra track open.

Sampled Non-Drum Sounds

Having a sampling keyboard (or at least a sample player) in your studio arsenal opens up all sorts of possibilities in terms of the sounds you can get on your recordings. No only can you get good facsimiles of keyboard sounds—piano, organ, vintage keys like the Wurlitzer and Fender Rhodes, and vintage synths—you can also add fairly decent sounds for strings, brass, woodwinds, and much more. How convincing these sounds will be in the end depends on three things: the quality of the samples themselves, the way you play or program them when recording, and how prominent the sound is in your mix. The quality of a sampled instrument—and by that I mean its likelihood of sounding like the real thing, regardless of how you play or record it—depends on the total amount of data that makes up each sample, such as the number of individual samples that make up the instrument, the sampling rate, and the bit resolution.

You could probably get away with a simple sampled brass-section riff in a dense mix, but if you try to put a sampled-trumpet solo in a sparse arrangement, you probably won't fool anyone (especially if you unwisely augment the performance with keyboard-specific things like pitch bends). Guitar, both electric and acoustic, usually doesn't come across well sampled, either. Because of the way it's played, the only thing that sounds like a guitar is a real guitar. An exception is if you've tailor-made the samples for the song you're recording. For example, if you need a riff to repeat over and over and actually playing the part is impractical (or impossible), a good solution might be to play it once and sample it. In contrast, building the riff out of existing power-chord samples and playing it on the keyboard will probably just sound like a lame attempt by a keyboardist to "play guitar."

Using a sampler or sample-player card with virtual tracks means you rarely need to actually record sampled sounds until the mixdown phase. But even if you aren't using virtual tracks, having a sampler at the ready gives you powerful options, simply because a modern sampler's sound quality is limited only by the samples themselves. Get great sampled instruments and you'll have great sounds on your tracks—it's as simple as that.

Naturally, when you aren't using virtual tracks, you'll need to record your sampler parts onto the multitrack. By now you probably know all you need to do this well. Just make sure you're gain-staging properly (see Chapter 2) so that your tracks will be clean and quiet. For sampled parts you usually don't need to add any compression—sampled sounds usually come pre-compressed.

Synth Bass & Other Synth Sounds

Synthesizer sounds are a mainstay of many popular-music genres. It's important to be able to tweak a synth's factory sounds or create your own programs, because rarely is a stock factory sound perfect for what you need on a specific song. Besides, you don't want other savvy keyboardists to know that you took the easy route and used recognizable, stock factory sounds. Synth programming is beyond the scope of this book; for an overview, I recommend Jim Aikin's *Power Tools for Synthesizer Programming* (Backbeat Books). It will give you plenty of background as well as specific information on synth programming, regardless of the gear you're using.

Recording a synth is straightforward: Just connect the synth's output(s) to one or two mixer-channel inputs using a standard shielded cable with ¼" jacks. As with any electronic device that outputs sound, make sure the synth's master volume is turned up; otherwise you'll need to boost the signal at the board's input, which will compromise your signal-to-noise ratio (see Chapter 2). Compression shouldn't be necessary, but expansion is useful to clean up the silence between passages, particularly from noisier synths.

If you're able to use virtual tracks for the synths and therefore avoid recording the synth parts, do so. It's much easier to tweak a sound on the synth itself during mixdown than to try fixing an already-recorded track, or to tweak the synth program and re-record the track. Just don't forget to store your sounds before you power down your gear!

Vocoder

You don't hear vocoder all that often on songs these days, but it's a cool retro sound that can be useful. A vocoder is a device that dynamically filters a sound based on the frequency characteristics of a second input's signal. The typical setup involves running a synth through the vocoder, with a mic plugged into the vocoder's MODULATOR (secondary) input. When you play the synth, you hear nothing—but if you also speak into the microphone, the synth comes through with speech-like characteristics, creating an '80s robot-like sound. (Think "Mr. Roboto" by Styx.) More creative applications involve using different modulation sources—for example, you can create catchy, rhythmic synth patterns by modulating a synth's sound with a drum track rather than a mic signal.

A vocoder can be difficult to record because it tends to be "peaky"—you set up your gain-staging, only to find that on certain notes or vowels the signal level goes through the roof, causing wild distortion. The solution is heavy compression to tame those peaks. Use a high compression ratio, such as 10:1, and listen to make sure the rest of the vocoder part isn't getting squashed to death by the compressor. (If it is, raise the compressor's threshold or lower the ratio.) If you need to EQ the vocoder sound—and you probably will—put the EQ before the compressor. This will allow you to tame the vocoder's most resonant frequencies somewhat, which should reduce the amount of compression you need overall to get a smooth, even sound.

GUERRILLA TACTIC

What If Your Voice Just Sucks?

Sometimes we Guerrilla recordists just have to make do with subpar vocal talent, whether it's ourselves or a guest singer in our studio. Or, regardless of talent, maybe you're just morbidly insecure about hearing yourself vocally struggle through a track. In these cases, your best friend is layering: double-tracking, triple-tracking, or quadruple-tracking identical (or at least similar) performances. Not only does this cause individual inaccuracies to disappear into the blend, but a layered vocal sounds richer and more supported.

At the very least, make sure you're singing in key. (If you can't do that, nothing may be able to help you—consider rapping instead.) Then build up a second and third layer. Each time you add a performance, monitor the previous ones at about 50 percent of the current performance's level. Pan previously recorded tracks to the left and right somewhat, with the current performance panned center. This will help your to ear distinguish between what's been recorded and what's being recorded. When you're done, blend the tracks at roughly the same level; if one performance is significantly stronger than the others, bring that one up a bit. Pan the tracks together, or almost together. If you'll need more tracks for background vocals or other instruments, bounce the vocals together (see Chapter 1).

Other techniques that can help the vocally challenged are track compositing and open-air recording; both are covered in Chapter 9.

Lead Vocals

As with drum tracks, the quality of a recording's lead vocal sound is extremely important. Drums (and bass) provide a foundational role, meaning that inadequacies in these areas weaken a recording the way a poor foundation weakens a building. But lead vocals are a song's emotional focal point and most obvious feature to most listeners, like the paint and windows on the outside of a building. Weak drums and bass will make a song sound bad to many listeners even if they can't put their finger on why—but if the lead vocals are bad, everyone will know why the song is hurting.

You may think the first requirement of a great lead-vocal track is that it be performed by someone who can sing really well. But there are many examples in rock & roll of distinctive, memorable songs performed by vocalists who don't necessarily have the strongest voices; Bob Dylan and Lou Reed are two names that come to mind. Usually, a sense of conviction is what gets these singers by—even if they aren't Placido Domingo, they put their heart and soul into the performance and they mean every word and inflection, and that's what connects with the listener. Since a thorough discussion of vocal technique is beyond our scope, let's just get you to make the best recordings of the vocals you or your musical collaborators have to offer, whatever they may be.

Lead vocals are often recorded with a condenser mic, as this type offers more top-end detail and clarity than dynamic mics. The classic studio vocal mic that you see in music videos is the Neumann U87 tube condenser—but if you're reading this book, you probably don't have a grand or two to spend on a single microphone, and that's okay. For years I've done well with an AKG C 414 (a perennial favorite that costs around $900 new), and in recent years several companies have introduced vintage-style condensers that sound great and cost considerably less.

Condenser mics often come with a slide-on windscreen, and there are also third-party pop filters that connect to mic stands; these protect the mic from bursts of breath resulting from plosive consonants like P's and B's. Aside from using one of these, avoiding "P-pops" is largely just a matter of technique: As long as you avoid singing directly into the mic at close range, you should be able to keep P-pops to a minimum. Angle the mic about 45 degrees away from your line of breath, and sing slightly *past* or over the mic. The mic will still "hear" you perfectly well—but it will be out of the line of fire of pops, spits, and other unsavory wind-related noises. As a side benefit, singing slightly off-axis in this way will soften sibilance, the harsh high frequencies that accompany "s" sounds. I don't know why so many people haven't figured this out, but when you hear a vocal filled with P-pops and sibilance blasts, you know the singer was aiming straight for the mic. Even worse is when an amateur recordist tries to correct the track afterward by rolling off all the lows (to tame the P-pops) and highs (to reduce the sibilance); the result is a dull, muted vocal with no bottom-end support. There's no reason to do this. Angle the mic properly and you'll get a natural sound that doesn't have to be wrestled into submission at mixdown.

I touched on another aspect of studio vocal technique in Chapter 4: adding "manual compression" to a vocal. When you're singing, be mindful of how your distance from the mic relates to your performance's dynamics. If you're singing along and you know a loud passage is coming up, stand back from the mic a bit as you deliver the passage. If you know you'll need to move forward and back to do this during a vocal performance, stand with your feet staggered somewhat; this makes it easier to lean into the mic or pull back. You can also turn your head a little more away from the mic, but not so much that your tone disappears. Experiment and learn what works best for you on any particular performance.

The signal chain. If any instrument can benefit from compression, it's vocals. Vocals are so dynamic and important, rarely does a totally uncompressed vocal work well in a recording. And it really helps to clean up the track if there's an expander in line as well. That's why I recommend putting all vocals through an insert sub-chain with a compressor/expander and EQ (see Chapter 3).

To set the compressor's parameters, get into your intended position in front of the mic and vocalize (you don't need to sing yet) at different dynamic levels while you watch the "compressor active" LED. I like to see the LED come on about one-third of the way between the quietest passage I'm about to sing and the loudest. A suitable compression ratio should be somewhere between 2:1 and 4:1—the louder the song and the more dynamic the vocal, the higher you should set the ratio. Still, unless you're going for a particular effect, you don't want to hear the lead vocal get "squashed" when the compression kicks in; it should sound as natural as possible. Whispers should still sound like whispers and screams like screams, only their actual level on the recording should be much closer to each other than they would be in a live, uncompressed performance.

As when recording any instrument through an expander, make sure the expander isn't cutting off the ends of words or phrases at all. The slightest noise you make vocally should open up the expander, but it shouldn't stay open or flutter open and closed due to background noise. If it does, adjust the expander settings and/or try to reduce the background noise.

As for EQ, you may not need to add any during the tracking stage. It often helps to give lead vocals a little "bump," or slight boost, at around 2kHz—but if you're unsure, you might as well wait until mixdown. You may want to cut frequencies below about 40Hz, however, as this will reduce wind noise as well as any rumble that happens to be transmitted from the floor to the mic by way of the mic stand. (Using a rubber shockmount to hold the mic helps in this regard, too.) Alternatively, the LOW CUT switch on many mixing boards' input channels is perfect for doing this—just don't forget to defeat this switch before you use the same channel to record bass or kick drum.

Performance. The time to be watching meters and LEDs is *before* you're recording a performance—not during. (This applies to any kind of recorded performance, not just vocals.) Make sure everything is set up properly, and when it's time to record, concentrate on the performance only, not the gear. If you find out afterward that something went technically wrong, such as clipping, just tweak your settings and go again.

I've found that my vocal performances generally get stronger after a few takes, so I record and keep each take until I've filled up four tracks. If I then determine that my first track is worthless compared to my last, I erase track 1 and record a fifth take over it. I've also noticed that when I compare four lead-vocal takes, usually one stands out as being the best for almost its entire duration—it's as if I were particularly "in the zone" for that performance. Still, sometimes a vocal track can benefit from the technique of *comping* or compositing—building one performance out of bits and pieces of several takes. I discuss comping in Chapter 9.

Naked or supported vocal? If you aren't a particularly strong singer, you may not like the "naked" sound of a single vocal track leading a song. This is where layering a vocal can improve your sound. At the same time, though, you might not want to hear four layers of yourself singing the lead vocals at equal volume—your song may benefit from the focus a single lead-vocal track provides. If so, as long as you have enough available tracks, augment one lead-vocal track with two support tracks, mixed 3dB to 6dB below the main track. Choose the best take as your main track, and then attenuate the levels of the others (perhaps eliminating the worst of four takes altogether); then blend them in at the same pan position, or have them "surround" the main vocal slightly. Aim to achieve an "ear candy" effect where you can't quite hear the support tracks distinctly, but the lead vocals sound different—specifically, thinner and weaker—when the support tracks are taken out.

Background Vocals

Well-done background vocals, or BVs, can do a lot to make your recordings sound fantastic. Few sounds are as pleasing as good vocal harmonies, and if you're making music by yourself, you have the advantage of instant perfect vocal blending—after all, whose voice could blend better with yours than your own? Still, plenty can go wrong when recording BVs, causing them to detract from a song rather than do what they're supposed to do: support the lead vocal and add power, shimmer, or sophistication to the mix.

Charting a course. Unless you have an unusually talented ear and/or significant harmony training, arrange and chart out your BVs before you start recording them. The best way to do that is on a musical staff with notation—but even if you can't read music, you can improvise a system by drawing lines on a piece of paper to represent notes (see Fig. 5). Sitting down with a keyboard, and playing bass notes with the left hand and chords with the right, may be the best way to figure out which notes work with the melody and which don't. And don't forget that sometimes, the best BV parts are not those that harmonize directly with the lead vocal but rather provide harmony

GUERRILLA TACTIC *Making BVs Bigger*

If you're laying down BVs and don't have many tracks to work with—or if you want your BVs to be exceptionally full and massive—thicken up each BV performance before it goes to the multitrack. The best way to do this is by adding a pitch-shift effect that can create two or more simultaneous small shifts (in the five-cent range, both up and down). If you don't have this capability, a delay set up with chorusing parameters (see Chapter 6) can suffice. Take an effect send from the mic's input channel and send it to the pitch shifter or delay, bring back the delay line with an effect return or another one or two input channels, and blend them together at roughly the same level. Then send this blend to the multitrack. Do this with each BV track, and your final BV blend will be bigger and richer than it would if you recorded each track dry.

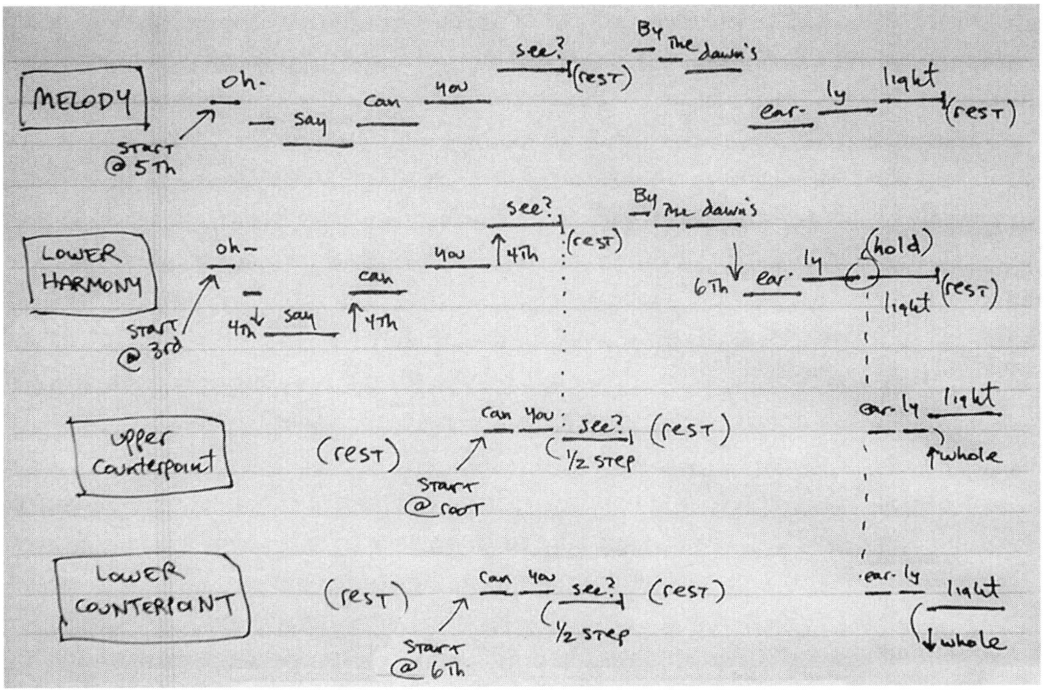

Fig. 5 Non-music-readers can use an improvised "notation" system to chart out background vocal parts, indicating approximately when and in what intervals the various parts move. This chart shows a four-part arrangement of part of "The Star-Spangled Banner" with the melody, one harmony, and two counterpoint lines.

counterpoint. The Beatles and Beach Boys were masters of this kind of arrangement. Dig out some of your favorite recordings and listen to the way the BVs augment the melody and create tension, release, and complexity in the arrangements.

How many parts? The term "three-part harmony" gets thrown around a lot, but don't feel you *have* to arrange elaborate three- or even four-part BVs for a song. In a lot of cases, just two parts—perhaps a double of the melody and one harmony a 3rd above—can do wonders. In any case, you'll get a thicker, more luxurious BV sound if you double-track or even triple-track each part. So, your BV arrangement may consist of two tracks of melody and two tracks of harmony. Three tracks of each, if available, will create a sound that's thicker still. Alternatively, coming up with a third part and only double-tracking each part will yield a "taller," more choral harmony sound.

The signal chain. It's convenient to record BVs right after finishing the lead vocals (or vice versa), because you can use the same signal chain: condenser mic, set up the same way, with a compressor/expander plus EQ insert sub-chain. BVs tend to sound better when you crank up the compression, however: The ratio can be somewhere between 3:1 and 6:1, and the threshold can come down a little compared to where it was for lead vocals. You also may want to EQ differently, too. While lead vocals need a certain amount of low mids to give the sound "body," BVs function higher and less broadly in the frequency spectrum. Also, as you add more and more layers to your BVs, the tracks will tend to muddy each other up. If you gently roll off a bit of the lows and low mids from each BV track, a blend of four or six voices will still sound crisp and clear enough to sit in the mix with little or no additional EQ at mixdown.

Performance. The manner in which you address the mic for a BV performance depends on the part itself. Is it a worded part with sibilant and plosive consonants? If so, then angle the mic and sing past it the same way you would with a lead-vocal part. But if all you're singing is "ahhhhh" or a worded part without any troublesome consonants, feel free to get close and sing right at (or at least next to) the microphone. Doing so will create a more intimate sound with more breath noise, which sounds great in BVs. You'll probably want to roll off the lows a little more heavily, though, because of something called the "proximity effect," which is the tendency of low frequencies to be accentuated when a sound source is close to the microphone. If you're building up six tracks, each sung two inches from the mic, you'll almost certainly need to roll off some lows to prevent your BVs from being weighed down by mud. For BV performances it's also nice to sing with a bright, airy tone with lots of extra breath—it helps to create a glossy sheen that really flatters the rest of the song.

Naturally, your BV performances should be as tight with each other as possible, both rhythmically and pitch-wise. I've found that regardless of where they'll end up in the final mix, when you're recording BVs it helps to turn down the BV tracks you've already recorded by several decibels and to pan them off to about 9:00 and/or 3:00. If you then pan your current performance straight-up center, you'll be able to monitor yourself effectively while still being able to hear the tracks you need to lock in with, on the sides. Your ears will be able to tell the difference between already-recorded performances and the new one, which is critical to performing the parts well.

Evaluating your work. If you're going for a slick BV sound, carefully scrutinize the tracks you've laid down before you move on to something else. Listen to the tracks together at roughly the same level. (Bringing down higher harmonies by a couple of decibels may help them blend better with lower harmonies.) If it sounds like one or more tracks aren't working for some reason, mute the tracks one at a time to find the offending track, and redo it. When you're satisfied with the performances, try to find panning positions for the BVs that you think will work well in the final mix. Sometimes it works better to pan BVs around the stereo field; sometimes they need to be bunched together. If you're spreading them out, you'll get a fuller, more lush sound if you balance doubled tracks on each side—for instance, putting the two lower harmonies at 10:00 and 2:00 and the higher harmonies at 11:00 and 1:00. On the other hand, panning the lower harmonies together on the left and the higher harmonies on the right (or vice versa) will result in a more "live" sound, because each harmony will appear to come from a single point in the stereo field, as opposed to being part of a broad mass of BVs. The choice is up to you.

Percussion & Other Miked Sounds

By now you should have a pretty good handle on how to mic up anything—from a guitar amp to a human voice—and set up a signal chain for it. For big, loud sounds use a dynamic mic, which is less likely to distort at high sound-pressure levels, and experiment to find a mic position that produces the sound you want. For woodwinds and miscellaneous acoustic sounds like percussion instruments, use a condenser mic. Rule of thumb: The more "rock & roll" a sound is, the more likely you should use a dynamic mic. For example, for a folksy, natural-sounding harmonica sound, use a condenser mic. But for a screaming blues-harp sound, pump that harmonica into a cranked-up amp and capture the amp's sound with a dynamic mic.

Adding a real shaker or maraca track can really liven up a sampled drum track or loop. Even better, record two acoustic percussion instruments and pan them left and right. But be careful, as things like shakers and tambourines can be extremely dynamic. Even if you think you've set up your signal chain with plenty of headroom, one hard shake could send your signal well above 0dB—which, of course, can mean nasty distortion.

Sound Effects

In some musical styles it's common to have voice-overs, pop-culture sound bites, and sound effects in songs. In the case of sounds that already exist on a DVD or CD (such as in a sound-effect collection), you can just play the CD and take a feed from your stereo receiver's headphone output, as described on page 133. To get sounds from a VCR, first disconnect any TV-signal cable that may be coming into it, either from a cable box or straight from the wall. (If you don't, the sound may be rendered unusable due to ground-loop noise—see Chapter 2.) Then take a feed from the VCR's RCA audio-out jacks and run them straight into one (for mono) or two (for stereo) input channels on your mixing board. Signals transmitted to TV and radio tend to be heavily compressed, but you may want to compress your sound some more to improve intelligibility, and/or add expansion to clean up its dynamic range's lower end. EQ often does wonders to make spoken-word tracks more intelligible. If a vocal track doesn't need a natural, full-range sound, EQ out the hissy highs and muddy, rumbly lows. They'll just clutter up your mix; besides, all of the information needed to get the words across is contained in the middle of the frequency spectrum, around 1kHz. The track will pop out even more if you create a niche in the mix for this frequency band through frequency slotting (see Chapter 5). If it's some other sound effect, like crowd noise or a train passing by, spend a little time thinking about where the sound's signature frequencies exist, and consider attenuating frequencies that don't fall in these areas. If you don't need them, removing them will make your mix that much cleaner.

Chapter 8

Humanizing Drum Patterns & Sequences

Much of the popular music from the 1980s—particularly music made between about 1982 and 1986—has a particular sound that's easy to recognize. From the Human League's "Don't You Want Me" to Prince's "Kiss," the era was known for mechanized dance beats and pulsating, metronomic synthesizers. It's no coincidence that 1982 was also the year that the world's first programmable digital drum machine, the LinnDrum, was released. By the time Peter Gabriel had a hit with "Shock the Monkey" (also in 1982), the world was hooked on the new sound of programmed drum machines spitting out samples of real drums in perfect time. And the following year, manufacturers began mass-producing the first MIDI-equipped musical instruments, which allowed drum machines, synthesizers, and digital sequencers to be hooked together and churn out rhythms in perfect lockstep.

Today, dance music and other electronic styles still incorporate the perfect rhythms that result from sequencing all of the musical parts and quantizing (time-correcting) them strictly to an eighth-note or 16th-note grid. However, in a lot of musical styles, that '80s sound can be dated and out of place. If you're making rootsy rock & roll, punk-rock, or even country music, you probably don't want a computer feel to dominate; you want the music to sound as if it had been played by human beings. Even hip-hop music can be livened up by a real drummer playing the drums and a real keyboardist playing the keys. Can we take advantage of this in the Guerrilla studio? You bet we can—that's what this chapter is about.

It is possible to reap the Guerrilla-friendly benefits of computers, samplers, and drum machines *and* make them sound real and human. Once you know how, it's actually quite simple. I believe this is the real secret to Guerrilla Home Recording, because without it, no matter how well you've recorded your sounds, your music will still sound like "one-man-band" drum-machine or computer music.

Lesson No. 1: Play It!

Naturally, different people have different skill levels on various instruments, and different levels of rhythmic sensitivity. If you're a guitarist, for instance, the most you

GUERRILLA TACTIC

MIDI Drums: The Interface Matters

Some people find it tough programming a drum machine in real time using the machine's small pads. Others have difficulty playing the parts from a keyboard controller. For programming drums, a MIDI drum controller is much more effective. A set of large velocity-sensitive pads that you hit with a stick is great for entering your drum parts in real time. Several years ago I bought a first-generation Roland Octapad on eBay for this purpose, for a very low price, and it was one of the best studio purchases I've ever made. The Octapad allows you to play kick and snare, or hi-hat and cymbals, or all of the toms at once. (With a little practice, you can play *all* of the drum parts in real time on such a controller.) There are a number of MIDI drum controllers on the market, spanning a variety of price ranges, and they're worth considering if you plan to do a lot of real-time drum programming.

might feel comfortable doing with a drum machine is choosing a stock factory pattern and hitting the PLAY button. But if you want to broaden your musical horizons and improve your music's feel (and ultimately its sound), I urge you to start trying a little harder and stretching yourself in musical ways that fall outside your primary instrument. If you're aiming only to create a karaoke-like backing track for your guitaristic genius, then that's what your music will sound like: a guitarist playing over a lackluster, stock backing track. Let's aspire to achieve something a bit better than that.

To begin, start playing your programmed (MIDI) parts into your sequencer or drum machine in real time—or at least in slow "real time." In other words, don't step-program them, and don't choose stock patterns—*play* your patterns instead! It doesn't matter that you aren't a drummer or a keyboardist. Just dive in—you can benefit from these techniques almost immediately, and they'll get easier with time as you continue using them. As a side benefit, your overall musicianship and rhythmic sensitivity will improve greatly, which can only help your playing on your primary instrument. With any luck, before long nobody will know that you didn't hire a live drummer to play on your songs.

Laying down drums. Let's say you're using a MIDI keyboard to enter a drum part into a sequencer program, and that the drum part will be "played" by a sampler loaded with drum sounds. First, set things up so that the keyboard is sending MIDI data to both the sequencer and the sampler. You can do this in various ways: with a MIDI splitter, by enabling the sequencer's MIDI Thru option (so that the sequencer passes all incoming MIDI data back out to the sampler), or by sending the MIDI into the sampler first and then out its MIDI THRU jack to the computer. In any case, you should be able to play a note on the keyboard, trigger the drum sound associated with that note, and record the event in the sequencer, all at once.

GUERRILLA TACTIC

The One-Key Undo

My deepest, darkest musical secret is that sometimes I labor for hours trying to get a programmed part just right. I've never counted, but I'm sure there are some short sections that I played, erased, and re-did 50 or more times. Stopping the sequencer, getting it to undo the recording, and then starting recording again is a three-step process that's both tedious and annoying (especially when things aren't going well). I was able to make this much more painless by putting a macro utility to work. This is a small computer program that runs in the background, allowing you to assign a single keystroke to perform a more complex string of keystrokes or actions. My "one-key undo" is the "0" key on my computer's numeric keypad. Whenever I'm recording within the sequencing program and I hit that "0" key, the program stops, performs an undo, and starts recording again, almost without missing a beat. This takes some of the tedium and frustration out of playing a tough section into the sequencer over and over.

Next, you'll need to be able to hear a click track so you'll know where you are in the pattern at all times. You can set it up so that the click track is a closed hi-hat—but this may be problematic when it's time to lay down the actual hi-hat part, so you may want to select another sound. Make sure it's a short one; a crash cymbal makes for a terrible click-track sound! A woodblock or cross-stick sound works much better. Set the tempo and give yourself one or two bars of countoff time before the part begins, or set up the sequencer to count off a similar time period before it begins recording.

Now you're ready to lay down a kick and snare. Get the sequencer to start recording, listen to the click and settle into its tempo, and start playing. If you aren't used to playing a rhythm instrument, try to get your body to move with the groove as you play—it really makes a difference.

The trickiest thing about playing a drum part is keeping track of where you are in the song. Sometimes it's easy to hear the as-yet-unrecorded parts in your head, and sometimes it isn't. If you're having trouble, one solution is to pause your efforts for a moment and lay down a scratch track to the click. A quick guitar and vocal track, recorded together in real time (they don't have to actually sound good), can make it much easier to keep track of your place in the song, and it will help you play things in the drums that are appropriate for the moment. Then again, if you haven't yet figured out the chords, song structure, etc., maybe it would be best simply to lay down a kick/snare backbeat, or something similar that captures the song's overall feel, for a few bars. You can then duplicate that segment of the sequence again and again until you have enough rough drums for the whole song. As long as you're using some kind of synchronization between the drum machine/sequencer and your multitrack

> **GUERRILLA TACTIC** ***Having Trouble Playing In Real Time?***
>
> After you've put down a pass of one or two drum sounds (such as kick and snare), listen back to what you've done, along with the click track. Depending on your skill level, you might be tight and solid with the click, or all over the place. If the latter is the case, here are some possible workarounds:
>
> 1. Slow down the sequencer's tempo to two-thirds or even half, and then record the part. When played back at full tempo, the drum parts you recorded at a slower tempo will be much tighter. It's harder, however, to keep the song's feel and form in mind when you're recording at a slow tempo in this way, and if you recorded a scratch guide track at full tempo, it will be useless now. One solution is to re-record a new guide track at the slower tempo. Or, if your sequencer allows you to time-scale an audio track—change its playback speed without altering its pitch—you can time-scale the existing guide track. (Be sure to keep the original guide recording so you'll be able to use it again once you return the song to full tempo.)
>
> 2. Record the part in short sections rather than all in one pass. You might have to put down only one or two bars at a time, but that's okay—it'll be our little secret. If it doesn't feel right, undo the recording and go again. This can be tedious, but in the end your efforts may pay off with a drum track that feels great.
>
> 3. If you're really struggling, combine methods (1) and (2) above.

recording medium, you can always lay down a more refined drum part after the other parts are down.

Let's assume you've laid down a kick and snare for the whole song. Next up is the hi-hat. Make sure the click will still play in record mode, and if you haven't switched the click sound over to something other than hi-hat, now would be a good time. When laying down a hi-hat part, it also helps for the click sound to be panned to the other side across from where the hi-hat is panned. That way, it will be easier for you to hear if your timing starts to drift off.

Unless the hi-hat part consists only of quarter-notes or slow eighth-notes, assign two black keys to the sound—for example, *C#* and *D#*. That way you'll be able to play the part with two fingers. I'm right-handed, so I like to play stronger beats on the higher key and weaker ones on the lower key. Hey—that's how a drummer does it; he'll tend to play downbeats with his dominant hand and offbeats with his weaker hand, which may explain why this method seems to give a programmed hi-hat a more natural feel.

For some songs, particularly if you're trying to throw together a quick song sketch, it can be pointless (and tedious) to lay down a hi-hat part for the whole song. Instead, lay down a hi-hat part for just four or eight bars. Once you're certain that it feels good and solid, duplicate the segment again and again for the entire song's length, or at least for parts of the entire song. In a computer sequencing program this is easy—it's a simple copy-and-paste job. On a drum machine or hardware sequencer, you'll have to improvise based on the system's capabilities.

Finally, with the kick, snare, and hi-hat done, finish the drum programming by adding tom fills, crashes, or whatever else is needed. To do this, it really helps to be able to play a little "real" drums, or at least to be familiar with what drummers do on drum kits. There are certain things that aren't physically possible for most drummers to do, such as hit the snare, hi-hat, and a tom at once, or two crashes and a hi-hat at once. It's not a serious problem if you leave such "impossibilities" in your drum programs, but if you edit them out (or don't play them in the first place), your drum programs will sound more authentic. For example, when a tom fill happens, drop out the hi-hat completely (perhaps replacing it with a pedal-hi-hat sound playing eighth-notes) and end the fill with a crash. You've heard these kinds of things on countless records, even if you don't know it—and it's subliminal details like these that will make your drum programs rise to a new level of authenticity.

If you've never played drums and don't really understand how drum parts work, I recommend spending some time listening closely to some great drum parts, and even transcribing them. The exercise called "re-production," described at the end of Chapter 1, is a great (and fun) way to do this.

The Importance Of Dynamics

In addition to timing subtleties, a big factor that separates programmed drums and live drums is dynamics. For example, only a machine could spit out a hi-hat part in which every event is at the exact same volume. No human can do this, because human muscles don't contract the exact same way each time. The ear is incredibly good at hearing subtle variations (or non-variations) in dynamics, so this is an area we can exploit to trick the listener's ear into hearing a live part, when in fact the part is programmed.

As an exercise, program a simple series of eighth-notes on the hi-hat. If you're able to play the part into the sequencer using a keyboard or MIDI drum pads, try to emphasize the strong beats and ease up on the weaker beats, the way a drummer would. Then check out the velocity values on the notes you played. You should be getting something like the values shown in Fig. 1. If the offbeat velocity values are close to the downbeats' values, you may be playing the part too stiffly. Programmed drum parts—hi-hat in particular—benefit from a lot of dynamic variation. For maximum human feel, even the strong beats should have some subtle variation among them (as in Fig. 1). If all of your strong beats are hitting the dynamic ceiling with the maximum velocity value of 127, it won't work as well; see if you can reduce the sensitivity of your MIDI drum pads or keyboard, or alter its velocity curve (check the owner's manual). This can make all the difference in translating a human performance on a

MIDI controller into a human-sounding part. On the other hand, if your velocity values are *too* inconsistent, that won't sound very good, either—in this case, see if you can increase your controller's velocity sensitivity.

When programming drums, people tend to underestimate the amount of dynamic variation that needs to go into creating more of a human feel. Consider the simple kick-and-snare part shown in Fig. 2. If that pickup 16th-note on the kick is anywhere near the velocity of the downbeat that follows, it's not going to sound like a real drummer, or at least a very good real drummer. The velocities shown in Fig. 2 will produce a much more realistic feel for this part. When in doubt, err on the side of overdoing the dynamics—but not to the extent that certain parts jump out or disappear from the mix altogether.

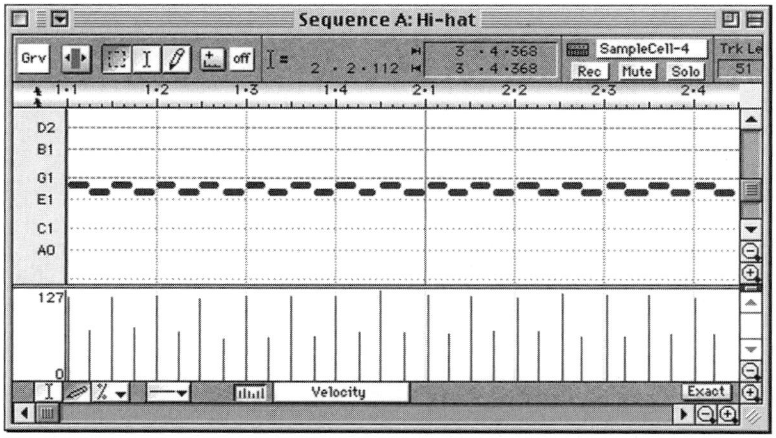

Fig. 1 The velocity strip (bottom) on this hi-hat part indicates how hard each event was played. The performance incorporates plenty of dynamic variation for a looser, more human feel.

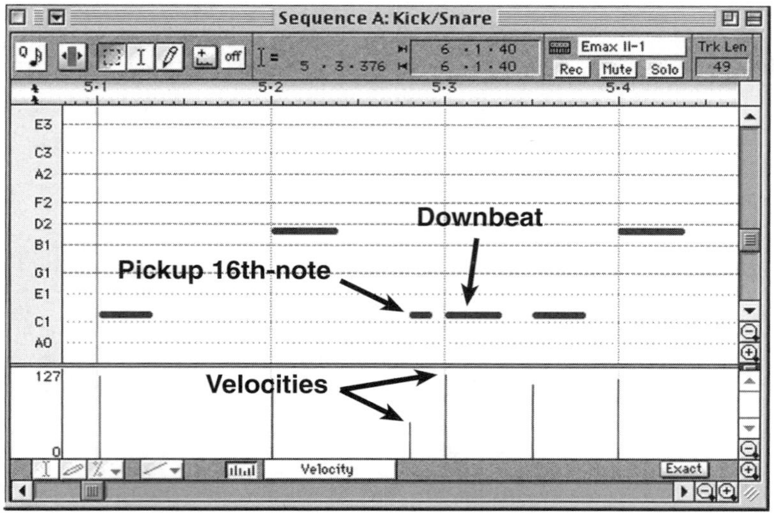

Fig. 2 In this drum part, the velocity of the kick drum's pickup 16th-note is much lower than the downbeat's velocity. If the pickup note's velocity were much higher, the part might sound less human—and if the velocity were as high as the downbeat's, it would sound like a badly programmed drum machine.

GUERRILLA TACTIC

Editing Dynamics Onscreen

If you're recording MIDI drum events into a sequencer program and the part comprises a consistent series of stronger and weaker beats (such as steady 16ths on the hi-hat), set it up so that you're playing the stronger beats with one drum pad or key, and the weaker beats with another drum pad or key. The sequencer should therefore record the stronger beats on one MIDI note and the weaker beats on another MIDI note, as in Fig. 1. That way, if you need to separately adjust the dynamics of either the stronger or the weaker beats, you'll be able to select one set but not the other. You can then scale that set's dynamics up or down by whatever amount you need, set a maximum velocity (effectively compressing the sound's dynamics), etc. You can also adjust a part's timing in this same way. For example, if you want the weaker beats to have a more laid-back feel, just select all of the weaker beats and move them later in time by a small amount.

The Beauty Of Partial Quantization

In the last chapter I stated unequivocally that quantization is evil. Actually, that's only half true—I was just trying to get a point across. More specifically, when you're trying to capture a human feel, *full* or *absolute* quantization is evil, because locking everything to a rigid time grid (which is what full quantization does) will suck the life right out of the part.

However, there's a kind of quantization called *partial quantization* that can be very useful, and it's a feature of many sequencing programs. When you partially quantize a performance, each MIDI event is moved earlier or later in time—but only part of the way, not all the way, to the nearest eighth-note (or 16th-note) value on the time grid. In other words, partial quantization makes a performance tighter, but it doesn't give it that rigid, metronomic feel where everything is exactly on the beat (see Fig. 3).

Partial quantization is usually expressed as a percentage. If you create a MIDI event in your sequencer that falls ten time units after the downbeat, performing a full quantize on the event would move it earlier by ten units, making the event occur exactly on the beat. But if you partially quantize by 50 percent (my sequencer refers to this parameter in the quantization window as "strength"), the event will be moved earlier by only five units. If your quantization strength were 30 percent, it would be moved earlier by only three units. So the MIDI event still isn't exactly lined up with the sequencer's time grid—but the performance is tighter, relative to the grid, than it was when you originally played it.

It should be clear how this can come in handy. In fact, for a non-drummer like myself with okay but not rock-solid time, partial quantization is a godsend. If I lay down a kick/snare performance and it sounds a little sloppy, I'll partially quantize it

Groove Quantization

Many sequencers incorporate a feature called *groove quantization*, which allows you to quantize a MIDI sequence based not upon the rigid time grid, but rather on a set of "groove templates." These are pre-existing patterns that emulate certain rhythmic feels; they may have names like "laid-back," "pushing," or "medium shuffle." The great thing about groove quantization is that it can affect not only each MIDI event's timing but also its velocity and even duration. Although groove quantization can be applied to any MIDI performance, it's especially useful when you're starting with a fully quantized sequence that has no variation in dynamics, which is what you usually get when you import a file from a music-notation program, for instance. Rather than manually playing the musical passage back into the sequencer to give it some feel and dynamics, sometimes all you need to do is select the notes and groove-quantize them. Try applying different templates to your sequence, groove-quantizing both partially and fully and with different values for note velocities and duration (where applicable), and listen to how they affect the feel. If it isn't right, choose Undo and try another template or set of parameters. Eventually you should hit on a combination that feels good—and it could very well be a vast improvement on the sequence you started with.

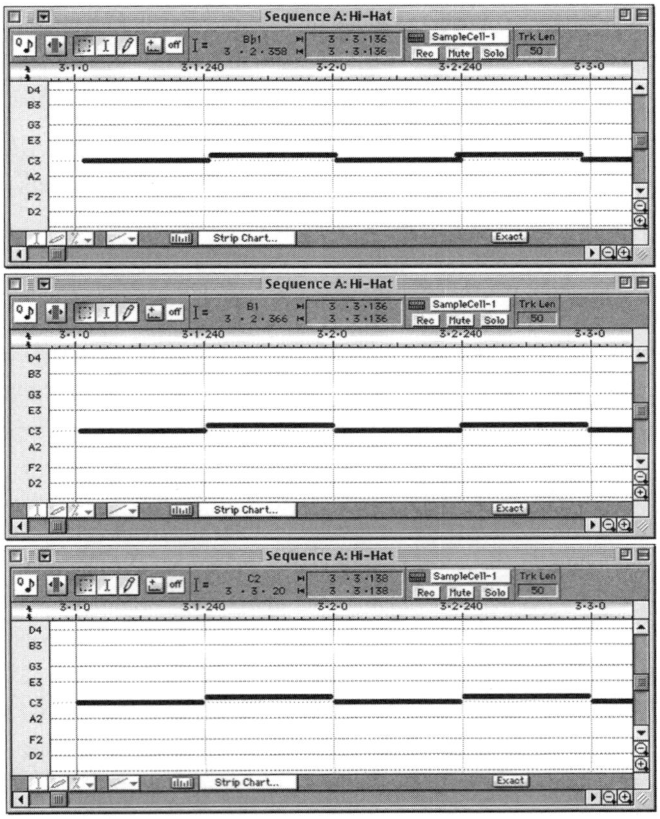

Fig. 3 An uneven hi-hat part played in real time (top). Partial quantization (center) tightens up the performance—but full quantization (bottom) goes too far, making the part rigid and machine-like.

LOOK ■ OUT!

Use Your Ears, Not Your Eyes

When you're scrutinizing a part you just laid down into a computer-based sequencer, it's extremely tempting to judge the part visually based on how all of the little MIDI events line up with the onscreen time grid. Even if a part sounds fine, if a kick-drum event is much farther away from the time grid than all of the others, sometimes every cell in your body wants to stop the playback, select the event, get it closer to that time-grid line. There's no need to do this! If it sounds fine, then it *is* fine! Only work on a part some more if it *sounds* wrong to your ears—preferably, before you've had a chance to see where it falls on the time grid. If you laid some of the world's greatest drum grooves onto an onscreen time grid, probably nothing would be visually "locked in." So give your eyes a break and just listen—*then* decide how to proceed.

by perhaps 40 percent. Or, since drum parts tend to feel tighter when the kick drum is quantized stronger than the snare, I might quantize the kick by 60 percent but the snare by only 30 percent. Once I'm happy with the kick and snare, I might lay down a hi-hat part and quantize that by 50 percent. If it still feels weak, I may quantize it again by 50 percent, which will move each event half again closer to the time grid.

With practice, you can become quite good at partial quantization—using your ears to determine what's needed to get a part tight, but not *too* tight. Laying down drum tracks is the perfect means to work on this skill, because with drums it's easy to hear when something is sounding loose and weird, or tight and groovy.

Swing Factor

Most drum machines and sequencers have a parameter called "swing factor," which, like partial quantization, is expressed as a percentage. Swing factor determines whether eighth-notes are to be played with a straight (evenly spaced) or triplet feel. The concept of swing factor recognizes that there aren't only two ways to play a series of notes; rather, there's a continuum between the straight feel and the triplet feel. In other words, some notes are straighter than others. Swing factor determines exactly how straight or how shuffled eighth-notes, or any other subdivision, are to be played.

Here's how it works: If swing factor is set to 50 percent and you were to fully quantize a MIDI performance of eighth-notes, that means the upbeat eighth-notes would fall exactly halfway between the downbeat eighth-notes (see Fig. 4). Those are very straight eighths—straighter, in fact, than real drummers typically play. In live drum feels, upbeat eighth-notes tend to drag a little compared to the downbeats, so they have a slight delay—this is what swing factor aims to emulate. So if you set swing factor to 54 percent and re-quantize, the upbeat notes will be moved a bit later in time so that they fall 54 percent of the way between the previous downbeat and the next one (see Fig. 5). If you set swing factor to 67 percent and quantize once more, the upbeats will produce an exact triplet feel, because now each upbeat falls two-thirds of the way to the following downbeat (see Fig. 6). Some people refer to this as "swing feel," but understand that real human feels (swing or otherwise) may fall anywhere between 50 and 67 percent, and even beyond.

A great example of notes that swing—but which aren't actually swung in triplet fashion—can be heard on the Beatles' "Hey Jude." Strictly speaking, the song has a straight (or duple) feel, but 1:32 into the song, a tambourine comes in with a loose,

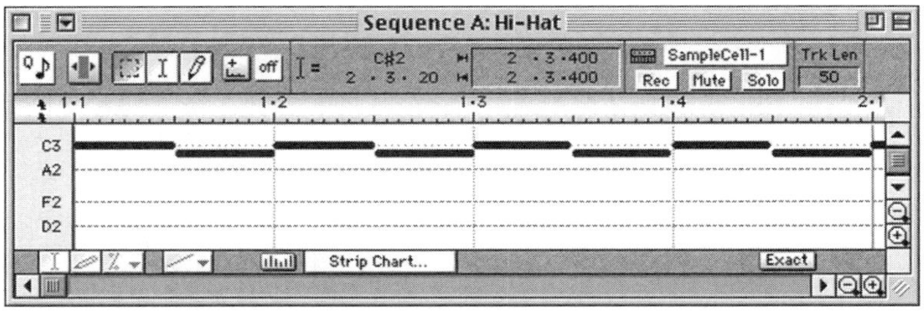

Fig. 4 Quantizing eighth-notes with swing factor set to 50 percent yields a very straight eighth-note feel.

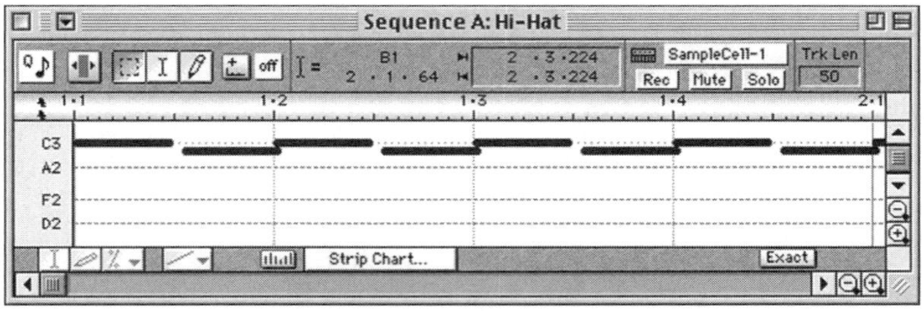

Fig. 5 With swing factor set to 54 percent, the offbeats fall slightly after the halfway point between the downbeats, for a looser straight-eighth feel.

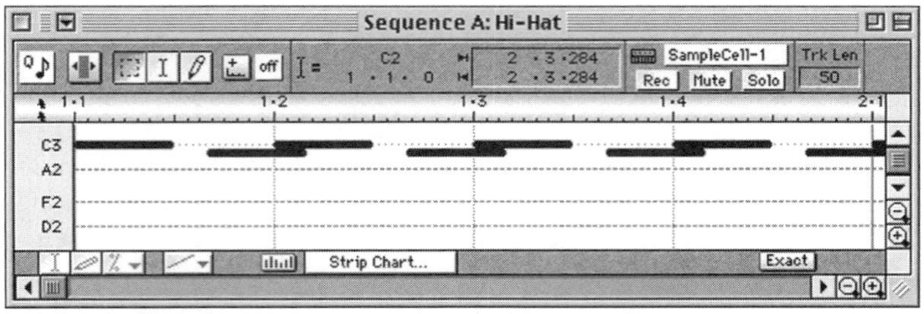

Fig. 6 With swing factor set to 67 percent, the offbeats end up at the two-thirds point between the downbeats, for a strict triplet feel.

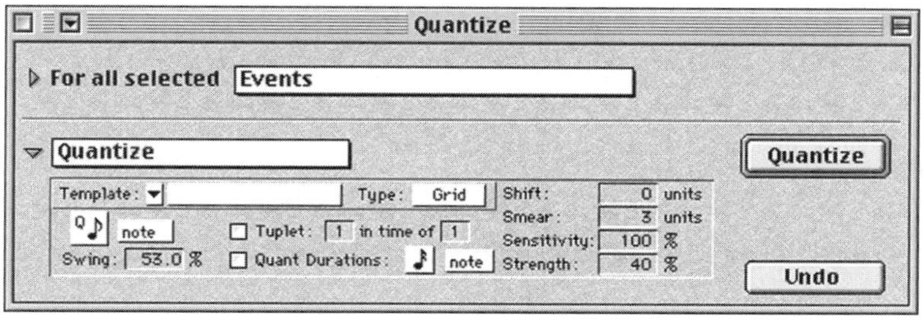

Fig. 7 This quantization window specifies that we're partially quantizing eighth-notes at 40 percent Strength, with a bit of swing (53 percent). In this program, the parameter Smear randomizes the placement of quantized notes slightly (in this case, up to three units away from the grid). The unused Shift parameter offsets all of the quantized events by a set amount, and Sensitivity applies quantization only to certain notes, depending on how far from the grid they are.

groovy 16th-note vibe. Listen to the track and see if you can hear how the offbeat 16ths are just a bit more laid-back than the stronger 16ths. By comparison, a drum-machine tambourine hard-quantized to 16ths with a 50 percent swing factor would sound stiff and totally different. At the song's 2:39 point, the tambourine comes back, this time swinging even harder. At this point it's quite obvious the tambourine isn't really playing straight 16ths.

As an exercise, try to reproduce these tambourine grooves on your drum machine or sequencer. You'll notice that even a strictly quantized part, if given a dash of swing (and varying dynamics), can come to life a little.

Swing factor + partial quantize. A great way to put swing factor to work is to combine it with partial quantizing. If you lay down a MIDI hi-hat part on a straight-eighths song, don't just partially quantize all the MIDI events to eighth-notes—also specify a bit of swing (see Fig. 7). This way, even if you fully quantized the part, you wouldn't suck out *all* of the life from the feel; it might actually still sound a little human. And by partially quantizing it, perhaps at 50 percent strength, you'll make it sound that much more human.

Flams

A technique that drummers use all the time is the *flam*—two hits on the same drum, a split-second apart. Flams are easy to work into a drum program, provided you're playing the part in, not step-programming. In a good flam, the two events kind of surround the beat they fall near, and the second hit is slightly stronger than the first (see Fig. 8). The flam is one of those nuances that people rarely program into drum patterns—but it's too bad, because flams make drum patterns more expressive and realistic-sounding.

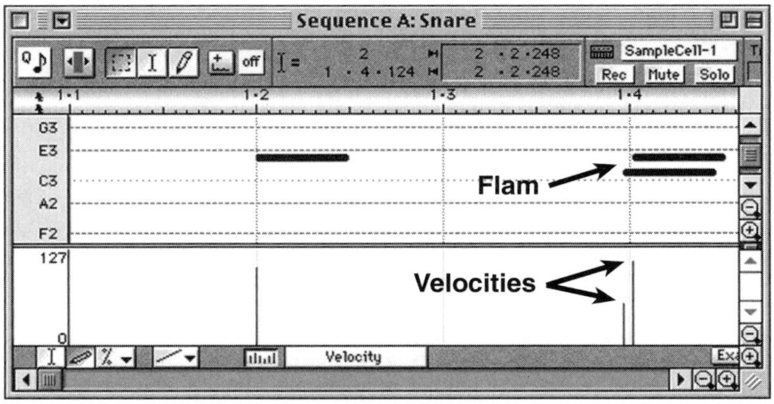

Fig. 8 In a flam, two drum events occur very close together in time, often with an increasing velocity. This mimics the way a drummer plays the first stroke with the weaker hand, followed by the second stroke with the dominant hand. Flams usually sound tightest when they straddle the grid line somewhat, as shown here. Since they're typically used as accents, they often reach a higher velocity than surrounding snares (like the note two beats earlier in this diagram).

Tempo Changes & Rubato Passages

Who says a drum pattern has to stay at the same tempo throughout a song? Subtle tempo changes, which most sequencers allow you to draw into the program, can really humanize a drum pattern. For example, songs sometimes speed up a bit as they head into the chorus. To reproduce this effect in a drum pattern, start ramping up the tempo in the last bar or two before the chorus begins, and have it reach its peak right at or shortly after the start of the chorus. In most cases, don't increase the tempo more than two or three beats per minute. The tempo change should only add a bit of intangible excitement; you shouldn't necessarily hear the song speed up.

Some songs call for passages that are *rubato*, or played freely without a specific tempo. There's no reason you can't include these in your programs as well—just defeat the click in the section of the song where you need to play the part in and, of course, perform the passage in real time. There's a slight complication, though: If the rubato passage ends and the song returns to tempo, unless you're very lucky, the downbeat won't fall on the start of a measure in your sequence. To solve this problem, after you've played in the rubato passage and established the next section's first downbeat, program a tempo change that lasts from the start of the last rubato note to the start of the first note at tempo. It doesn't matter how extreme this tempo change is—the listener will never hear it. The goal is merely to get the song's downbeats to coincide once again with the downbeats in the sequence. If a tempo change isn't enough to make this happen, insert a meter change, such as a single bar of 1/4 time, at the end of the rubato section.

Programming Non-Drum MIDI Parts

Most of what I've said about programming real-sounding drums applies to recording any real-sounding MIDI part. Wherever possible, play parts into the sequencer in real time, and don't fully quantize anything unless you want it to have that rigid feel. Utilize partial quantization and swing factor if you need to tighten up your performances, and if it's a velocity-sensitive sound (such as piano or Wurlitzer keyboard), build dynamic variations into the part in a way that's appropriate and that enhances the part's human feel.

For non-keyboardists, there's nothing that says you have to play both the left-hand and right-hand components at the same time. Trying to do so can be frustrating and pointless. Make a few passes to get the left-hand part down into your sequencer, and then overdub the right-hand part on top. If you do it right, you'll sound just like Elton John. Nobody needs to know that you cheated!

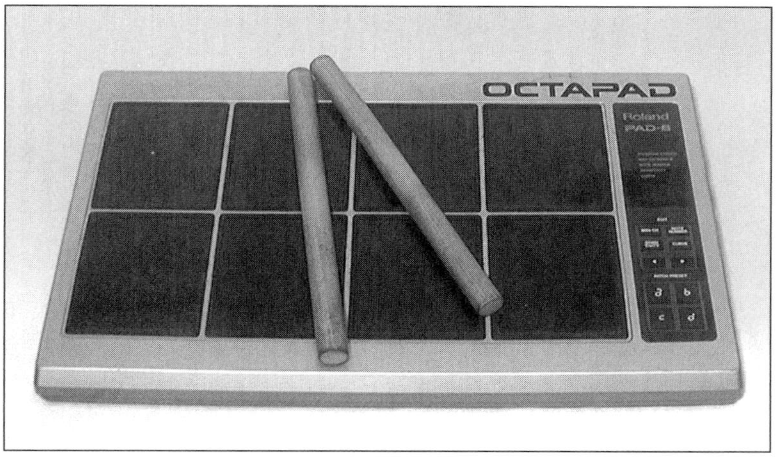

Even the most obsolete MIDI drum controller, such as this 1980s-era Roland Octapad, can make it easy to lay down a MIDI drum performance—and with far better results than with a keyboard.

CHAPTER 9

Miscellaneous Techniques

Guerrilla Home Recording is all about creating the illusion of several different live musicians playing at once, together in a solid groove, and recorded in a professional facility by a skilled producer. As you've already seen, this involves magician-like tricks and other devious acts of deception. But there's more you can do to stretch what you can get, in terms of sound and performance skill, out of your Guerrilla studio. Understand, though, that some of these aren't just Guerrilla tricks—they're used by the pros, too, to help achieve that slick and seamless sound. Why not use every tool available to get the most out of your studio?

Punching In & Out

Aside from multitracking itself, this is perhaps the most basic studio trick. Punching in is the technique of switching a multitrack machine or recording program from playback mode to record mode on the fly. My old Tascam 38 8-track had a ¼" jack on the back for a footswitch, and hitting the footswitch while the machine was playing toggled it into record mode; hitting the footswitch again toggled it back into play mode. Most hardware multitracks use a similar footswitch setup, although many digital systems—including most desktop computer systems—allow you to automate punch points: The machine or program will be playing along, and when it gets to a pre-specified point in the song, it will switch over to record mode, or back to play.

In case you've never used this essential home-recording technique (which the pros also use all the time, by the way), punching in is a way to fix mistakes or finish an uncompleted track. It allows you to start recording in the middle of a song; you can hear (and play along with) the song for a while, taking a moment to settle into the groove, before the recording actually begins—which happens before the point of the mistake or where you stopped playing. If done properly, the result is a seamless edit that sounds like you played the performance straight through the first time. Dastardly studio trickery!

Manual punching. If you're using an analog multitrack, you'll probably have to punch in and out manually, using a footswitch. This takes a little practice, but it's easy once you get the hang of it. It's important that your recorder be able to provide seamless punch-ins; if the machine leaves any kind of click, drop-out (a brief silence), or other glitch at the punch-in point, that's no good. My guess is that *any* multitrack system sold these days—analog or digital—can perform seamless punch-ins, although that wasn't always the case. Still, even the best recorder may not give you a great punch-in if it happens at the wrong moment—particularly in the middle of a note, or during a note's attack. That's why you need to be skillful in exactly where you punch in. It's usually best to punch in a split-second before a new note starts, preferably in a place where there's at least a momentary rest before the new note. If you're doing this with a footswitch, make sure you don't hit the switch right on the beat, as if you were tapping your foot to the tempo; if you do, you may miss your ideal punch-in point and/or cut off the attack of the first new note you record. Work on hitting that switch just before the downbeat; there should be a tiny time lag between hitting the switch and playing the first note, and you shouldn't play the note late as a result of hitting the switch. Again, this just takes practice.

Punching out on an analog system is a whole different question. Because analog tape needs to pass over the erase head before it passes over the record head, there will be a slight gap after the point where you punched out. While you were in record mode, the erase head was clearing the way for the new performance, and by the time you punched out, a short segment of tape had already passed over the erase head, thereby erasing that segment of the track and leaving a hole in the audio. Because of this phenomenon, on an analog recorder you can seamlessly punch out *only* if the part you're recording has a rest right after the point at which you want to punch out. Also, you need to punch out early enough during this rest so you don't erase any portion of the existing track that you want to keep. On a reel-to-reel machine, the rest might need to last only one-tenth of a second; on a cassette deck you might need up to a half a second. I always thought punching out was too tricky to do on an analog system, so I rarely did it. If I was laying down a track and made a mistake, I'd stop the tape, punch in before the error, and try to finish the track, rather than finish a take that I knew would have to be punched into (and out of) later.

Automatic punching. Digital systems allow you to specify exact, stable punch-in and punch-out points, which means you can just start playing—and continue to play—with the punching automatically done for you. The precision of auto-punching, and not having to worry about hitting a footswitch at a particular moment, makes it possible to overwrite just one or two bad notes while you blaze through a performance. Also, because digital recording doesn't use record-and-erase-head technology, there's no gap of silence after the punch-out point. Some digital systems go so far as to incorporate slick automatic crossfade algorithms, making even mid-note punches less audible. Still, try to place your punch points in between notes for the best punch-point transitions.

Compositing A Track

Compositing, or *comping*, refers to building a track by piecing together parts of other tracks. This technique, which can be somewhat laborious, is most often used on lead vocals to get a "perfect take" built out of several less-than-perfect takes.

Let's say you're recording a lead vocal and have four tracks available. First, get a solid take on each of the first three tracks. Next, listen back to each phrase of the vocal, one track at a time, and decide which take has the best performance of that phrase. Do this for the entire song. Typically, most of the best-performed phrases will come from the same track. If that's the case, you'll need the other takes only to shore up a few weak phrases in the best take.

On analog systems, the second phase of comping involves bouncing the entire performance to an available open track. (For more on bouncing, see Chapter 1.) In most cases, this means putting up all three tracks on three of the board's input channels, and working either the board's faders or its MUTE buttons to select which track is getting bounced at any particular moment. You might start the bouncing process with track 1's fader up, and halfway through the verse you might pull down that fader as you bring up track 3's fader, then returning to track 1 after just one vocal phrase. Obviously, this is a lot easier when there are pauses between the vocal phrases. Otherwise, you have to make quick, skillful crossfades between takes, minimizing the amount of overlap at the transition points. Using the MUTE buttons is another approach, but you need to be careful not to cut off the beginnings or ends of vocal phrases, and because the transitions are sudden, they're more likely to end up being audible. When I comped on analog, I preferred using the faders. Working the faders gives you a chance to even out the levels a bit from phrase to phrase, as well as within phrases; in other words, it allows

GUERRILLA TACTIC

Make A Take Report Card

When comping a track, an alternative to judging several takes one phrase at a time is to make a "take report card." For a lead vocal, for example, write the lyrics down the page's left side, one phrase on each line. Then draw vertical lines down the page to delineate columns, one column representing each take. Next, listen to each take in its entirety, and scrutinize the quality of each phrase from that take. In the appropriate spot on your page, grade the phrase either with an A (great), B (good enough), or C (not worth using). Add plusses and minuses to the grades if you want. Do this for all of the takes you recorded, and use the report card to choose which phrases from the various takes should make it into your comp. This approach is a slightly less tedious way to do a comp—and perhaps best of all, it provides a visual map that you can follow if you need to work the board's faders or mute buttons while bouncing the comp track.

you to "compress" the vocal slightly by pulling down the level for louder passages and bringing it up for softer passages, perhaps in places where a word or two might otherwise get buried. When comping, if you make a mistake or miss a transition, you can always punch in on the composite track to get it just right.

With a digital system, once again it's a different process. On a desktop computer system as well as some standalone digital systems, there's no need to bounce. Using a computer system, for example, you can just split each take into individual phrases and then drag the phrases from the original tracks to the comp track, one at a time (see Fig. 1). If transitions aren't quite working, you can adjust the transition points or try using other takes, and if need be, you can set up crossfades between takes. On numerous occasions on digital systems, I've brought in just a single *consonant* (such as a "t" sound at the end of a word) from another take, perhaps because it wasn't audible on the otherwise best take.

Comping isn't only for lead vocals. Many of rock & roll's most famous guitar solos were pieced together from several improvised takes, one phrase at a time. If a track needs to be as good as it possibly can be—and lead vocals and guitar solos certainly qualify—it makes sense to put this technique to work.

As you might imagine, comping can get incredibly nitpicky, but the goal is to create the sound of a single, unified performance that just *kills*. If done well, you can put together a performance that's better than anything you could actually perform in one piece—and for the Guerrilla recordist (or the pro producer, for that matter), that's a very powerful tool.

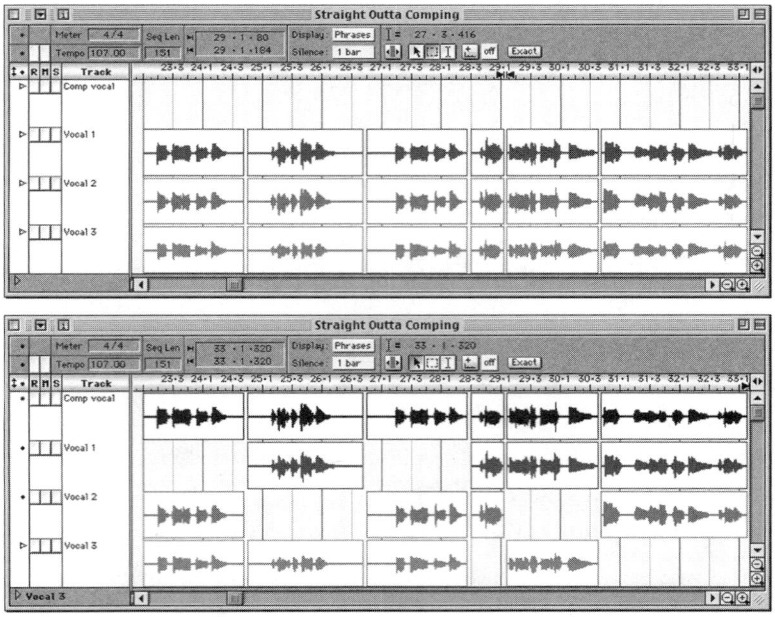

Fig. 1 On a digital system, creating a composite track is easy. At top, three takes of a lead vocal are split into phrases. Making the comp (bottom) involves simply dragging the best phrases to an open track—here, a track labeled "Comp vocal." The original tracks are then muted, allowing only the best phrases to be heard.

Open-Air Vocals

If you have trouble singing with headphones on, and a lot of people do, there's no reason to record all of your vocal tracks that way. I've noticed that sometimes I have a tendency to sing slightly sharp with headphones on—but I can avoid this problem by singing "open air," or listening to the backing tracks over speakers rather than headphones. This is how I do lead vocals that are particularly full-voice and rocked out, as my pitch problem is worse on these types of songs, for whatever reason.

The downside of recording open-air vocals is that the sound from the speakers tends to bleed into the vocal mic, contaminating the tracks slightly and reducing instrument separation. But you should be able to minimize bleed-through if you use a cardioid (directional) mic, position the mic so that it's pointing directly *away* from the speakers, and keep the speakers as quiet as possible. The speaker volume should be *just* high enough so that you can accurately keep your place in the song and sing in tune with enough energy. Unfortunately the reduced monitor levels can make it hard to really rock, but that's the compromise you have to make with this technique.

Re-Amping

As I mentioned in Chapter 7, one way to get an amplified guitar sound on tape is to record a clean direct sound first, and then play the track back out of the recorder and into a guitar amplifier (perhaps with effects placed between the multitrack and amp). By miking the amp at this stage rather than during the actual performance, and recording the mic signal to an open track, you can get the guitar sound at the amp just right. It's a great technique for the do-it-yourselfer, because you don't have to be both a guitarist and a producer at the same time; you can concentrate on playing a great performance first, and then you can go back and work on getting the perfect sound.

You probably won't get a good re-amped sound if you record the guitar's direct track through a direct box and later send this track straight from the recorder to an amp. This is because direct boxes are designed to create a broad-frequency, high-fidelity guitar tone—and believe it or not, that isn't the kind of sound that you deliver to an amp when you plug a guitar into it. Plugging a guitar into an amp creates an electronic interaction between the two known as *loading*, which causes a significant shift in tone. When a tone is loaded, the highs get rolled off somewhat, but there are other changes as well. The loaded tone, when run through distorted circuitry, is what we recognize as a normal distorted guitar sound. In contrast, sending a crisp, broad-frequency direct line to a distorted amp can result in a nasty, brittle type of distortion.

One solution is to load your tone before you record it, by recording your direct track through a direct box that offers variable impedance. If your DI has this feature, turn down the impedance knob until you get a significantly muted or dulled tone—

> ### *Plug-In Re-Amping*
>
> If you're recording on a computer, you may want to look into bundles of recording-software plug-ins that use modeling technology to simulate amplification signal chains. Rather than setting up a "real" signal chain during the re-amp phase to get your sound, you can just try different plug-ins and different parameters after you've recorded your direct track. Unlike with conventional re-amping, plug-ins allow you to quickly and easily tweak your sounds right until mixdown time. Naturally, this has a few limitations. For example, you won't be able to get real amplifier feedback. If nothing else, you can use these kinds of plug-ins to broaden and thicken your conventionally recorded or re-amped guitar sounds, for absolutely monstrous tones.

that's the sound you want. (Don't worry—to an amplifier input, that sounds like a nice, bright tone.) If you don't have one of these boxes for the recording phase, another solution is to load the tone as it's passing from the multitrack to the guitar amp during the re-amping phase. Several companies offer boxes built specifically for this task—they turn a direct-recorded guitar signal into a signal optimized for the amp's input. If you don't have one of these boxes, check your direct box—if it's the passive type (i.e., it doesn't require a battery to operate), try using it "backwards": Run your clean, high-fidelity direct signal from the multitrack into the direct box's output jack, and then send the signal out of the box's input jack into the guitar amp's input. It should hit the amp's input properly loaded.

If neither of these methods is feasible, when you record the track initially, try plugging the guitar into a ¼" instrument or line input jack on one of your board's input channels. It might not sound pretty, but this may load the signal sufficiently so it will sound fairly "normal" when you send this recorded sound to your guitar amp. As a last resort, try rolling off the highs quite a bit during either the recording phase (before the multitrack) or during the re-amping phase (before the amp). Although this won't sound exactly like a properly loaded guitar tone, you should be able to reduce the amount of harsh distortion coming out of the amp.

By the way, re-amping isn't just for guitar tracks. For instance, if you want a sampled organ sound to be more rock & roll, try running it into a guitar amp that's turned up loud (but not necessarily distorted), and mic it onto an open track. You can even do this with drums, vocals, and other sounds. Experiment and see what you come up with—if it works for the song, then it works, period.

Printing MIDI Instruments

Setting up sequenced instruments like sampled drums and MIDI keyboards as virtual tracks (see Chapter 1) not only results in the cleanest possible sound, it also allows maximum flexibility for making last-minute changes. However, sometimes it's useful to "print" these sounds—i.e., record them onto the multitrack along with other audio tracks like vocals. Here are a few reasons why you might want to print a MIDI instrument:

1. No sync. If you can't use a sync tone (see Chapter 1) for whatever reason, you can't use virtual tracks. So you'll need to print the MIDI instruments' audio signals. How many tracks you use is a tradeoff: Printing them to just two tracks in stereo saves tracks, but you'll never be able to adjust the instruments' blend afterward. But using up four or five tracks may not leave you much room to work with for recording other audio.

2. Not enough MIDI instruments. If you want a sequenced organ sound *and* an electric piano on your song, but you have only one keyboard and it can't do both sounds at once, print one of them. Set up your sequence to play one of the sounds via MIDI, and connect the keyboard's audio out(s) to one or two input channels on your board; then run the sequence while recording the keyboard's audio to an available track or tracks. For the rest of the tracking process and during mixdown, let the other keyboard sound run as a virtual track, and blend the first keyboard's audio track into the rest of the mix.

3. Sound not thick enough. Printing can also be used to thicken up a sound. For example, you could make a more complex string sound by printing several different string sounds that are playing the same notes, and blending them with a virtual-track string sound during mixdown. Pan the various string sounds differently if you want the strings to sound broader overall. Just make sure the sounds are sufficiently different from each other; if one sound is just a slight variation on another sound, frequency cancellation could result, which is almost always a bad thing.

4. Effect needs. Suppose you want a cavernous reverb on a string sound, but you have only one reverb unit and want to use it on the vocals, too. The solution: Print the string sound onto two tracks in stereo, along with the cavernous reverb. Alternatively, you could print *just* the cavernous reverb and run the dry strings as a virtual track. This would allow you to easily alter the blend of dry strings and reverb whenever you need to. The tradeoff is a minor one: If you need to mute the string sound, it's a two-step process, because you have to mute the dry strings and the reverb separately.

5. Simplify mixdown. Maybe you have some fader, pan, or EQ moves on a virtual track that you can only perform manually on the board during mixdown. Rather than repeating these moves each time you make a pass at mixing the song down, perform them while printing the instrument to two tracks in stereo. That way, each time you run the song, the moves will be there—almost as if you had automated them. This is especially useful if the moves are an important part of the song's arrangement, as hearing them can affect your subsequent playing and/or arranging choices. Actually, this technique applies to any tracks—not just MIDI instruments. For example, if you want a lead vocal's reverb to undergo complex panning and level changes, consider printing the reverb to two tracks with these moves in place. Then they'll be there each time you run the song.

Whatever the case, don't delete the MIDI tracks for any instruments you print; instead, simply mute them. You never know when you'll want to go back, tweak a sound or a blend, and re-print it. Keep your options open; a muted MIDI track takes up virtually no disk space or processing power, so why erase it?

Flying In Bounced Tracks

This is a powerful, if laborious, technique for people working on linear systems (analog or digital tape), or those who don't have enough available tracks. Before I owned a real sampler, I'd often want to build up a complex backing-vocal part on my Tascam 38, but with only eight total analog tracks, I'd run out quickly—and short of numerous layered bounces (an idea that never appealed to me), there was no way I could get the part down and into the mix. My solution was to get the drums and keyboards together first as virtual tracks, and then record the background vocals as the first audio tracks. That way, I'd have six full tracks to work with. Then I'd mix down *only* the background vocals to two channels in stereo, recording them onto a different ¼" reel-to-reel (and later, a DAT machine). Finally, after erasing the six original tracks, I'd run the reel-to-reel machine and record the vocals in stereo back onto the 8-track. The tricky part is getting the two machines synchronized. It was basically trial and error, although after a while I got pretty good at knowing where and when I needed to start the reel-to-reel so it would lay the tracks into the right spot on the song. In terms of timing, things like background vocals are somewhat forgiving. In contrast, you'd probably drive yourself crazy trying to fly in something like a percussion part this way.

A side benefit to flying in tracks is that you can duplicate them in various parts of

GUERRILLA TACTIC *Flying In Tracks With A Sampler*

If you have a stereo sampler with plenty of memory, you can use it to fly in tracks. Compared to an analog tape or DAT machine, it's much easier to control a sampler's timing—and if you can trigger the sampler with a sequence, you can get the timing both exact and perfectly repeatable. In that case, you can fly in pretty much anything, no matter how accurate the timing needs to be. And if you're strapped for tracks, maybe you don't need to fly them back to the recorder after all—keep them on the sampler as virtual tracks, triggered by the sequencer. Also, for the track-challenged, why devote two tracks to just the flown-in part? Blend in something else—like bass or guitar—while the sampler is flying the part in. Be sure to save the flown-in part to disc; that way, if you later need to redo the live-played instrument or adjust the blend, you can just load the part back into the sampler and go at it again.

the song. If all three choruses have the same background-vocal part, for instance, just fly your BVs into each of the three choruses, one at a time. Of course, this works only if the tempo is the same from chorus to chorus.

Digital Editing

The rest of this chapter deals with techniques specific to computer recording systems. A large part of digital recording's appeal is the ease and speed with which songs and tracks can be edited. For anyone who uses one of these systems, a technique like flying in vocals from a reel-to-reel machine sounds downright archaic (maybe even crazy). On a computer, duplicating a vocal arrangement into the next chorus can be as easy as selecting the tracks, holding down a key, and dragging the tracks wherever they need to go.

As soon as you start working on a computer system, get familiar with the essential techniques: selecting tracks, dividing them into segments (such as phrases of a vocal), shortening and lengthening these segments, and moving and copying segments, both to different time locations on a track as well as to other tracks. Also, learn what kind of DSP (digital signal processing) your system allows you to perform on the sound files. DSP functions may include level change, pitch change, time scale, EQ, and reverse.

Armed with these basic tools, you can improvise all sorts of techniques. For example, if one note in a vocal is decidedly flat and you don't have another take to pilfer notes from, here's how to fix it. Find the wrong note and select it. To give yourself some room to work with, start the selection a little before the note's beginning, and select slightly past the end of the note. Isolate this segment from the rest of the track (my program calls this function Separate). With this isolated segment selected, bring up the pitch-change DSP dialog box, and estimate how much you need to adjust the pitch to get it in tune (30 cents up or down might be a good place to start). The computer will

LOOK ■ OUT!

Don't Overdo It

In some circles, digital recording programs have gotten a bad reputation because digital editing is so easy to abuse. Some perfectionist types just will not rest until they've edited every last note into submission. But in many musical styles, rock & roll among them, this is a bad idea. As with absolute quantization, you can suck the life and energy out of something by performing numerous time and pitch corrections. Real music is never perfect; the mild inaccuracies are what make it human and (we hope) interesting and exciting. So perform your edits judiciously, know when to say when, and always use your ears—not your eyes—when deciding what to keep and what to change.

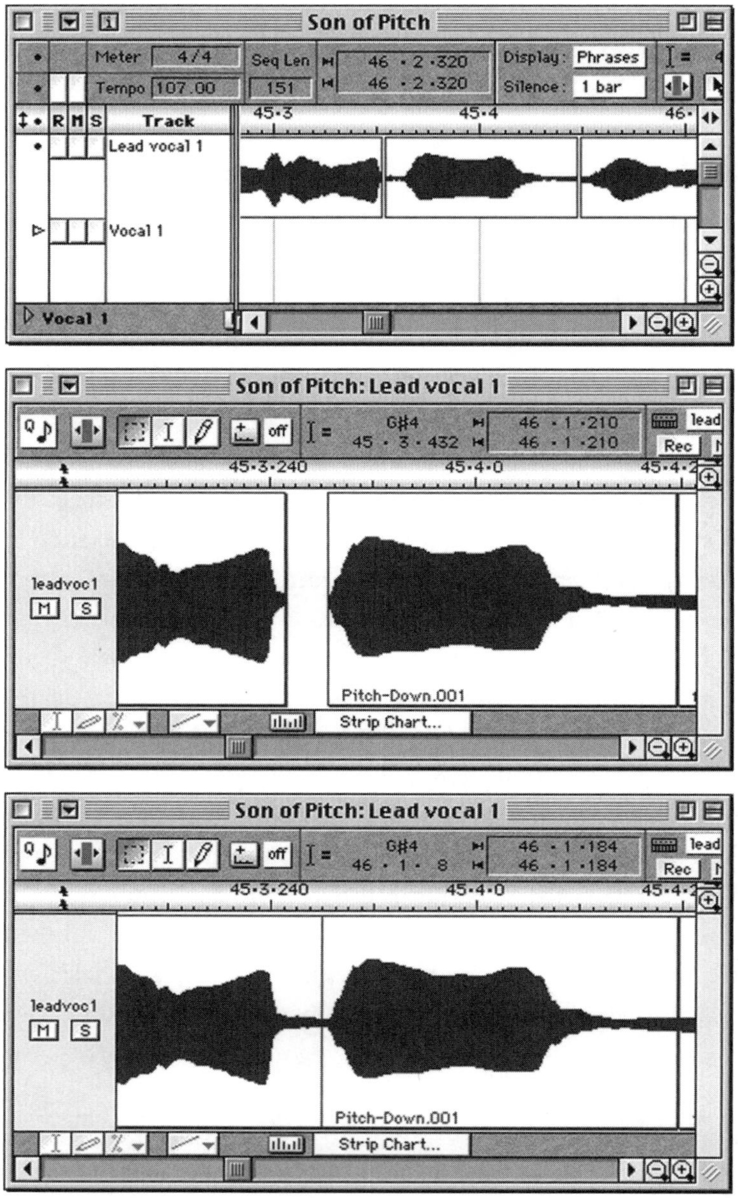

Fig. 2 Correcting a single note's pitch using DSP: First, isolate the note slightly beyond its beginning and end, and perform the pitch-change operation (top). Zoom in and truncate the pitch-changed segment so that it starts at the beginning of the note (center). Then, lengthen the previous segment to overlap the pitch-changed segment, and adjust the endpoints until the transition sounds smooth (bottom). Finally, repeat this process for the end of the note and its transition into the next segment of the track.

perform the processing and will create a new sound file of this segment only. Listen to the note—ignore any clicks or other weirdness for now—and decide whether the note is sufficiently in tune. If not, undo the operation and try again. Once you've gotten the rogue note roughly in tune, zoom into the segment's start and end points and truncate the segment so it consists of only the formerly out-of-tune note; then lengthen the ends of the surrounding segments so that they touch or slightly overlap the pitch-shifted seg-

LOOK OUT!

Don't Erase The Audio!

If you want to record automation moves into a track of audio that you've already laid down, you need to disengage the program's audio-recording capability; otherwise you'll erase the audio while you're recording your automation moves. In other words, you need to set up the program so the track is record-enabled, but you aren't actually recording audio onto it. In my program, I do this by clicking a button next to the appropriate track in a "record monitor" window. See your documentation to learn how to do this with your own program.

ment. To make sure the note fits seamlessly into the original take, zoom way into the transitions and, if necessary, adjust the endpoints and beginning points so that the ends of the wave shapes meet from one segment to another. (If there's a discontinuity, it will show up in the audio as a click or pop at that point—not good.) If you have to move the pitch-shifted segment a bit to get the end points to match, or if you have to smooth over the transitions with crossfades (see the documentation to learn how to do this), go ahead. When you're done, the pitch-corrected note should fly by and fit into the take perfectly—only in tune now (see Fig. 2).

Some recording programs, such as Pro Tools, allow you to redraw wave shapes with a pencil tool. This can be helpful in getting the ends of wave shapes to match up, as well as for getting rid of other momentary anomalies in the wave. Just be sure to zoom in really close, and keep the shape smooth and flowing at the corrected point, just like the wave shape around it.

Digital Automation

Besides digital's editing capabilities, one of its most valuable functions is its ability to automate mixdown moves like level changes, pan sweeps, and even changes to EQ and plug-in parameters. This is especially valuable for the Guerrilla recordist: Pro studios often use $500,000 consoles to automate mixdowns, but with a desktop recording system you can automate many of the same functions right in your home studio.

This kind of automation is normally done using the program's "virtual console," or whatever other name the software company uses. This is an onscreen depiction of a mixing board complete with channels, faders, pan knobs, etc. If you switch a track into record mode and then begin recording, any changes you make to that track's fader or other controls on the virtual console will probably be recorded. If you then play back the song from the same spot, you should see the fader magically move as you had moved it previously. Welcome to automation! It's probably obvious how powerful this functionality can be. In addition to getting mixdown moves *exactly* the way

GUERRILLA TACTIC

Automating Virtual Tracks

Audio tracks aren't the only things you can automate with a computer's recording software. Things like drums and keyboards, recorded during the tracking process as MIDI information, can be automated to a certain extent as well. However, you'll need to draw the changes in the appropriate windows representing the MIDI parameters for volume and panning, which aren't the same windows as those representing audio levels and panning. If you draw a ramping increase in an electric piano track's MIDI volume window, for instance, the sequence will send the electric piano module not only MIDI information for notes and velocities but also for MIDI volume values—which will cause the electric piano to get gradually louder as the sequence plays.

you want them, they're stored right in the computer file along with the song itself, so the exact same moves will still be there when you open the song a year from now.

Dragging virtual faders and knobs with the mouse can be a little awkward, so do a little digging into your recording program to find out how you can program automation moves in other ways. For example, if you want a track to fade in smoothly over the course of a whole verse, there's probably a way to draw a straight line in some window representing the track's fader level. If you're a perfectionist, you may find yourself spending hours in these windows adjusting and readjusting automation moves, listening to portions of a song over and over, until everything is just right. It may sound obsessive, but such attention to detail can make your productions very slick, if that's the sound you're going for. It can give you a huge advantage over other home recordists who spend just a few minutes setting levels and are done with it.

Automation even allows you to create effects that might otherwise be impossible. For example, in a guitar track's panning window, you might be able to draw a triangle-wave shape that cycles once every quarter-note, perfectly synchronizing the instrument's panning with the song's tempo. By doing something similar in a level window, you can create a tremolo effect that's perfectly synchronized to the song.

In addition to setting automation moves for individual tracks, your program probably also allows you to create busses, or groups of tracks, on the virtual console—and you can automate these as well. For example, if you want eight background-vocal tracks to fade in slowly, don't program a move on each of the eight tracks; instead, create a bus that groups them together, and program the move for just the single bus.

GUERRILLA TACTIC *Create An Automated Reverb Bus*

On a desktop recording system, it's incredibly powerful to be able to automate the level, panning, and EQ for every audio track. But depending on your program's features, you may also be able to automate the levels of outboard reverb and other effects. Here's how: First, your recording program must allow you to set up both busses and effect sends in a "virtual console" (pretty standard these days). In the virtual console, for each audio track that needs reverb, set up an effect send. If you'll need its reverb level to go up and down independent of the dry signal's level, switch the effect send to pre-fader (see Chapter 3). Next, set up a mono bus channel named "reverb bus," and specify that all of the virtual console's effect sends be routed to this reverb bus. Then, assign an unused output on your audio interface or soundcard to the reverb bus, and bring that output's audio signal into an unused input channel on your mixing board. (If your board doesn't have a spare input channel, you can plug a cable straight from the audio interface's output jack to the reverb's input jack. Just make sure the level going to the reverb isn't so high or low that you get distortion or excess noise.) Bring the board channel's fader all the way down, and switch its effect send to pre-fader. Finally, turn up the appropriate effect-send knob to provide a pre-fader signal to your outboard reverb unit. At this point, whenever there's audio on a track where you set up a virtual effect send, some of that signal will be sent to the program's reverb bus, out the reverb bus's output, into your mixing board, and out to the reverb unit.

Now, here's the cool part: If your recording program allows you to automate changes to its virtual effect-send levels, you can simply draw ramps and curves into the appropriate window to tell the program when the effect-send levels need to go up or down: up for more reverb on that track, down for less. If you can't do this on your program, you can probably at least automate the level of the reverb bus (see Fig. 3). The downside of this system is that you can't change the reverb levels independently for each track; if you want the vocal's reverb level to go down, the guitar's will go down as well. The

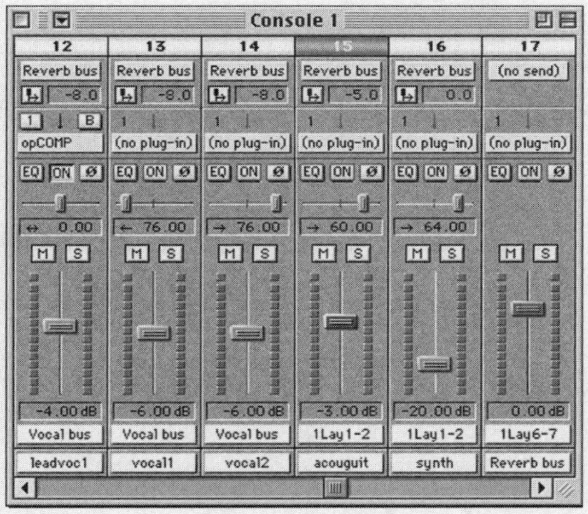

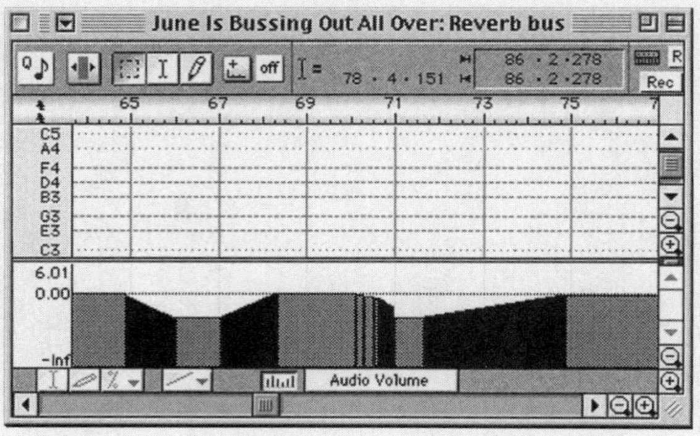

Fig. 3 An automated reverb bus in the recording program's "virtual console" (top, toward the right); note the reverb bus sends at the top of the other console channels. Automated changes to the reverb bus level are reflected in the bus's volume window (bottom).

workaround: Set up a separate bus for just the reverb you need to control independently (perhaps named "vocal reverb bus"), with the other reverb sends going to a separate bus (perhaps "misc reverb bus"). *Then* route both of these busses to a third bus (perhaps "master reverb bus"), and tell it to feed your audio interface's output jack. Draw your automation on your vocal reverb bus track and your overall reverb level on your master reverb bus track, and you'll have all of the reverb levels automated, independently of each other.

By the way, if you want to automate two different reverb units or one reverb and another effect, just set up a separate bus for the second effect unit. You'll need to send this bus out of its own audio-interface output jack, though; if one isn't available, you may not be able to automate that other effect. But don't let that discourage you—put on your Guerrilla Home Recording thinking cap and see if you can dream up a way to improvise! It seems like there's always a way to get the job done if you just employ some good ol' ingenuity.

Chapter 10

Mixing & Mastering

We've reached the end of the line: Mixing is your last chance to finalize all of a song's individual sounds, levels, and pannings, and mastering is your last chance to make sure the final mix sounds balanced and has the proper overall dynamics for maximum impact once it's burned onto CD.

Mixing Goals

In many recording sessions, especially in pro studios, it can take longer to mix a song than it took to record it. That's a testament to the importance of this step—it's absolutely critical. However, if you've been following the Guerrilla Home Recording "mix as you go" concept (see Chapter 1), most of your work is already done by the time you get to mixdown. In pro studios it's common to "wipe" the board, or zero out all of its settings, before beginning a mixing session. But if you've been mixing the song all along, the mixing process becomes simply a matter of fine tuning, listening closely, and asking yourself questions about what you're hearing and what you'd like to be hearing.

When you go into final-mix mode, the first thing to consider is: What kind of emotional effect do you want this recording to have on the listener, and which of its ingredients contribute the most toward creating this effect? Does the song have a strong impact because of its beautiful melody and great lyrics? Is it a party-hearty rock & roll tune with a catchy instrumental riff? Does its infectious beat make you want to dance your butt off? Having an objective view of the big picture is a great way to start this process, as it will inform the fine-tuning (or perhaps not-so-fine tuning) decisions you'll make in your quest to maximize the song's strengths.

In any song with vocals and instruments, there's always a bit of a tradeoff between the two. On one hand, you don't want the instruments to overshadow the vocals such that they detract from the vocals' visceral impact. Plus, if the lyrics are important, you don't want the instruments to obscure them. But on the other hand, prominent vocals can make the music behind them sound small—in effect, detracting from the instruments' impact as well. This isn't an exact science; even among world-class mixing engineers, there are no standard levels at which vocals and instruments are set against each other. It's always an artistic decision, but it helps at least to ask these questions. That way you can decide where on the continuum, from vocal-heavy to instrument-heavy, you'd like your mix to fall in order to best achieve your goals for the song.

Have A Frame Of Reference

Before you start a mixing session, play a song from a professionally mixed and mastered CD at a moderate volume through your studio monitors. Ideally, choose something in the same genre as the song you're about to mix, and/or with a sound similar to what you'd like to achieve with your song. It's hard to mix in a vacuum, so it can help greatly to have a sonic frame of reference before you begin. It may also inspire you to try a few new things in your mix. And by all means, don't be afraid to bring up that reference song *during* your mixing session. It can be humbling (especially since the reference song has been mastered and yours hasn't yet), but putting your music up against professionally recorded music is an important part of the Guerrilla Home Recording process. Since the beginning, you've been trying to get your song to sound as if it had been professionally recorded, right? So why stop now? Do your best to get your own mix to sound as smooth and balanced as your reference mix. The extra effort will pay off.

The Importance Of Monitor-Dimming

We tend to love the music we record, and we tend to play music we love *loud*. That's fine for listening enjoyment (as long as you aren't hurting your ears), but in the studio we have a job to do—so don't combine too much pleasure with your business. Understand that few people are going to play your song as loudly as you'd like them to. That's why it's important to frequently "dim" your monitors, which is a fancy way of saying, *turn down the volume*. And when I say down, I mean way down—to the point where you could easily have a quiet, even whispered, conversation over the music. It may feel silly to mix a song this way, where you can't even hear some of the instruments. But consider this: You play the music loud because you want to hear all the little details, right? Well, that's valuable for sure—but it is just as valuable to be able to *zoom way out* and take a very broad listen of the song. That's what dimming the monitors does. You'll find out what's jumping out too much, as well as what's completely inaudible. For instance, often when I'm monitoring loud, I'll think a vocal is totally buried and unintelligible under the music—but then I'll dim the volume way down, and surprise, I can hear every word. That tells me turning up the vocals is unnecessary—maybe even an outright bad idea.

When mixing, try to have the monitors dimmed about 50 percent of the time. In addition to having a more varied perspective on mixing, you'll experience considerably less ear fatigue—and your neighbors may thank you, too.

Make A Mix Card

Shortly after you finish a mix—particularly a difficult one with a lot of manual moves on the board—document what you've done on an index card. Note which recorded tracks or track routings are associated with your board's channels, and anything unusual about other routings, such as effect-send assignments. Also indicate critical points in the song and any mix moves that you needed to make at these points. If you have a digital camera, shoot the board from above with all controls at their positions for the start of the song; label the channels as necessary with masking tape and a black marker. Documenting these details will save a lot of time should you need to go back and mix the song again—something that always seems to happen more often than you expect.

Headphones Vs. Speakers

Throughout this book I've mentioned that a good pair of headphones can be very useful during the tracking process. They're also useful for the mixing stage. However, as with loud and dimmed monitoring, if you use headphones during mixdown you should balance it out with speaker listening. Consider the strengths and weaknesses of each method: Headphones (good ones, anyway) offer a very "up close" listening perspective; they let you hear every subtle detail, and if you turn your head slightly, the stereo image won't change as it will with speakers. But headphones can play weird psychoacoustic tricks on your ears and brain, and you often can't get a true read of the low frequencies through headphones. Speaker monitors provide a more accurate low end—at least the good ones do. However, they're subject to acoustical interactions with their immediate surroundings as well as with the room, which can seriously affect your perception of a mix. For example, placing monitors close to a wall causes bass frequencies to build up, making the monitors (and consequently your mix) sound boomier than they really are. This effect is more pronounced if the speakers are near the corners of a room, or, worst of all, near the corners *and* the ceiling or floor. Also, the louder you monitor, the worse the bass buildup. So, for more accurate mixing, try to get some room behind your speakers, and if possible, put something heavy (but not rigid) between the speakers and the wall. And remember, dim those monitors frequently!

Triple-Check Your Mixes

In addition to listening at different levels through both your studio monitors and headphones, it's always a good idea to burn a CD of rough mixes and listen to them on at least two other stereo systems. The car, for instance, is a great place to listen to rough mixes. At least one of your listening systems should be something with small speakers, such as a boombox or a personal computer. Small speakers react differently than large ones and therefore provide an alternative listening perspective. For example, if one of your songs has a particularly midrange-heavy sound, such as a telephone-like filtered vocal, it may sound fine on a home stereo while it jumps out too much on a boombox. In this case, you might try bringing down the vocal's level by 3dB or 4dB; you can then dim your studio monitors and determine whether the vocal is still sufficiently present and audible in the big speakers. It probably will be.

Besides being extra work, the downside to listening on several systems is that the results can almost be overwhelming—kind of like a "too many cooks" effect. On one system you might be hearing all guitar; on another, all vocals; and on another, all bass. The trick is to strike compromises so that your mix is optimally satisfactory on all the systems you check it through. Your mix can't please every listening system all of the time, so the best you can do is find a middle ground for everything.

The Listen-Back Checklist

If you don't have a lot of mixing experience, you might simply set an approximate level for each instrument, decide the mix sounds fine, and leave it at that. Unfortunately, that's not good enough. In order to get more professional-sounding mixes, push yourself to scrutinize them more carefully. Consider the dynamics, frequency content, and pan position of *every* instrument or sound, as well as the mix relationships between related sounds, such as keyboards and rhythm guitar or lead vocals and background vocals. As you gain experience, you'll find yourself becoming increasingly precise with your mix settings.

I learned a valuable lesson about ten years ago when I was recording a demo for a singer/songwriter who went on to join a multi-platinum band. When we were mixing his songs, he was asking me to adjust the background-vocal levels by what seemed like ridiculously small degrees—nudging the faders by just a millimeter or so. He explained that the vocals just weren't "sitting in the mix" exactly right. Eventually he was satisfied, and the recording turned out really well. After that experience, I found that I began scrutinizing levels in my own mixes much more carefully, looking for that "sweet spot" for each instrument where it fit perfectly into the mix. This is what you should strive to do, because getting every single instrument "seated" just right can make an enormous difference. It's often what makes a mix sound like a real *record*, as opposed to a mix that sounds like a thrown-together demo.

To help you improve your critical listening skills, here's a checklist you can follow when listening back to a rough mix. Keep in mind these are only guidelines for achieving a fairly conventional popular-music sound; your own aesthetics may be wildly different, which is a good thing. Also, requirements change depending on the style. In a punk-rock song, for example, a half-open hi-hat may be a major energy

> ### *What's Wrong With This %@!#& Mix?*
>
> Sometimes, mixes simply go bad. Everything seems to be going fine, and then you make some adjustments, then some more—and all of a sudden everything sounds like total garbage, but you have no idea why. Everything you try to fix the problem only makes the mix sound worse, and you just want to throw out the whole thing and start over. Well, often that's the best thing to do—you just have to start mixing a song again, from scratch.
>
> If you've reached wits' end, "wipe" the board—set all faders to zero and EQs flat—and start over. Begin with the kick and snare, keeping in mind that the kick often needs to be louder than the snare at this point in order for the two to balance each other in the final mix. Bring in the hi-hat next; don't overdo it, as setting the hi-hat too loud is one thing that can make a whole mix sound mysteriously wrong somehow. Next comes the bass; spend a little time massaging the EQ so it speaks clearly and blends well with the kick drum. Next, bring in the other rhythm instruments—keyboards and guitars. Finally, bring in the background vocals and the melodic lead instruments: lead vocals, lead guitar, etc. With any luck, your mix will have a smoother, more balanced sound than the one that was giving you so much frustration. With the heavy lifting done and the major problems solved, you can get to work fine-tuning your mix to perfection.

provider, so in that case you'd probably treat the hi-hat differently than you would otherwise.

Kick drum. Is the attack sufficiently audible? Does the drum sound's "body" provide a subtle feeling of power? Or, does the kick pop out of the mix too much, causing your meters to peak every time the kick drum sounds? The kick usually causes the meters to jump somewhat; that's unavoidable. But if they jump too much, it suggests that the kick is too loud and is robbing your other instruments of dynamic range—they all need to be quieter in order to keep the overall mix from being too loud.

Snare drum. Can you hear it? Is it providing enough of a backbeat sound to fulfill its function? Does it have enough "body" to prevent it from sounding tinny, with enough top-end "crack" to balance the rest of the sound? Or, is it (or its reverb) too loud—are you getting an '80s sound like an old INXS record, when you actually want the snare to sound more contemporary? Listen to the snare on a small-speaker system: Is the sound's "body" causing the snare to pop out too much? Inexperienced recordists tend to mix the snare too loud. Set it just loud enough that it fulfills its function and doesn't step on the other sounds.

Hi-hat. Is it bright enough? Or, is it *too* bright? The hi-hat's unique high-frequency domain means that it can usually cut through even dense mixes at low to moderate levels. Considering this, is it too loud? When the hi-hat level is too high, you tend to want to pump up everything else; you keep reaching for faders and turning them up, and eventually the whole mix becomes too loud, when all you had to do in the first place was bring down the hi-hat. Make sure it's there providing a pulse in the background; that's usually all the hi-hat needs to do.

Toms. Do they have enough punch? Do they attract your attention when they occur? Or, are they bombastically loud? Toms should be bold and assertive—but when they come in, they shouldn't blow away the other sounds.

Crash cymbal. Is it moderately audible? Crashes don't need to be much more than just somewhat audible to be effective. Is the crash blasting out of the mix? Nothing is more annoying than crash cymbals that obliterate everything else when they occur.

Ride cymbal. Similar to the hi-hat, is it sufficiently bright and audible? The lower-frequency "body" of a ride is a component of its overall sound, but this is not what you should hear when a ride part comes in; you should notice only the "ping" of its attack. Otherwise, either the ride is too loud or it needs to be EQ'd.

Bass. Does the level provide enough of a solid low-end foundation to keep the mix from sounding thin and top-heavy? Still, it shouldn't overwhelm other instruments with low- to mid-frequency components. Also important, can you hear the individual notes' pitches? If they're more or less indistinguishable, you may need to bring up the low mids and perhaps temper the lows. Blurry pitch may also be a sign that the instrument you used is inferior. Finally, does the bass blend well with the kick drum? Ideally, they should both mesh together somewhat to provide a unified sense of foundation and power, but you should still be able to distinguish their sounds from one another.

Clean electric guitar. Is it sufficiently audible? Is it bright and crisp enough? Keep in mind this is often an ornamental background instrument, so it usually doesn't need to be very loud. Are its high frequencies distracting from the vocals? If so, consider reducing its level and/or changing its pan position to give the vocals a little more room to work with.

Acoustic guitar. Are the highs bright without being annoying and clangy? Is there enough body in the sound to keep the instrument from sounding tinny? A tinny clean electric guitar can often work fine, but a tinny acoustic guitar usually doesn't sound like an acoustic guitar—the body is an important sonic characteristic. Then again, if the body is muddy or woofy and is disproportionate to the top, it may be time to adjust the EQ.

Crunch rhythm guitar. This is often mixed at a bold, aggressive level. If you'd like the instrument to be aggressive (which is usually the case), does it achieve this function in the mix, or is it wimpy? Perhaps the problem is in its bottom end: Does the guitar have enough heavy bottom to complement the bass and kick drum, without having so much that it competes with these instruments for the lowest frequency band? Or, do its high-frequency components detract from the low end in a buzzy, annoying way? Check the pan positions—does the guitar obliterate the vocals, or does it need to be panned apart from the vocals so both can be mixed sufficiently up-front?

Lead guitar. If there's a guitar solo, is it roughly on the same level as the lead vocal? Often, both sounds provide the same function: a melodic, up-front performance. So, when the lead vocal ends, it should sound like it's "handing off" to the lead guitar. The lead guitar shouldn't sound like it's saying "Step aside!" when it comes in, 6dB hotter than the vocal. Then again, the solo is probably the song's focal point for that stretch, so it shouldn't sound timid or weak. (If guitar is your primary instrument, my guess is that you *never* mix your guitar solos too low!)

Piano, organ & other keyboards. Can you hear the notes sufficiently without the instruments overpowering everything else? Keyboards are an important part of the low-mid to middle part of the frequency spectrum, so make sure they aren't being shortchanged in these bands. Do the keyboards exhibit power in the frequency spectrum's lower half, without being so thick that they're muddy?

Background vocals. Remember that background vocals are just that—they often sound best in the background. Inexperienced recordists frequently mix the BVs too forward in the mix, perhaps because they're often a mix's slickest-sounding component. But ask yourself: Are they *supporting* the lead vocal, or does it sound like the lead vocal is supporting the BVs? Also, if there are harmonies, are they blended in the proper proportion? Higher harmonies pop out more than lower harmonies, so you may need to balance them apart by 3dB or so. (If you've bounced or otherwise premixed your BVs, oh well—better get 'em next time!) Finally, are the BVs sufficiently crisp, or are they muddying each other up? BVs don't need very much low mids at all; as long as they don't sound irritatingly tinny, you can let the lead vocals fill in the lower end for the vocals department.

Lead vocals. Finally we come to this all-important ingredient. If applicable, can you hear all of the words? If not, you may need to work a little harder during mixdown tweaking the level. Is the top end crisp, without hissing and spitting like a pan of frying bacon? Is there enough "body" to the sound to give the performance warmth? Listening at several different volume levels and on different listening systems, scrutinize the way the lead vocal sits in the mix. Is the level at a comfortable place, appropriate for how you want the lead vocal to function in the song? If you're having trouble setting the lead vocal's level—if it's popping out one minute and buried the next—it may be under-compressed. Consider running it through your compressor again during the mixdown stage, and set your compressor to a fairly low threshold and a low ratio (2:1 should be plenty). Take your time setting the lead-vocal level; it can make or break a song. When your ears get really dialed in, you may find yourself going back to remix a song days later just to bring up (or down) the lead vocal by as little as 1dB.

Riding The Faders

If you've ever watched a professional mixing engineer at work, you probably noticed that the faders rarely remain stuck at their levels as the song runs. A good mixing engineer makes constant adjustments—kind of like the way you constantly adjust the steering wheel's position as you drive down a road, even if it's straight. This is called "riding the faders." Learning how to do this well can take years, but here are a few suggestions for good fader-tending during a mixdown. Keep in mind that fader-riding can involve very subtle changes, such as moving a fader up and down by only a couple of millimeters in either direction.

Even out overall levels. If a song starts out quietly—perhaps with no drums—then it may be a good idea to boost the overall (master) level at the beginning, and then bring down the master fader(s) when the louder instruments, such as drums, kick in. It's important for a song to begin with strength and presence; otherwise the listener's first impression may be that the song is wimpy and weak—even if it could crush cars once the acoustic-guitar intro is over. Later in the song, if some of the louder instruments drop out and the overall level goes down, consider bringing the master level back up again, but don't bother if doing so may sacrifice a sense of drama created by the varying dynamics.

Work the emotion. If a vocal or instrumental track reaches an emotional peak during the course of a song, you may be able to enhance its impact by creating a subtle dynamic arc that matches the emotional arc. But like most other aesthetic decisions, don't overdo it—if the listener can sense that you're milking the performance with overly dramatic level changes, the effect can go from subtle and effective to ham-handed and embarrassing.

Bring out obscured phrases. Sometimes certain things just aren't as audible as you'd like, requiring some fader-riding help. Maybe a vocal goes into a lower register, or some instruments collide right at the moment of your most brilliant lyric. You can bring out these things with a bit of fader-riding.

Explode entrances. A mix can sound more bold if you "explode" entrances: When a new part comes in, start it 1dB or 2dB louder (a fairly small boost), and then have it settle into its optimal level after just a couple of seconds. Done properly, this can create a subtle but exciting effect where new instruments seem to be saying "Listen here!" whenever they enter. Without this treatment, the listener's ear kind of has to wander around the mix, unsure exactly of what deserves focus and attention.

Don't neglect drum dynamics. Sampled drums can seem lifeless, or unforgiving and relentless, if their mix dynamics aren't handled with some sensitivity. Don't be afraid to bring up the drum levels as the song's energy increases, and bring them down as the energy subsides. Real drummers respond to a song's energy by varying their dynamics—try to get this element into your sampled drums as well.

How To Splice Analog Tape

Splicing analog tape requires practice, so do a few dry run-throughs on rough mixes before you start cutting up your perfect mixes. Use only splicing tape made for that purpose, and use a proper splicing block; these are inexpensive, save a lot of hassle, and make your splices more precise. Carefully rock the reels of your mixdown tape machine to find easy-to-locate transient moments (such as the downbeat at the beginning of that guitar solo), mark the point on the back of the tape with a white splicing pencil, and cut *just* before that point. The transient will help disguise any imperfections in your splice. Keep in mind that if any prominent sound exists on both sides of the splice point, you need to mix it similarly on each side of the splice; otherwise you'll be able to hear the edit. Once you've spliced the previous section together with the current section, fast-forward and rewind the splice back and forth across the heads a few times; this will loosen up and flatten the splice joint, making it play more seamlessly.

On digital systems, of course, you can build fader-riding into your automation. Still, sometimes there's nothing like real hands on real faders, responding to the music in real time, to squeeze a little extra humanity and feel into a mix.

Mixing In Sections

If you're working on a linear format such as analog or digital tape, it can help to mix a song in sections rather than in one piece—especially if your mix is complicated. After all, if you need to move five faders and three pan knobs all to new settings just as the chorus ends and the guitar solo starts, you're going to have trouble. Rather than getting things just the way you want them, you'll have to compromise just to make your mixdown physically feasible. That's not the case if you mix in sections, though: You can get the verse mix just right, stop the tape, set up the board for the guitar solo, and then mix that section. When you're finished, you splice together the pieces of tape, or edit them together digitally. On one of the last songs I mixed on my old 8-track analog system, I ended up splicing together over 15 pieces of tape. It meant having to do some extra work, but the result—a wild, schizophrenic chop job of a mix—simply would not have been possible otherwise.

Mastering: The Essential Finishing Touch

It's amazing how many home recordists are still unaware of the importance of *mastering*. Mastering is the process of making slight EQ adjustments to an entire mix, optimizing the dynamics for maximum impact, and making EQ and dynamic adjustments so your mixes are more uniform and balanced from one song to the next. Professional mastering engineers get paid handsomely to massage entire CD projects for major labels. Once upon a time, when everything was analog, nobody else could do what they do—if you made a record, you had to take it to a mastering facility before it could get pressed. With the digital revolution and the invention of the CD burner, though, now we can master our own projects at home—to a certain degree of success, anyway. Pro mastering engineers still get the big bucks for their finely tuned listening abilities and arsenal of super-expensive gear, but at least we home recordists can now do a few mastering operations ourselves to improve our projects.

If you're recording on an analog medium, you'll need to digitize your music at some stage (assuming you intend to burn it onto CD), so it makes sense to do your mastering after it has been digitized. If you don't have a computer with a good soundcard and sound-processing software, it probably doesn't make much sense to upgrade just for mastering purposes. Ask around to find out if someone you know has a digital recording system, preferably with a collection of plug-ins, and see if they'd be willing to help you finish your project. Mastering is a good way to get your feet wet with digital recording and sound processing.

Mastering for levels. A raw, unmastered mix will not be able to compete with commercially recorded music that has gone through the mastering process. The unmastered mix will sound small and wimpy in comparison, because the mastered mix's dynamic range has been optimized to make the music sound bigger and louder. As I mentioned back in Chapter 2, louder almost always sounds better—and because of this phenomenon, mastering engineers try to get mixes to sound as loud as possible without significantly compromising the sound. To do this, they put the mix through compressors and limiters designed for this task; these units bring the music to the top of digital's dynamic range, so that its dynamics get very close to the 0dB top—sometimes for the duration of the entire song (see Fig. 1). There's a tradeoff, though, as piling on too much compression and limiting can flatten out a song's natural dynamics and can make the song sound like it's pushing too hard. Part of the mastering process involves knowing how much of this processing is too much.

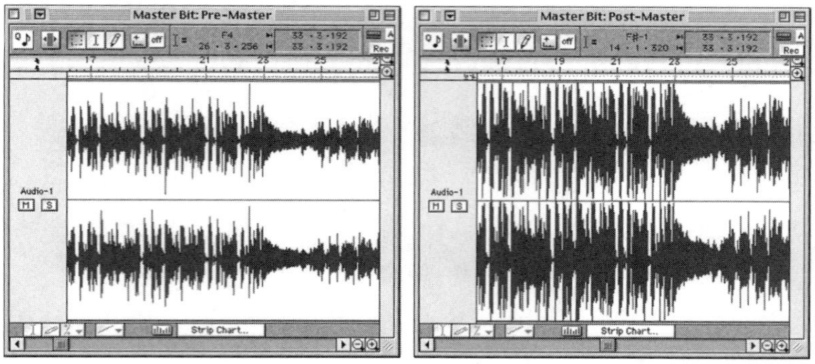

Fig. 1 You can usually tell whether a song has been mastered just by looking at its waveform. At left is a few seconds of an unmastered song; note that its dynamics reach a maximum only occasionally. At right is the same segment after mastering. Notice how the overall level is higher, making the song sound bigger and louder.

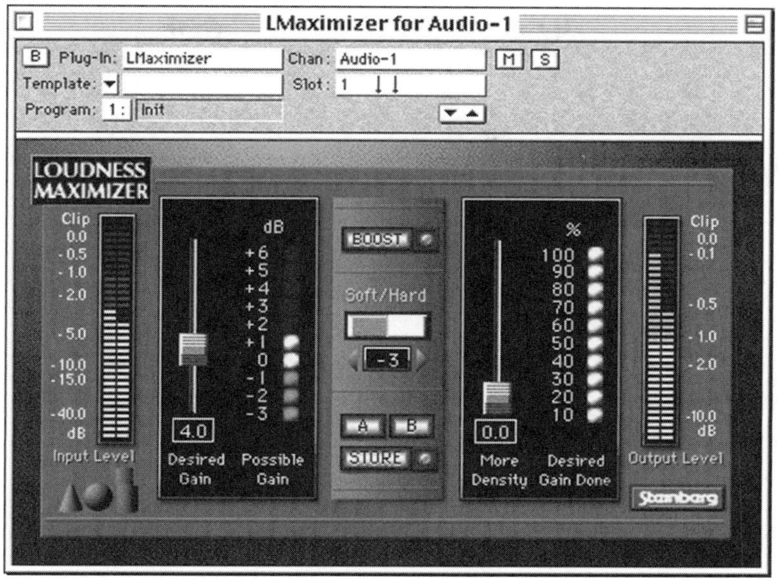

Fig. 2 Steinberg's Loudness Maximizer is a simple-to-use plug-in that brings up a song's level without going over 0dB or clipping the waveform.

On a computer recording system, mastering for levels is usually done with a plug-in. I usually use a basic plug-in by Steinberg called Loudness Maximizer (see Fig. 2); while you run your mix through the plug-in, it analyzes the signal and indicates how much gain is available, moment by moment. A slider allows you to specify how much gain the plug-in actually performs. On the right side of the window is an indicator showing how close to 0dB your post-Maximizer levels are. Loudness Maximizer is quick and easy to use, but for more serious projects I bring my mixes to someone who has more sophisticated mastering plug-ins. Still, it's remarkable how much you can improve a mix's punch and presence with a basic plug-in like this.

Mastering for EQ. Inevitably, if you mix ten songs over a period of time, they won't all have the same balance of frequency components from one song to the next. Some will be brighter than others, some will have a boomier low end, and some will have more midrange presence. A big part of mastering an entire CD project involves achieving an overall consistent sound among the songs. On a computer, you can usually perform this mastering-process component simply with the EQs in the recording program's virtual console: Just import the final mix into the program, assign it to a track, call up the track's virtual console channel, and then open up the channel's EQ windows and load the mastering plug-in into the channel. Now you're ready to start mastering the song.

Mastering tips. Do mastering work when your ears are fresh—not after a long day of recording or mixing. As when you're mixing, start out the session by getting a frame of reference. Put up a professionally recorded and mastered CD on your studio

> LOOK ■ OUT!
>
> ## *Mind Your Digital Signal Chain*
>
> When you're mastering, make sure the various digital processes happen to your mix in the proper order. The mix should encounter the EQ algorithms first, followed by the mastering (compression/limiting) plug-in, and, finally, a global level cut, if there is one. If the EQ comes *after* the mastering plug-in, you'll compromise the plug-in's effectiveness. And if there's a boost in the EQ, even a very slight one, the mix will likely go over 0dB, resulting in nasty digital clipping. If you find that the processing order is wrong, you may need to set up an extra one or two busses in the virtual console, give each bus a processing task, and route your mix through them in sequence. However, don't confuse this digital signal chain with the order that you follow when you're doing a mastering job: Set up your mastering plug-in first, then add EQ, and, finally, configure the global level cut if necessary.

monitors at a moderate (not loud) level, and listen to a song or two before you get to work on your own material.

The first decision to make is how much gain to apply to your mix. This depends partly on how "hot" you mixed the song. If for most of the mixdown your input meters were peaking at only –3dB, you have more room to work with than if your meters were consistently hitting –1dB (2dB of additional room, to be exact). The Loudness Maximizer plug-in defaults to 6dB of gain—but unless I'm doing a song that needs to sound *very* loud and in-your-face, or if I didn't mix the song very hot to begin with, 6dB usually sounds like too much. At 6dB of gain, many mixes start to sound "puffy" or "over-inflated," like they're about to burst at the seams, which isn't always the sound you want. About 4dB is often a good compromise between getting the mix to the top of the dynamic range and pushing it too much. But if a song has a quiet nature, such as a solo acoustic guitar and vocal arrangement, you may need just 1dB or 2dB of gain, or even none at all. On the other hand, if a song was mixed at a low level for one reason or another, you may need to pump it up by 7dB or 8dB to bring the sound to the front where you want it.

Usually when you push a song like this with a mastering program, the frequency balance is affected—it can sound much brighter, often too bright, with several decibels of gain applied. So, you need to control that high end with some EQ. Start by rolling off the high end quite a bit—say, 6dB of cut above 8kHz. The song should now sound overly muted; that's okay. Go back to your reference CD and listen for 15 seconds or so to get that sound into your head. Then return to your mix and tweak the high-end EQ parameters until it sounds like the right amount of highs has returned to your mix, relative to the other frequency bands. Check your mix once more against the reference CD, and tweak your mix's high end some more if necessary.

CD-Burning Options

If you own a computer that can burn CDs, it probably came with a program that can create audio CDs from audio files. This is fine for putting together a collection of rough mixes, or for testing out song sequences and the spaces between songs. But if you intend to have the CD duplicated professionally, you'll need to use a CD-creation program made specifically for pro audio. Such a program will also allow you to make last-minute level adjustments to the songs and allow you to set up things like segues, where one song blends into the next while the track number changes. Most important, the program will create a CD that conforms to the Red Book standard—the CD will be encoded so that it can be interpreted correctly by any CD-duplicating manufacturer. Duplicating plants require master CDs to conform to these Red Book specs.

Finally, scrutinize all of your mix's other frequency bands against the reference CD, one at a time: high mids, mids, low mids, and then lows. Keep the studio monitors at a low to medium volume level, and, if possible, "A/B" your mix and the reference CD—quickly switch back and forth between them, at the same general volume. This is an excellent way to hear if certain frequency bands need taming or are deficient. If you do need to boost a band, it should get only 2dB or 3dB at most; otherwise, you're better off going back and mixing the song over, this time with a flatter frequency profile. Also, be careful that when you boost a band (particularly the lows), you aren't causing the mastering plug-in to clip. In its window you'll probably see a CLIP indicator; make sure this doesn't light while your EQ'd song is playing through it.

Nix the subsonics. Mastering engineers often apply an extreme cut of very low frequencies—for example, –12dB below 25Hz—to ensure that any subsonic frequencies that got onto the recording, for whatever reason, don't mess up the mastering job. Lows carry a lot of energy; if these subsonics are in your mix, you won't be able to hear them, but they will show up on meters. As a result, you'll have to master the song at a lower level, and the song will have a lower apparent volume than the meters suggest—all because of something you can't even hear. So, if you're able, pull these frequencies out.

A final cut. Sometimes mastering engineers apply a global cut of –0.1dB to the mix. The reason is that some professional CD-burning software will balk if it detects that your mastered mix hit and stayed at exactly 0dB—even for just an instant—as this is a sign that the song tried to go over the 0dB ceiling and digitally clipped, even if it's harmlessly inaudible. But you'll never hear a –0.1dB cut, either, so it's not a bad idea. Make sure this cut comes *after* the EQ and gain stages in the computer's digital signal chain.

Last touches. Finally, mastering is a good time to add fade-ins and fade-outs: Just draw a ramp on the mix track's volume-automation window. And sometimes, for aesthetic reasons, you need a song to sound quieter than its neighboring songs on the CD. The mastering step is the time to make this happen: Just add a global level cut of a few decibels at the end of the digital signal chain.

... And It's A Wrap

When you're happy with your mastering job, select the block of audio representing the song in the recording program, and choose the appropriate Export function—probably under the File menu. Make sure that all level changes, EQ, and plug-ins are taken into account (check the documentation), and export the song as a single stereo-interleaved AIFF file, at the CD-standard 44.1kHz sampling rate and 16 bits of resolution. That's it! Burn the song to CD, and you're done.

APPENDIX A

Twenty Songs In One Day

Introducing Volume Recording

When I first started recording my own music, I'd come home from college classes and bang out a song in one evening, no problem. And the songs *sounded* like they were banged out in one evening. As I continued recording and my skills got increasingly sophisticated, I noticed something: I was becoming a perfectionist, spending more and more time on each song, and as a direct result I was recording less and less music. Eventually I found myself spending a whole evening just choosing drum sounds, and several days programming the part—just for the drums. Starting up a new recording became a drag: When the first task involves scrolling through several dozen kick-drum sounds on a computer screen, how much room is there for spontaneity and inspiration? I started letting go of countless song ideas almost as fast as they came to me, just because I knew that turning one into a finished recording could be a month-long process. And if I did follow through and a song turned out poorly, it seemed like such a waste of time, it was that much more difficult to get up the energy to try recording something new. At one point, I think I recorded two new songs in the space of three years. Was I in a rut? You bet.

Then my close friend and former bandmate, the composer Steven Clark, told me of a new group he was invited to join called the Immersion Composition Society. Founded by local musicians Nicholas Dobson and Michael Mellender, ICS met once a month at one of the members' homes. The members—all self-sufficient songwriter/recordists—were to spend the entire day by themselves doing nothing but writing and recording original music, with the ultimate goal of composing, recording, and mixing 20 songs in the space of 12 hours. Even though members rarely achieved the 20-song goal, most showed up with at least five or ten, no small feat for a day's work. After participating a couple of times, Steven was so enthusiastic that he decided to start his own ICS chapter, and he invited me and several other musician friends to join.

During my first ICS session, within only an hour or two, I realized that I had forced myself into a very different recording mode: When you're "volume recording" and the clock is ticking down, there is no time to waste—to redo a flawed take, to fuss over a sound, or even to think about what to do next. There is also no time for writer's block:

Not having an idea is simply never an option. No matter what you recorded last or how you are feeling, you have to pick up an instrument, start recording, and *just play.* It's a given that some ICS songs will be failures, but that's okay. The point is that you just plow ahead—and with some luck, at the end, you'll find a few gems among the rubble.

By the end of my first session, I had finished ten songs. Even though during the process I had no time even to think about what I was doing, when it was all over I was amazed at what I had accomplished. I had no idea I was capable of this kind of output; it was easily the most creatively productive day of my life. Best of all, the volume-recording mindset resulted in music that was very "me": Liberated from the nagging internal voices of self-criticism and self-doubt, my musical personality was free to flow forth at its most authentic, to explore complete, playful abandon, and to run wild. I was immediately hooked.

I and my fellow members of the ICS "Wig Lodge" have done over two dozen sessions since; none of the members from the first meeting has dropped out. Several other "lodges" have formed across the U.S. and even in Canada. We've circulated compilation CDs, had a live show, and had theme sessions, joint-lodge sessions, and collaborative sessions. I have reached the 20-song goal on two occasions—and while grueling and painful, those sessions were without a doubt my most rewarding and successful. Four- and five-song sessions are okay (and far less stressful), but they never achieve the incandescent inspiration of the sessions where I completely let go and follow through all the way. And now, with over 100 rough songs in the can, I never have a shortage of material when I want to go into the studio and give something the full-on polished treatment.

Since I began doing volume recording, I've noticed that a similar mindset exists in other disciplines. When I tutored writing in college, "freewriting"—essentially a 15-minute exercise in volume writing—was a way to loosen up nervous young writers who lacked confidence. I've visited improvisational workshops where people learned to cut loose and be free to make fools of themselves in front of others. Even business consultants who teach brainstorming techniques aim for similar goals. One thing ties all of these endeavors together: In each case, participants learn to open up, feel free to go out on a limb, and, most important, celebrate failure. If failures are okay and have no negative consequences, particularly if you and your fellow participants can laugh at them together, your potential to create freely—and ultimately, to create something of beauty and excellence—becomes that much greater.

I encourage you to give volume recording a try. I think you'll find it a valuable, even life-changing, experience. Almost as a side benefit, you'll learn how to get things done faster in the studio and to put together a reasonable-sounding production in just a few minutes. And the next time you read about how Joe Famous Rock Star has been holed up in some rented mansion for a month without coming up with any new songs, you'll think, Jeez—just get over yourself and *start making some music!*

For more information on the Immersion Composition Society, go to **www.ics-hub.com**.

APPENDIX B

Re-Production

A Guerrilla Home Recording Exercise

Since Guerrilla Home Recording aims to get a professional sound, it makes sense for us to look to professional recordings for guidance and inspiration. The best way to do that is to try to copy, as closely as you can, an actual professional recording that you admire. In other words, make a sound-for-sound (or even note-for-note) cover recording. This may seem like a silly proposition; after all, why would anyone be interested in hearing your karaoke-like clone of someone else's song? Well, that's not the point—maybe they *shouldn't* hear it. This kind of recording is just for you; it's a production exercise, not necessarily a great work of art. That's not to say you can't have some fun and put your own touches on the recording—you can change the words or insert a guitar solo or a new instrumental bridge if you want. But the real goal of "re-production," as I call it, is to listen to each sound and challenge yourself to reproduce it, using the Guerrilla Home Recording approach: Achieve the sounds you want to hear by any means possible.

About ten years ago, I took my shot at doing a note-for-note re-production of one of my favorite recordings, Donald Fagen's "New Frontier." The end of the tune features a tasty harmonica solo—and since I can't play harmonica, nor do I know anyone who does, I had to come up with a way to approximate the sound. Simply trying to get my old Ensoniq Mirage sampler to approximate the part would have been hopeless; there were just too many hand-muting and mouthwork nuances. I ended up rigging together probably the craziest signal chain I've ever done. I started with a MIDI sequence of the part, which drove a harmonica sample on the Mirage. I thought I might be able to approximate the performance nuances by using a "talk box" concept, but I didn't have a talk box. (A talk box is a guitar effect that pumps an amplified sound into a tube, which you place in your mouth; mouthing vowels and consonants causes your mouth to emit vocal-like guitar sounds, which you then capture with a microphone.) I ran the Mirage signal into a reel-to-reel tape deck that had a particularly powerful headphone amplifier, got an adapter, and plugged a pair of Walkman-style headphones onto the jack. I then wrapped one of the earpieces with plastic wrap, secured the wrap with a rubber band, and then placed this contraption in my mouth. When I clicked PLAY on my MIDI sequencer, the harmonica line started coming out of my mouth, and I was able to mimic the original's nuances, capturing the sound with a carefully compressed and gated microphone.

Re-production yields plenty of challenges like this, but nothing is more effective for teaching yourself how to record good sounds. You quickly learn what your pile of cheap studio gear—along with a large helping of creativity and ingenuity—is really capable of. If something is a little off from the original, try to figure out why, and then try to get it closer. Perhaps even more beneficial than improving your studio ear, this kind of exercise is great for your *musical* ear. It was tough for me to suss out the subtle harmonies of "New Frontier," but I wrestled with the original for hours, going back over the keyboard parts again and again. And after that, I found it was a lot easier to deconstruct chords, progressions, vocal arrangements, you name it.

Even if nobody ever hears your re-productions—and you might not want anyone to—aiming for a pro sound in this way is incredibly rewarding. And it makes sense why: You won't know what pro sound really is until you actually study pro sounds closely.

Acknowledgments

I would like to thank Richard Johnston, Amy Miller, and the rest of Backbeat Books for the opportunity to write *Guerrilla Home Recording*. Thanks also to Bill Leigh and the staffers of *Bass Player* magazine, past and present—not only for teaching me much over the years, but also for helping me get to the point where I can live the life of a bum without a job. Thanks to Rich Leeds for a great book cover (and, indirectly, a great title), to Dave and Jennifer Goldwag, and to Steven Clark, Nicholas Dobson, Michael Mellender, and everyone else involved in the Immersion Composition Society. A special thank you to my technical editor, Gino Robair, who tidied up plenty of loose ends and made me feel 100 percent better about this book. Finally, thank you to all the readers of *Guerrilla Home Recording*—keep your ears open and your listening skills growing. Even if your music never makes it to satellite radio, just know that as long as you get pleasure from making and listening to your own creations, the time and effort is well worth it.

—*KC*

About the Author

For 14 years Karl Coryat was an editor at *Bass Player* magazine, where he was the staff recording guru and wrote a series of columns on recording and technology. He is also the editor of *The Bass Player Book* (Backbeat Books). Under the names Eddie Current, the Progeny of Sodomy Featuring Lumpy Fatt, and several other obscure monikers, he has been a prolific creator of original music since the mid 1980s—first on cassette 4-track, then analog 8-track, and currently a digital system. He is a founding member of the Immersion Composition Society's Wig Lodge (www.wiglodge.com), and he has also worked in the studio with the late Kevin Gilbert (Giraffe, Toy Matinee), Eric Valentine (Smash Mouth), Dan Vickrey (Counting Crows), and others. Karl is currently a consulting editor for *Bass Player* as well as a freelance writer and editor.

Index

WHEN IT COMES TO MAKING MUSIC, WE WROTE THE BOOK.

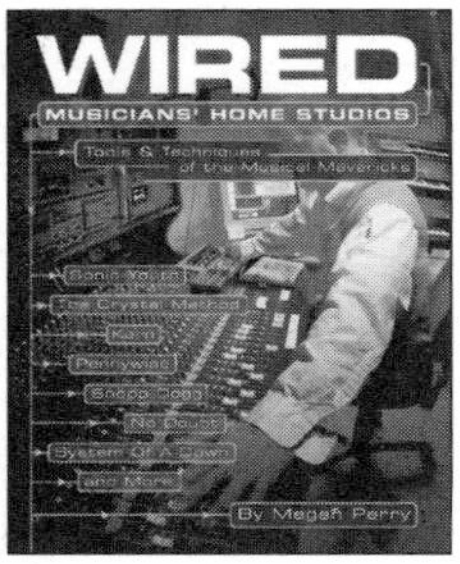

Wired: Musicians' Home Studios

Tools & Techniques of the Musical Mavericks

By Megan Perry

Helping musicians become better producers, stars such as No Doubt, Sonic Youth, Crystal Method, Snoop Dogg, BT, 311, and Korn open their homes to reveal their personal studio setups. Everything a musician wants to know is covered in this insightful book, including artist profiles, studio construction, gear, consoles, and new Pro Tools hubs.

Softcover, 192 pages, ISBN 0-87930-794-3, $22.95

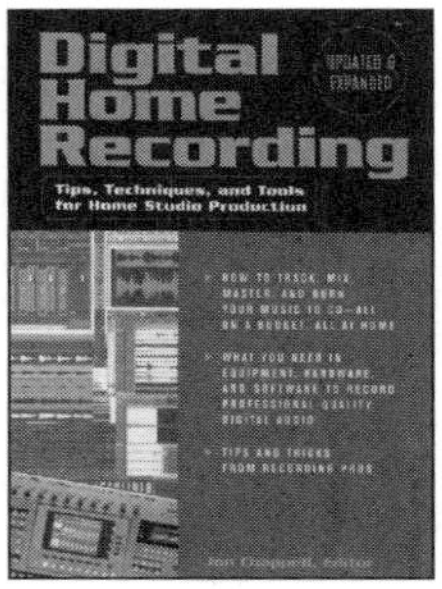

Digital Home Recording

Tips, Techniques, and Tools for Home Studio Production

2nd Edition

Edited by Jon Chappell

This practical guide is packed with tips and techniques for creating and operating a cost-effective, professional-level digital studio at home. Now you can be your own recording engineer, producer, and CD mastering facility—right in your own home—with today's affordable digital audio technology and *Digital Home Recording.*

Softcover, 256 pages, ISBN 0-87930-732-3, $24.95

Behind the Glass

Top Record Producers Tell How They Craft the Hits

By Howard Massey

George Martin, Glen Ballard, Phil Ramone, and 34 other world-class producers share their creative secrets and nuts-and-bolts techniques in this prime collection of firsthand interviews. These masters of the trade offer tips and tricks you can use in the studio—professional or at home—whether you're a musician, producer, engineer, or student, or just want to know how the hits are made.

Softcover, 328 pages, ISBN 0-87930-614-9, $24.95

The Art of Digital Music

56 Artists and Insiders Reveal Their Creative Secrets

By David Battino and Kelli Richards

Through a dynamic blend of in-depth interviews, hands-on production tips, inspiring case studies, and extensive graphics, this book explores the creative freedom today's music tools afford. This entertaining volume features lively discussions with technological pioneers—the artists, producers, engineers, software wizards, and Internet visionaries who are shaping the sound of the future.

Softcover w/DVD, 272 pages, ISBN 0-87930-830-3, $27.95

Make Music Now!

Putting Your Studio Together, Recording Songs, Burning CDs, Distributing Online

Edited by Mitch Gallagher

If you're starting to set up a home studio or making one better, here's all the information and inspiration you need. This easy-to-read guide is a fun introduction to how to use computers for making and distributing original music. From the basics of MIDI, to choosing and using gear, putting your music online, burning CDs, and more, you get the guidance you need to make music now!

Softcover, 192 pages, ISBN 0-87930-637-8, $17.95

Confessions of a Record Producer

How to Survive the Scams and Shams of the Music Business

2nd Edition

By Moses Avalon

If you're a musician, producer, engineer, or any other recording professional, this practical, provocative guide will help you protect your rights and assets. Using real-life examples drawn from 20-plus years' experience, this book reveals how producers dip into budgets, artists steal songs, labels skim royalties, and other unfortunate truths—and how you can survive them.

Softcover, 256 pages, ISBN 0-87930-660-2, $19.95

Backbeat Books

AVAILABLE AT FINE BOOK AND MUSIC STORES EVERYWHERE, OR CONTACT:

Backbeat Books • 6600 Silacci Way • Gilroy, CA 95020 USA
Phone Toll Free: (866) 222-5232 • Fax: (408) 848-5784
E-mail: backbeat@rushorder.com • Web: www.backbeatbooks.com